MICROBIOLOGY & BIOTECHNOLOGY

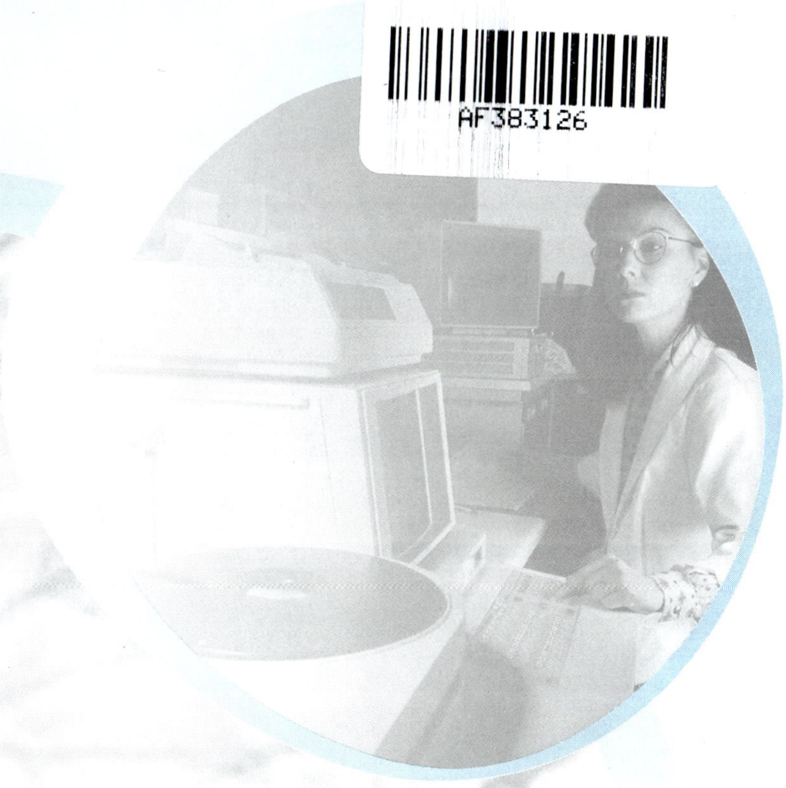

MICROBIOLOGY & BIOTECHNOLOGY

Biology **Modular Workbook**

First Edition 2006
Second edition 2007
Third edition 2013

Third printing
ISBN: 978-1-927173-72-5

Distribution Offices:

Head office (New Zealand)
Biozone International Ltd, NZ
Telephone: 07-856-8104
Fax: 07-856-9243
Email: sales@biozone.co.uk
Website: www.biozone.co.uk

United Kingdom & Europe
Biozone Learning Media (UK) Ltd, UK
Telephone: +44 (0)1746 250006
Email: sales@biozone.co.uk
Website: www.biozone.co.uk

Australia
Biozone Learning Media Australia, Australia
Telephone: 07-5535-4896
Fax: 07-5508-2432
Email: sales@biozone.com.au
Website: www.biozone.com.au

USA
Biozone Corporation
FREE phone: 855-246-4555
FREE fax: 855-935-3555
Email: sales@thebiozone.com
Website: www.thebiozone.com

Front cover photographs

Micrograph of irregularly shaped macroconidia of the
fungal pathogen *Microsporum distortum*.
Image courtesy of CDC ©2006

Gene information
Image ©2005 JupiterImages Corporation www.clipart.com

Meet the writing team

Tracey Greenwood
I have been writing resources for
students since 1993. I have a Ph.D
in biology, specialising in lake
ecology and I have taught both
graduate and undergraduate biology.

Tracey
Senior Author

Lissa Bainbridge-Smith
I worked in industry in a research
and development capacity for eight
years before joining BIOZONE in
2006. I have an M.Sc from Waikato
University.

Lissa
Author

Kent Pryor
I have a BSc from Massey University
majoring in zoology and ecology and
taught secondary school biology and
chemistry for 9 years before joining
BIOZONE as an author in 2009.

Kent
Author

Richard Allan
I have had 11 years experience
teaching senior secondary school
biology. I have a Masters degree
in biology and founded BIOZONE
in the 1980s after developing
resources for my own students.

Richard
Founder & CEO

Biology **Modular Workbook** Series

The BIOZONE *Biology Modular Workbook Series* has been developed to meet the demands of customers with the requirement for a flexible modular resource. Each workbook provides a collection of visually interesting and accessible activities, catering for students with a wide range of abilities and background. The workbooks are divided into a series of chapters, each comprising an introductory section and a series of write-on worksheets ranging from paper practicals and data handling exercises, to activities requiring critical thinking and analysis. Page tabs identifying "**Related activities**" and "**Weblinks**" help students to find related material within the workbook and locate online support that will enhance their understanding of the topic. During the development of this series, we have taken the opportunity to develop new content, while retaining the basic philosophy of a student-friendly resource, which spans the gulf between textbook and study guide. Its highly visual presentation engages students, increasing their motivation and empowering them to take control of their learning.

MICROBIOLOGY & BIOTECHNOLOGY

Microbiology & Biotechnology covers what is an overwhelmingly extensive topic area, encompassing not only gene technologies and their applications, but fermentation technology, cloning and tissue culture, bioremediation, enzyme technology, and genome research. Microorganisms play a central role in many biotechnological processes, and a knowledge of microbial structure and diversity is necessary background to an understanding of the topic. This workbook comprises five chapters, each of which corresponds to a broad area of either microbiology or biotechnology. These areas are explained through a series of one and two page activities, each of which explores a specific concept (e.g. dilution plating or restriction enzymes). *Microbiology & Biotechnology* is a student-centered resource. Students completing the activities, in concert with their other classroom and practical work, will consolidate existing knowledge and develop and practise skills that they will use throughout their course. This workbook may be used in the classroom or at home as a supplement to a standard textbook. Some activities are introductory in nature, while others may be used to consolidate and test concepts already covered by other means. BIOZONE has a commitment to produce a cost-effective, high quality resource, which acts as a student's companion throughout their biology study. Please do not photocopy from this workbook; we cannot afford to provide single copies of workbooks to schools and continue to develop, update, and improve the material they contain.

ACKNOWLEDGEMENTS & PHOTO CREDITS

Royalty free images, purchased by Biozone International Ltd, are used throughout this workbook and have been obtained from the following sources: Corel Corporation from various titles in their Professional Photos CD-ROM collection; IMSI (International Microcomputer Software Inc.) images from IMSI's MasterClips® and MasterPhotosTM Collection, 1895 Francisco Blvd. East, San Rafael, CA 94901-5506, USA; ©1996 Digital Stock, Medicine and Health Care collection; ©Hemera Technologies Inc., 1997-2001; © 2005 JupiterImages Corporation www.clipart.com; ©Click Art, ©T/Maker Company; ©1994., ©Digital Vision; Gazelle Technologies Inc.; PhotoDisc®, Inc. USA, www.photodisc.com. The authors would also like to thank those who have contributed to this edition: • Bioengineering AG Switzerland for their photograph of a bioreactor • Bio-Rad Laboratories, Inc. for allowing us to photograph the Helios gene gun **EliLily:** ©2002 EliLily and Co. for the photo of humalog • Pharmacia (Aust) Ltd for photos of the DNA gel sequencing • Stacey Farmer and Greg Baillie, Waikato DNA Sequencing Facility for their assistance with material on DNA sequencing and PCR • Rosie Bradshaw, Institute of Molecular Biosciences, Massey University, for assistance in the gene technology section • Roslin Institute for their photo of Dolly • Raewyn Poole, University of Waikato, for information provided on transformation of *Acacia* • Genesis Research and Development Corp. Auckland, for the photo used on the HGP activity • ©1999 University of Kansas, for the photo of the incubator for culture of cell lines • David Wells (AgResearch) for photos on cloning • Liam Nolan, Leo Sanchez, and Burkhard Budel for contributions to the activities on the genetics of Antarctic springtails • Kapiti Cheeses NZ, for information and photos of cheese production • Villa Maria Wines (NZ) for their photos of wine production • Greenpeace for use of GMO ethics images • Totem Graphics, for their clipart collection of plants and animals • TechPool Studios, for their clipart collection of human anatomy: Copyright ©1994, TechPool Studios Corp. USA (some images were modified by R. Allan and T. Greenwood) • Corel Corporation, for clipart of plants and animals from the Corel MEGAGALLERY collection • 3D models created using Poser IV, Curious Labs.

We also acknowledge the photographers that have made their images available through **Wikimedia Commons** under Creative Commons Licences 2.0, 2.5. or 3.0: • Eric Erbe • Peter Halasz • Jan Christian • Dual Freq • Romain Behar • Georgetown University Hospital

Photos kindly provided by individuals or corporations have been identified by way of coded credits as follows: **BOB**: Barry O'Brien (Uni. of Waikato), **BH**: Brendan Hicks (Uni. of Waikato), **CDC**: Centers for Disease Control and Prevention, Atlanta, USA, **CF**: Conan Fee (Uni. of Waikato), **EII**: Education Interactive Imaging, **HGSI**: Dena Borchardt at Human Genome Sciences Inc., **MPI**: Max Planck Institute for Developmental Biology, Germany, **NIH**: National Institute of Health, **RA**: Richard Allan, **RCN**: Ralph Cocklin, **TG**: Tracey Greenwood, **USDA**: United States Department of Agriculture, **VMW**: Villa Maria Wines, **WMU**: Waikato Microscope Unit

Other titles

SKILLS IN BIOLOGY

HEALTH & DISEASE

GENES & INHERITANCE

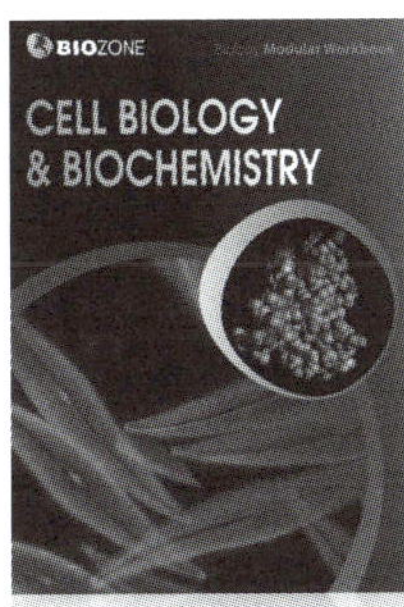

CELL BIOLOGY & BIOCHEMISTRY

See the whole series at:
www.theBIOZONE.com

Contents

CODES: △ **Upgraded** this edition ★ **New** this edition **Activity** is marked: ⬚ to be done; ☑ when completed

Features of the Chapter Topic Page

An understanding of the microbial world, and a working knowledge of the place of microorganisms in modern biotechnology are important in many biology curricula. *Microbiology and Biotechnology* aims to provide material in a way that will help you to acquire the knowledge and skills needed for this course of study. This workbook is suitable for biology students grades 10-12 and will reinforce and extend material covered by your teacher. Its aim is to complement the main text for your course.

Key terms

A list of important key terms used throughout the chapter. These will help you focus on important ideas.

Key concepts

The important key ideas in this chapter. You should have a thorough understanding of the concepts summarized here.

Page references

The page numbers for the activities covering the material in this subsection of objectives.

Chapter 1

Microorganisms and Biotechnology

Key terms

antibiotic
antibiotic resistance
Archaea
aseptic technique
batch culture
bacterium (pl. bacteria)
binary fission
biofuel
bioreactor
bioremediation
continuous culture
dilution plating
enzyme immobilization
food preservation
fungus (pl. fungi)
Gram stain
growth curve
lag phase
log (exponential) phase
microbe (=microorganism)
plasmid
primary metabolite
protist
secondary metabolite
sewage treatment
stationary phase
strain isolation
streak plating
virus

Key concepts

▶ The microbial world includes viruses and bacteria, as well as representatives from Fungi and Protista.

▶ The industrial-scale culture of microorganisms requires bioreactors, which provide optimum growth conditions, either in continuous or batch culture.

▶ Microbial products can be produced as primary or secondary metabolites.

▶ Microbes are widely used in industrial processes, in food production, in bioremediation, and in medicine.

Learning Objectives

☐ 1. Use the **KEY TERMS** to compile a glossary for this topic.

Introduction to Microorganisms pages 9-24

✓ 2. Recognize microbial groups, including the Archaea, in a named classification system. Describe the distinguishing features of **viruses**, **bacteria**, **fungi**, and **protists**. Comment on the role of these microbial groups in biotechnology.

✓ 3. Describe the life cycles of selected representative viral types, including representative viral replication in the host cell. Examples could include HIV, the bacteriophage lambda (λ), or an enveloped virus such as *Influenza*.

◉ 4. Describe the structure of a bacterial cell, as illustrated by *E. coli*. Identify cell surface membrane, nuclear zone, 70S ribosomes, flagella, and plasmid.

◉ 5. Describe the **growth curve** of a bacterial population. Explain why growth usually continue exponentially and identify exceptions to this.

◉ 6. Describe the role of **antibiotics** in inhibiting bacterial growth. Explain the mechanisms by which **antibiotic resistance** arises and how it spreads.

You can use the check boxes to mark objectives to be completed (a **dot** to be done; a **tick** when completed).

Microbial Culture pages 25-27, 32-36

☐ 7. Identify some of the safety issues associated with working with microorganisms. Identify safe working practices and explain why they are necessary.

☐ 8. Describe the *in vitro* growth requirements of bacteria and fungi, including reference to carbon and nitrogen sources, mineral requirements, temperature, pH, and oxygen.

☐ 9. Describe or demonstrate the use **aseptic technique** to prepare and inoculate nutrient broths and nutrient agar plates, and use **streak plating** for **strain isolation**.

☐ 10. Describe the growth curves of fungi and bacteria in culture. Suggest how bacterial and fungal cultures might be maintained in the rapid phase of growth.

☐ 11. Describe the use of **dilution plating** to measure the density of a bacterial culture.

☐ 12. Annotate a diagram of an industrial scale fermenter (**bioreactor**), identifying the features associated with providing optimum culture conditions. Compare and contrast the features and applications of **batch culture** and **continuous culture**.

Applications of Microbes pages 28-31, 36-50

☐ 13. Using named examples, describe the use of microbes in industrial processes, e.g. in producing alternative fuels, in **sewage treatment**, in **bioremediation**, and in mining.

☐ 14. Describe the production and use of microbial enzymes.

☐ 15. Describe the use of mircroorganisms in the food industry including in bread making, brewing, wine making, and the production of cultured milk products.

☐ 16. Describe how microbes themselves can be used as a food source (e.g. mycoprotein).

☐ 17. Recognize the importance of genetically modified microorganisms in the large scale production of valuable commodities including human proteins (e.g. insulin).

☐ 18. Recognize that methods of **food preservation** (e.g. drying, salting, canning) are important in many aspects of food biotechnology to prevent microbial growth.

Weblinks:
www.thebiozone.com/
weblink/MnB-3725/

The Weblinks on many of the activities can be accessed through the web links page at:
www.thebiozone.com/weblink/MnB-3725/
See page 4 for more details.

The objectives provide a point by point summary of what you should have achieved by the end of the chapter. They can also be used to derive **essential questions** for this chapter.

Features of the Activity Pages

The activities make up most of the content of this book. Your teacher may use the activity pages to introduce a topic for the first time or you may use them to revise ideas already covered by other means. You can use the activities in the classroom, as homework exercises and topic revision, and for self-directed study and personal reference. You may wish to read the related material in your textbook before you attempt the activities or use simpler activities as an introduction to your textbook reading. Model answers for this modular workbook are available on CD-ROM, or as a download from our website.

Introductory paragraph: The introductory paragraph provides essential background and provides the focus of the page. Note words that appear in **bold**, as they are 'key words' worthy of including in a glossary of terms for the topic.

Easy to understand diagrams: The main ideas of the topic are represented and explained by clear, informative diagrams.

Write-on format: Your understanding of the main ideas of the topic is tested by asking questions and providing spaces for your answers. Where indicated by the space available, your answers should be concise. Questions requiring more explanation or discussion are spaced accordingly. Answer the questions adequately according to the questioning term used (see the introduction).

A tab system at the base of each activity page identifies resources associated with the activity on that page. Use the guide below to help you use the tab system most effectively.

Perforations allow easy removal so that pages can be submitted for grading or kept in a separate folder of related work.

26

Strain Isolation

In nature, bacteria exist as mixed populations. However, in order to study them in the laboratory they must exist as pure cultures (i.e. cultures in which all organisms are the same species). The most common way of separating bacterial cells on the agar surface is the **streak plate method**. This provides a simple and rapid method of diluting the sample by mechanical means. As the loop is streaked across the agar surface, more and more bacteria are rubbed off until individual separated organisms are deposited on the agar. After incubation of the streak pattern will show conflu continuous sheet), while the area nea should show discrete colonies. Isolat removed from the streak plate using transferred to new sterile medium. After in the new culture will be descendants a pure culture).

When approximately 10 to 100 million bacterial cells are present, colonies become visible. Note the well-isolated colonies in the photo above. A single colony may be removed for further investigation.

A swab containing a single strain of bacteria is used to inoculate additional nutrient plates to produce pure cultures of bacteria.

To test purity, a sample of a culture can be grown on a selective medium that promotes the growth of a single species. The photo above shows a positive encapsulation test for *Bacillus anthracis*.

1. Explain the basis by which bacteria are isolated using streak plating: ______

2 Discuss the basic principles of aseptic technique, outlining why each procedure is necessary: ______

3. Explain the importance of aseptic (sterile) technique in streak plating: ______

4. State how many bacterial cells must be present on the plate before the colony becomes visible to the naked eye: ______

5. Explain when it might be necessary to use **selective media** to culture bacteria: ______

KNOW

Related activities: *Techniques in Microbial Culture, Serial Dilution*
Weblinks: *How to Streak a Plate*

© BIOZONE International 2006-2013
ISBN: 978-1-927173-72-5
Photocopying Prohibited

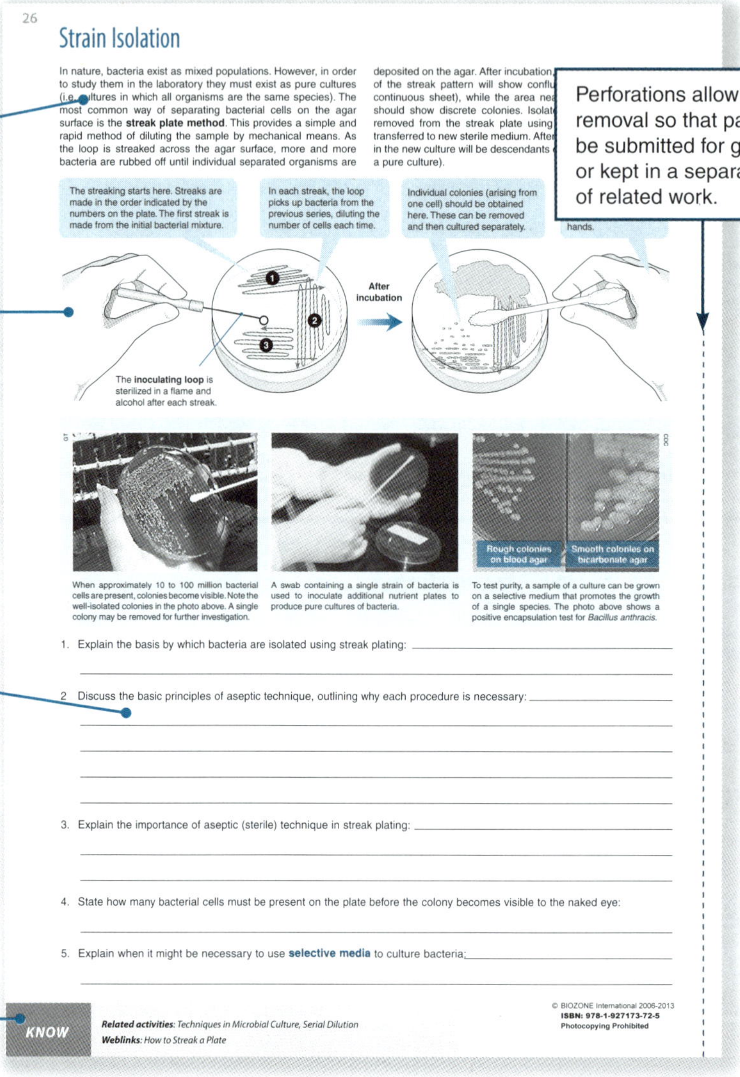

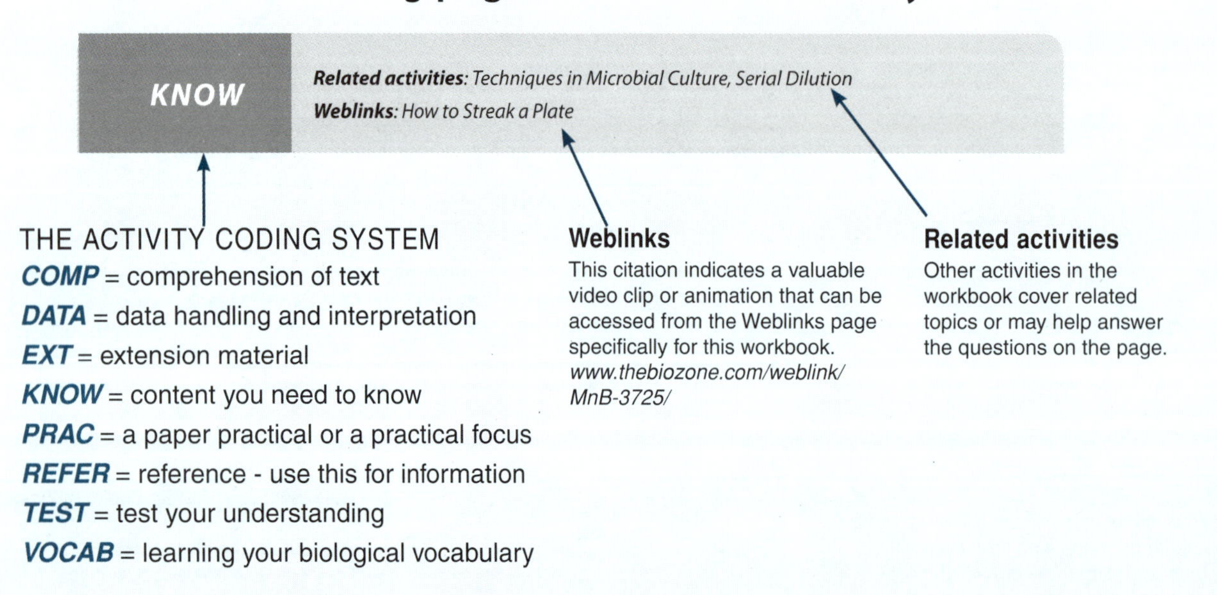

Using page tabs more effectively

KNOW

Related activities: *Techniques in Microbial Culture, Serial Dilution*

Weblinks: *How to Streak a Plate*

THE ACTIVITY CODING SYSTEM

COMP = comprehension of text
DATA = data handling and interpretation
EXT = extension material
KNOW = content you need to know
PRAC = a paper practical or a practical focus
REFER = reference - use this for information
TEST = test your understanding
VOCAB = learning your biological vocabulary

Weblinks

This citation indicates a valuable video clip or animation that can be accessed from the Weblinks page specifically for this workbook. *www.thebiozone.com/weblink/MnB-3725/*

Related activities

Other activities in the workbook cover related topics or may help answer the questions on the page.

Questioning Terms

Questions come in a variety of forms. Whether you are studying for an exam or writing an essay, it is important to understand exactly what the question is asking. A question has two parts to it: one part of the question will provide you with information, the second part of the question will provide you with instructions as to how to answer the question. Following these instructions is most important. Often students in examinations know the material but fail to follow instructions and do not answer the question appropriately. Examiners often use certain key words to introduce questions. Look out for them and be clear as to what they mean. Below is a description of terms commonly used when asking questions in biology.

Commonly used Terms in Biology

The following terms are frequently used when asking questions in examinations and assessments. Students should have a clear understanding of each of the following terms and use this understanding to answer questions appropriately.

Account for: Provide a satisfactory explanation or reason for an observation.

Analyze: Interpret data to reach stated conclusions.

Annotate: Add **brief** notes to a diagram, drawing or graph.

Apply: Use an idea, equation, principle, theory, or law in a new situation.

Appreciate: To understand the meaning or relevance of a particular situation.

Calculate: Find an answer using mathematical methods. Show the working unless instructed not to.

Compare: Give an account of similarities and differences between two or more items, referring to both (or all) of them throughout. Comparisons can be given using a table. Comparisons generally ask for similarities more than differences (see contrast).

Construct: Represent or develop in graphical form.

Contrast: Show differences. Set in opposition.

Deduce: Reach a conclusion from information given.

Define: Give the precise meaning of a word or phrase as concisely as possible.

Derive: Manipulate a mathematical equation to give a new equation or result.

Describe: Give a detailed account, including all the relevant information.

Design: Produce a plan, object, simulation or model.

Determine: Find the only possible answer.

Discuss: Give an account including, where possible, a range of arguments, assessments of the relative importance of various factors, or comparison of alternative hypotheses.

Distinguish: Give the difference(s) between two or more different items.

Draw: Represent by means of pencil lines. Add labels unless told not to do so.

Estimate: Find an approximate value for an unknown quantity, based on the information provided and application of scientific knowledge.

Evaluate: Assess the implications and limitations.

Explain: Give a clear account including causes, reasons, or mechanisms.

Identify: Find an answer from a number of possibilities.

Illustrate: Give concrete examples. Explain clearly by using comparisons or examples.

Interpret: Comment upon, give examples, describe relationships. Describe, then evaluate.

List: Give a sequence of names or other brief answers with no elaboration. Each one should be clearly distinguishable from the others.

Measure: Find a value for a quantity.

Outline: Give a brief account or summary. Include essential information only.

Predict: Give an expected result.

Solve: Obtain an answer using algebraic and/or numerical methods.

State: Give a specific name, value, or other answer. No supporting argument or calculation is necessary.

Suggest: Propose a hypothesis or other possible explanation.

Summarize: Give a brief, condensed account. Include conclusions and avoid unnecessary details.

In Conclusion

Students should familiarize themselves with this list of terms and, where necessary throughout the course, they should refer back to them when answering questions. The list of terms mentioned above is not exhaustive and students should compare this list with past examination papers / essays etc. and add any new terms (and their meaning) to the list above. The aim is to become familiar with interpreting the question and answering it appropriately.

Using BIOZONE's Website

Use the menu to browse products or check on the latest news from BIOZONE.

Access the **BIOLINKS** database of web sites directly from the homepage of our new website. Biolinks is organized into easy-to-use sub-sections relating to general areas of interest. It's a great way to quickly find out more on topics of interest.

Contact us with questions, feedback, ideas, and critical commentary. We welcome your input.

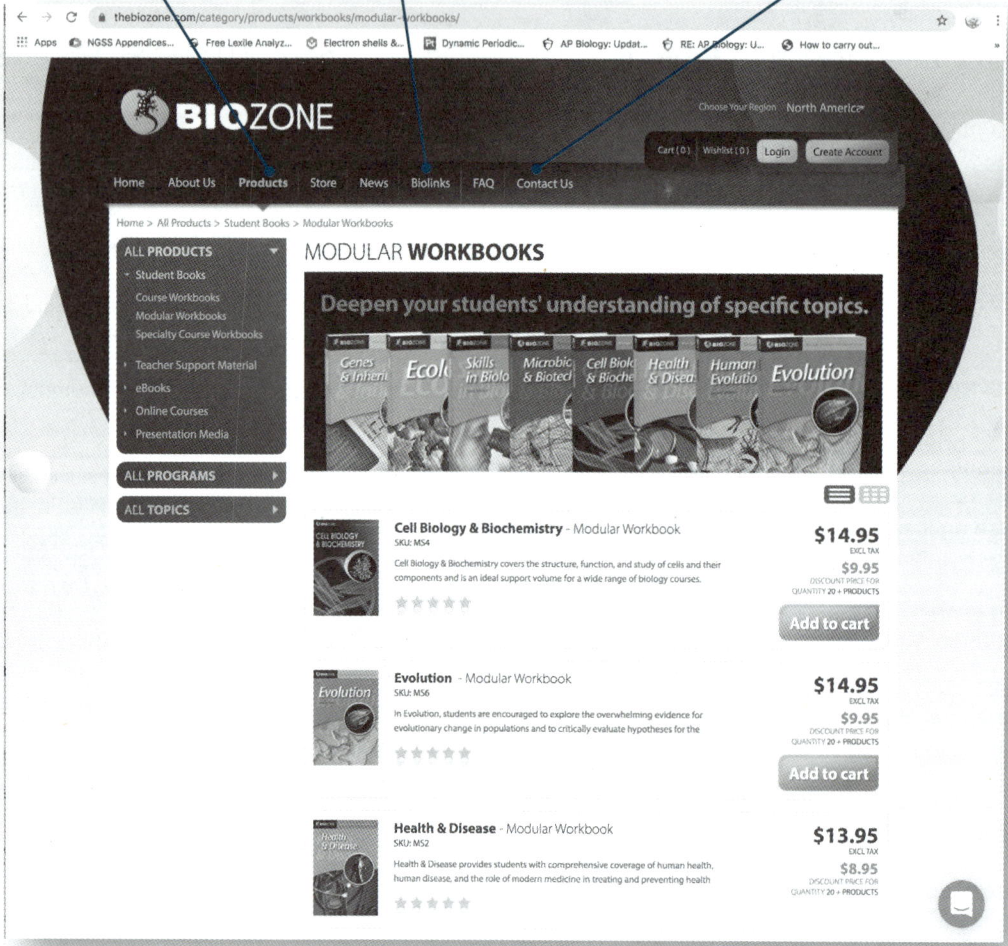

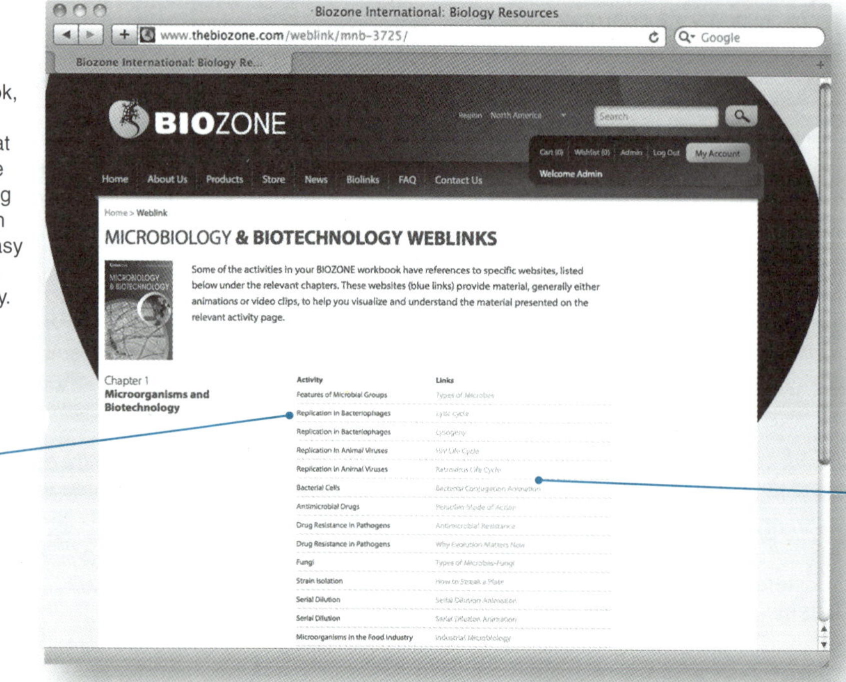

Weblinks: www.thebiozone.com/weblink/mnb-3725/

BOOKMARK WEBLINKS BY TYPING IN THE ADDRESS: IT IS NOT ACCESSIBLE DIRECTLY FROM BIOZONE'S WEBSITE

Throughout this workbook, some pages make reference to websites that have particular relevance to the activity by providing an explanatory animation or video clip. They are easy to use and a very useful supplement to the activity.

Activity reference
The activity on which the weblink is cited.

Weblink
Provides a link to an **external web site** with supporting information for the activity. If there are any additional activities, these are also listed here as links.

Concepts in Microbiology and Biotechnology

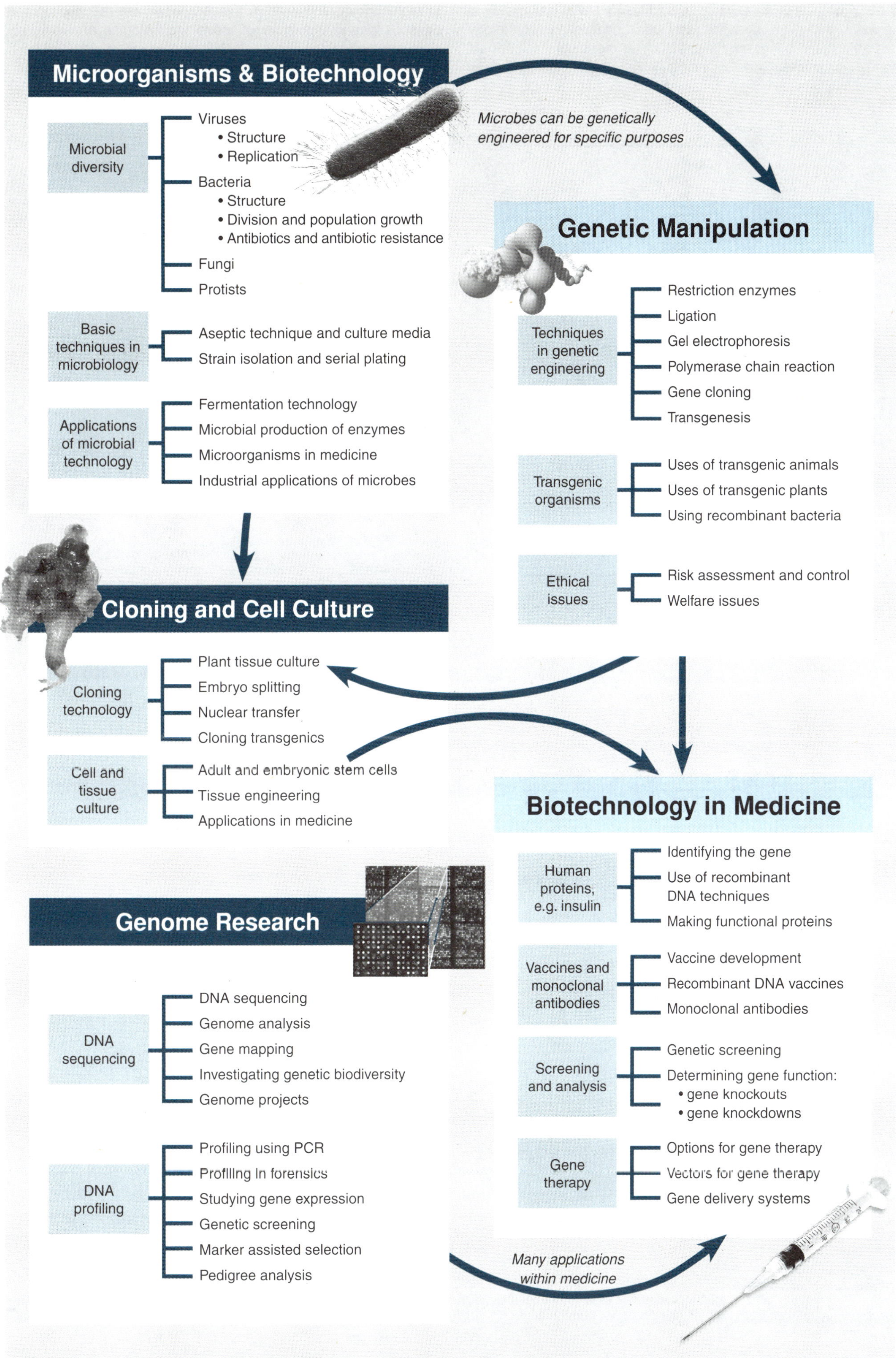

Landmarks in Biotechnology

Biotechnology is an area of applied science that has grown at an astonishing rate over the last three decades. Biotechnology has a profound effect on our use of other organisms, our impact on the environment, and our health. Some of the important areas of biotechnology covered in this workbook are mapped on the previous page. A number of these technologies are relatively new, while others are well established but progressing rapidly.

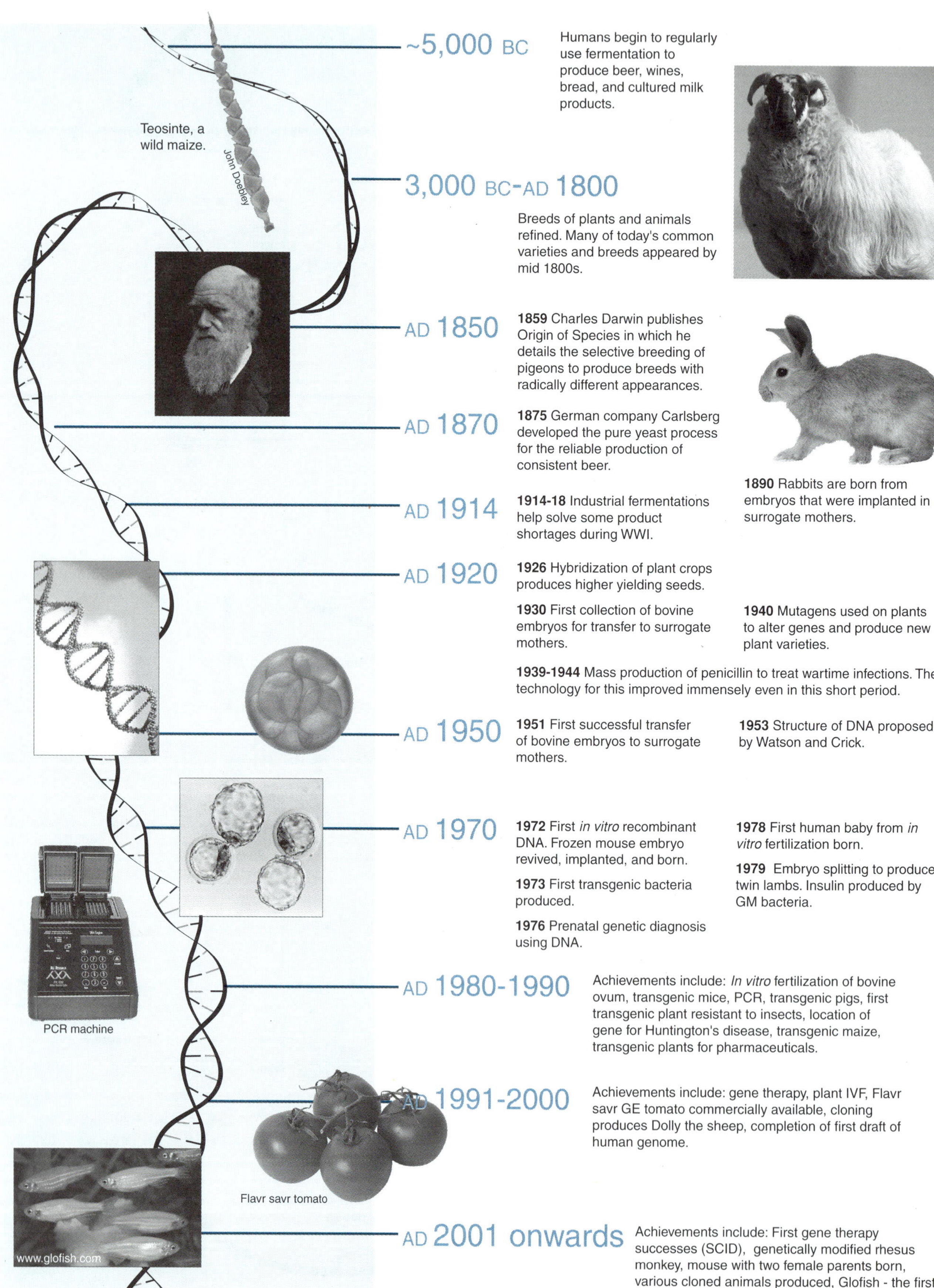

Teosinte, a wild maize.

John Doebley

~5,000 BC Humans begin to regularly use fermentation to produce beer, wines, bread, and cultured milk products.

3,000 BC-AD 1800 Breeds of plants and animals refined. Many of today's common varieties and breeds appeared by mid 1800s.

AD 1850 **1859** Charles Darwin publishes Origin of Species in which he details the selective breeding of pigeons to produce breeds with radically different appearances.

AD 1870 **1875** German company Carlsberg developed the pure yeast process for the reliable production of consistent beer.

1890 Rabbits are born from embryos that were implanted in surrogate mothers.

AD 1914 **1914-18** Industrial fermentations help solve some product shortages during WWI.

AD 1920 **1926** Hybridization of plant crops produces higher yielding seeds.

1930 First collection of bovine embryos for transfer to surrogate mothers.

1940 Mutagens used on plants to alter genes and produce new plant varieties.

1939-1944 Mass production of penicillin to treat wartime infections. The technology for this improved immensely even in this short period.

AD 1950 **1951** First successful transfer of bovine embryos to surrogate mothers.

1953 Structure of DNA proposed by Watson and Crick.

AD 1970 **1972** First *in vitro* recombinant DNA. Frozen mouse embryo revived, implanted, and born.

1978 First human baby from *in vitro* fertilization born.

1973 First transgenic bacteria produced.

1979 Embryo splitting to produce twin lambs. Insulin produced by GM bacteria.

1976 Prenatal genetic diagnosis using DNA.

PCR machine

AD 1980-1990 Achievements include: *In vitro* fertilization of bovine ovum, transgenic mice, PCR, transgenic pigs, first transgenic plant resistant to insects, location of gene for Huntington's disease, transgenic maize, transgenic plants for pharmaceuticals.

AD 1991-2000 Achievements include: gene therapy, plant IVF, Flavr savr GE tomato commercially available, cloning produces Dolly the sheep, completion of first draft of human genome.

Flavr savr tomato

www.glofish.com

AD 2001 onwards Achievements include: First gene therapy successes (SCID), genetically modified rhesus monkey, mouse with two female parents born, various cloned animals produced, Glofish - the first genetically engineered pets commercially available.

Resources Information

Your set textbook should always be a starting point for information, but there are also many other resources available. A list of some readily available resources is provided below. Please note that our listing any product in this workbook does not, in any way, denote Biozone's endorsement of that product and Biozone does not have any business affiliation with the publishers listed herein.

Supplementary Texts

Chenn, P., 1997.
Microorganisms and Biotechnology, 176 pp.
ISBN: 0-71957-509-5
Good coverage of the nature of microorganisms, their culture and growth, and their roles in biotechnology. It includes chapters on the genetic engineering of microbes and enzyme technology.

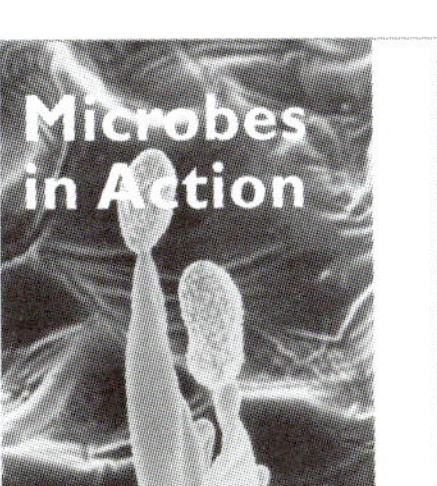

Clegg, C.J., 2002.
Microbes in Action, 92 pp.
ISBN: 0-71957-554-0
Microbes and their roles in disease and biotechnology. It includes material on the diversity of the microbial world, microbiological techniques, and a short account of enzyme technology.

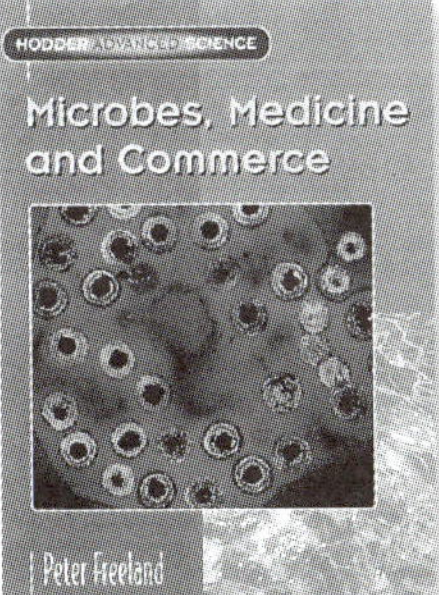

Freeland, P., 1999
Hodder Advanced Science: Microbes, Medicine, and Commerce, 160 pp.
Publisher: Hodder and Stoughton
ISBN: 0340731036
Comments: *Coverage of biotechnology, microbiology, pathology, and immunity.*

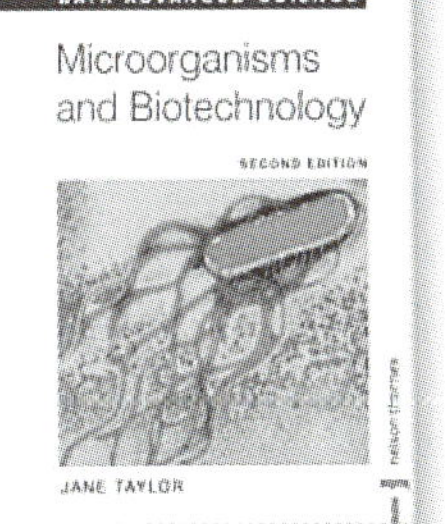

Taylor, J., 2001.
Microorganisms and Biotechnology, 192 pp.
Publisher: NelsonThornes.
Available in Australia through Thomson Learning
ISBN: 0-17-448255-8
Comments: *Good coverage of this topic, including pathogens and disease, defence, and the use of microbes in industry and medicine.*

Biology Dictionaries

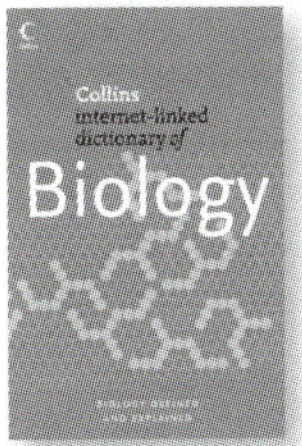

Hale, W.G. **Collins: Dictionary of Biology** 4 ed. 2005, 528 pp. Collins. **ISBN**: 0-00-720734-4.
Updated to take in the latest developments in biology and now internet-linked. (§ This latest edition is currently available only in the UK. The earlier edition, ISBN: 0-00-714709-0, is available though amazon.com in North America).

Henderson, I.F, W.D. Henderson, and E. Lawrence. **Henderson's Dictionary of Biological Terms**, 1999, 736 pp. Prentice Hall. **ISBN**: 0582414989
An updated edition, rewritten for clarity, and reorganized for ease of use. An essential reference and the dictionary of choice for many.

Periodicals

Biological Sciences Review: *An informative quarterly publication for biology students.* Enquiries:
Philip Allan Publishers, Market Place, Deddington, Oxfordshire OX 15 OSE
Tel: 01869 338652
Fax: 01869 338803
E-mail: sales@philipallan.co.uk

New Scientist: *Widely available weekly magazine with research summaries and features.* Enquiries:
Reed Business Information Ltd, 51 Wardour St. London WIV 4BN **Tel**: (UK and intl):+44 (0) 1444 475636 **E-mail**: ns.subs@qss-uk.com
or subscribe from their web site.

Scientific American: *A monthly magazine containing specialist features. Articles range in level of reading difficulty and assumed knowledge.* Subscription enquiries: 415 Madison Ave. New York. NY10017-1111 **Tel**: (outside North America): 515-247-7631 **Tel**: (US& Canada): 800-333-1199

Microorganisms and Biotechnology

Key concepts

▶ The microbial world includes viruses and bacteria, as well as representatives from Fungi and Protista.

▶ The industrial-scale culture of microorganisms requires bioreactors, which provide optimum growth conditions, either in continuous or batch culture.

▶ Microbial products can be produced as primary or secondary metabolites.

▶ Microbes are widely used in industrial processes, in food production, in bioremediation, and in medicine.

Key terms

antibiotic
antibiotic resistance
Archaea
aseptic technique
batch culture
bacterium (pl. bacteria)
binary fission
biofuel
bioreactor
bioremediation
continuous culture
dilution plating
enzyme immobilization
food preservation
fungus (pl. fungi)
Gram stain
growth curve
lag phase
log (exponential) phase
microbe (=microorganism)
plasmid
primary metabolite
protist
secondary metabolite
sewage treatment
stationary phase
strain isolation
streak plating
virus

Weblinks:
www.thebiozone.com/
weblink/MnB-3725/

Learning Objectives

☐ 1. Use the **KEY TERMS** to compile a glossary for this topic.

Introduction to Microorganisms
pages 9-24

☐ 2. Recognize microbial groups, including the Archaea, in a named classification system. Describe the distinguishing features of **viruses**, **bacteria**, **fungi**, and **protists**. Comment on the role of these microbial groups in biotechnology.

☐ 3. Describe the life cycles of selected representative viral types, including reference to the process of viral replication in the host cell. Examples could include the retrovirus, HIV, the bacteriophage lambda (λ), or an enveloped virus such as *Influenzavirus*.

☐ 4. Describe the structure of a bacterial cell, as illustrated by *E. coli*. Identify the cell wall, cell surface membrane, nuclear zone, 70S ribosomes, flagella, and **plasmids**.

☐ 5. Describe the **growth curve** of a bacterial population. Explain why growth does not usually continue exponentially and identify exceptions to this.

☐ 6. Describe the role of **antibiotics** in inhibiting bacterial growth. Explain the mechanisms by which **antibiotic resistance** arises and how it spreads.

Microbial Culture
pages 25-27, 32-36

☐ 7. Identify some of the safety issues associated with working with microorganisms. Identify safe working practices and explain why they are necessary.

☐ 8. Describe the *in vitro* growth requirements of bacteria and fungi, including reference to carbon and nitrogen sources, mineral requirements, temperature, pH, and oxygen.

☐ 9. Describe or demonstrate the use **aseptic technique** to prepare and inoculate nutrient broths and nutrient agar plates, and use **streak plating** for **strain isolation**.

☐ 10. Describe the growth curves of fungi and bacteria in culture. Suggest how bacterial and fungal cultures might be maintained in the rapid phase of growth.

☐ 11. Describe the use of **dilution plating** to measure the density of a bacterial culture.

☐ 12. Annotate a diagram of an industrial scale fermenter (**bioreactor**), identifying the features associated with providing optimum culture conditions. Compare and contrast the features and applications of **batch culture** and **continuous culture**.

Applications of Microbes
pages 28-31, 36-50

☐ 13. Using named examples, describe the use of microbes in industrial processes, e.g. in producing alternative fuels, in **sewage treatment**, in **bioremediation**, and in mining.

☐ 14. Describe the production and use of microbial enzymes.

☐ 15. Describe the use of mircroorganisms in the food industry including in bread making, brewing, wine making, and the production of cultured milk products.

☐ 16. Describe how microbes themselves can be used as a food source (e.g. mycoprotein).

☐ 17. Recognize the importance of genetically modified microorganisms in the large scale production of valuable commodities including human proteins (e.g. insulin).

☐ 18. Recognize that methods of **food preservation** (e.g. drying, salting, canning) are important in many aspects of food biotechnology to prevent microbial growth.

Microbial Groups

In order to distinguish organisms, it is desirable to classify and name them (a science known as **taxonomy**). An effective classification system requires features that are distinctive to a particular group of organisms. Revised classification systems, recognizing three domains (rather than five kingdoms) are now recognized as better representations of the true diversity of life. However, for the purposes of describing the groups with which we are most familiar, the five kingdom system (used here) is still appropriate. The three kingdoms commonly associated with microbiology are described below in summaries and diagrams.

SUPERKINGDOM: PROKARYOTAE (Bacteria)

- Also known as prokaryotes. The term moneran is no longer in use.
- Two major bacterial lineages are recognized: the primitive **Archaebacteria** and the more advanced **Eubacteria**.
- All have a prokaryotic cell structure: they lack the nuclei and chromosomes of eukaryotic cells, and have smaller (70S) ribosomes.
- Have a tendency to spread genetic elements across species barriers by conjugation, viral transduction, and other processes.
- Asexual. Can reproduce rapidly by binary fission sex.

- Have evolved a wider variety of metabolism types than eukaryotes.
- Bacteria grow and divide or aggregate into filaments or colonies of various shapes. Colony type is often diagnostic.
- They are taxonomically identified by their appearance (form) and through biochemical differences.

Species diversity: 10,000+ Bacteria are rather difficult to classify to species level because of their relatively rampant genetic exchange, and because their reproduction is asexual.

Eubacteria

- Also known as 'true bacteria', they probably evolved from the more ancient Archaebacteria.
- Distinguished from Archaebacteria by differences in cell wall composition, nucleotide structure, and ribosome shape.
- Diverse group includes most bacteria.
- The **gram stain** is the basis for distinguishing two broad groups of bacteria. It relies on the presence of peptidoglycan in the cell wall. The stain is easily washed from the thin peptidoglycan layer of gram negative walls but is retained by the thick peptidoglycan layer of gram positive cells, staining them a dark violet color.

Gram-Positive Bacteria

The walls of gram positive bacteria consist of many layers of peptidoglycan forming a thick, single-layered structure that holds the gram stain.

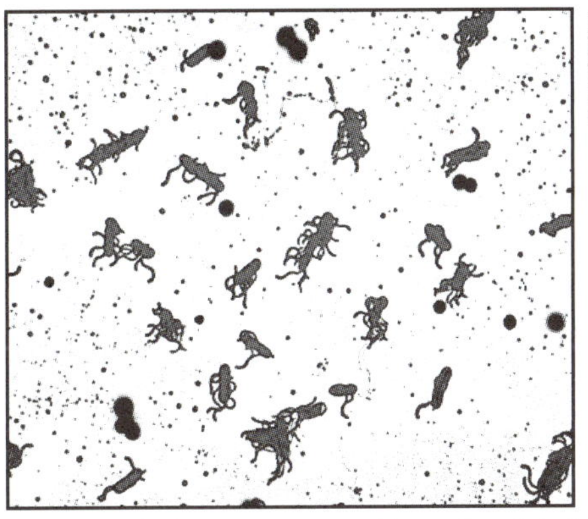

Bacillus alvei: a gram positive, flagellated bacterium. Note how the cells appear dark.

Gram-Negative Bacteria

The cell walls of gram negative bacteria contain only a small proportion of peptidoglycan, so the dark violet stain is not retained by the organisms.

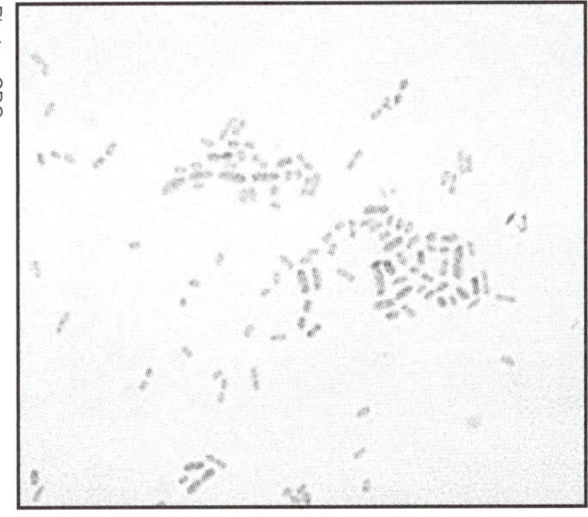

Photos: CDC

Alcaligenes odorans: a gram negative bacterium. Note how the cells appear pale.

SUPERKINGDOM EUKARYOTAE
Kingdom: FUNGI

- Heterotrophic.
- Rigid cell wall made of chitin.
- Vary from single celled yeasts to large multicellular organisms.
- Mostly saprotrophic (ie. feeding on dead or decaying material).
- Terrestrial and immobile.

Examples:
Mushrooms/toadstools, **yeasts**, truffles, morels, molds, and lichens.

Species diversity: 80,000 +

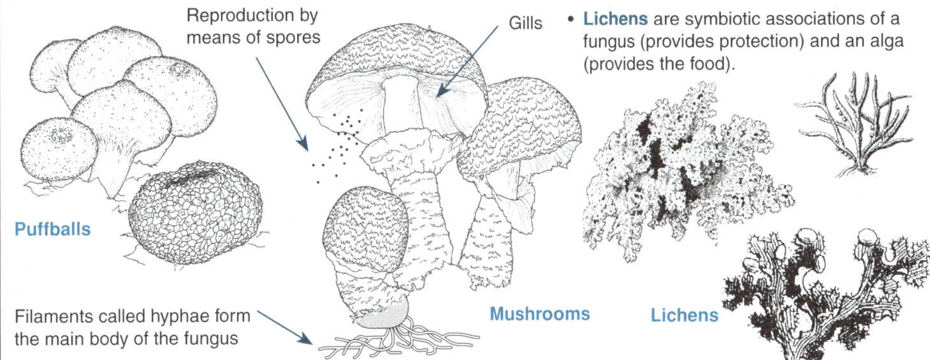

- **Lichens** are symbiotic associations of a fungus (provides protection) and an alga (provides the food).

Kingdom: PROTISTA

- A diverse group of organisms which do not fit easily into other taxonomic groups.
- Unicellular or simple multicellular.
- Widespread in moist or aquatic environments.

Examples of algae: green, red, and brown algae, dinoflagellates, diatoms.
Examples of protozoa: amoebas, foraminiferans, radiolarians, ciliates.

Species diversity: 55,000 +

Algae 'plant-like' protists

- Autotrophic (photosynthesis)
- Characterized by the type of chlorophyll present

Cell walls of cellulose, sometimes with silica

Diatom

Protozoa 'animal-like' protists

- Heterotrophic nutrition and feed via ingestion
- Most are microscopic (5 µm - 250 µm)

Move via projections called pseudopodia

cell walls

Amoeba

KNOW

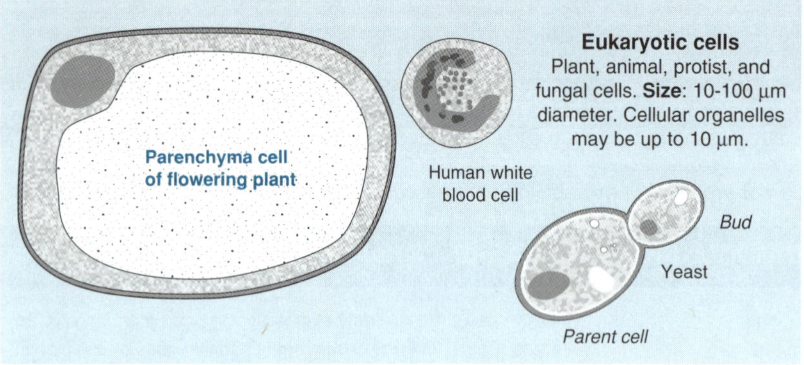

Unit of length (International System)

Unit	Meters	Equivalent
1 meter (m)	1 m	= 1000 millimeters
1 millimeter (mm)	10^{-3} m	= 1000 micrometers
1 micrometer (μm)	10^{-6} m	= 1000 nanometers
1 nanometer (nm)	10^{-9} m	= 1000 picometers

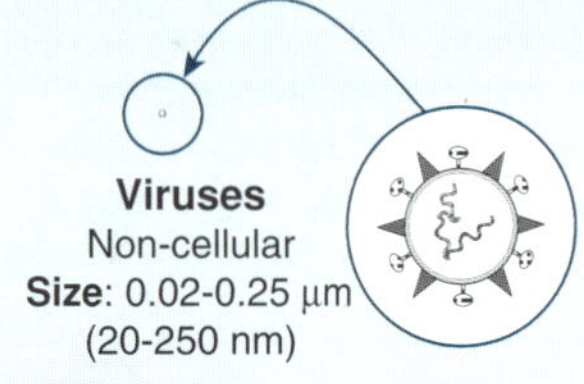

Micrometers are sometime referred to as microns. Smaller structures are usually measured in nanometers (nm) e.g. molecules (1 nm) and plasma membrane thickness (10 nm).

Many of the organelles within eukaryotic cells are the same size as bacterial cells. Viruses, which are non-cellular, are often called viral particles or virions. Although technically they are often thought to be non-living, they are an important and active component of the microbial world.

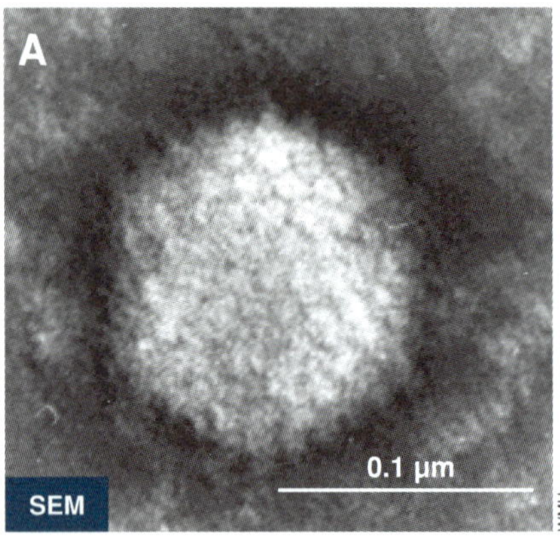

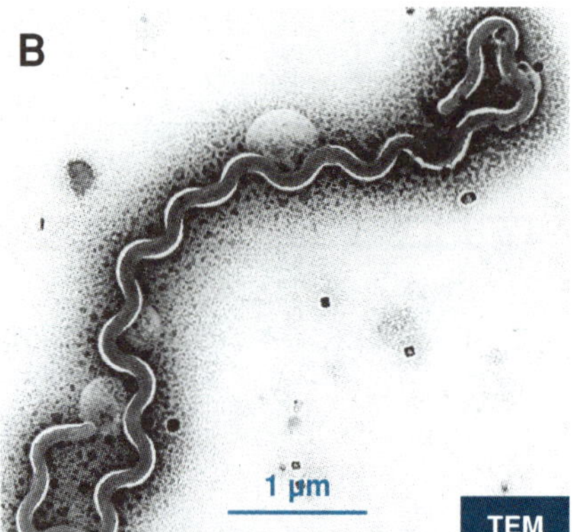

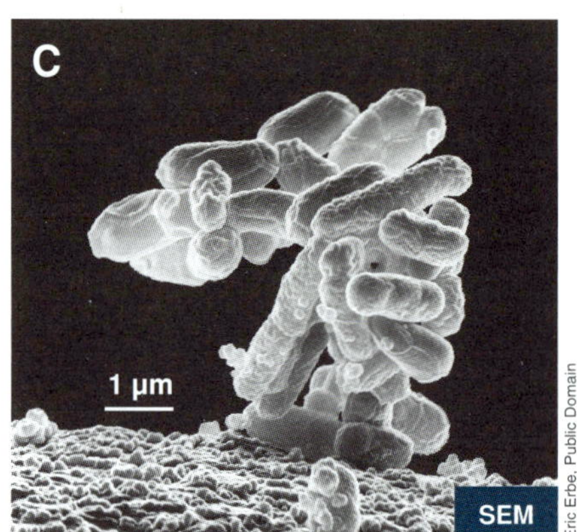

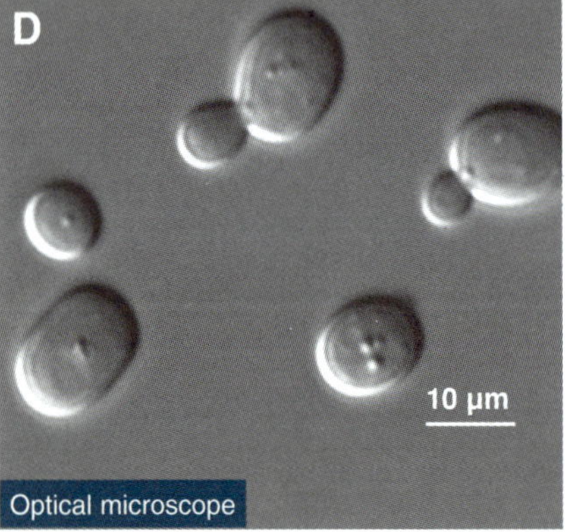

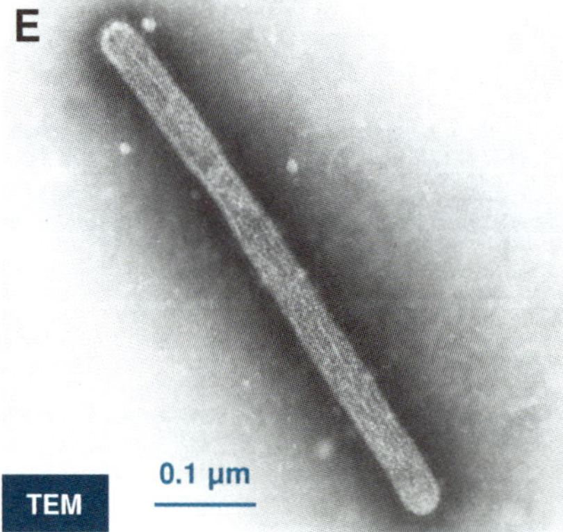

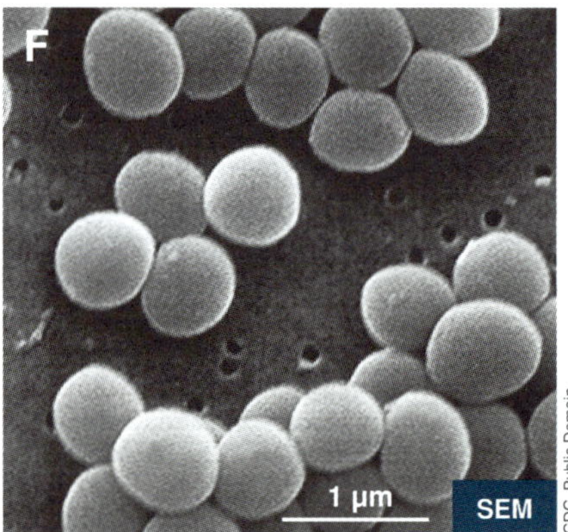

1. Identify each of the photographs (A-F) above as virus, bacterium, or fungus, and state the reason for your choice:

   (a) A: ____

   (b) B: ____

   (c) C: ____

   (d) D: ____

   (e) E: ____

   (f) F: ____

2. Bacterial cells often appear similar morphologically, e.g. as rods or cocci. Describe one way to easily categorize bacteria into one of two broad groups:

   ____

   ____

Features of Microbial Groups

A **microorganism** (or microbe) is literally a microscopic organism. The term is usually reserved for the organisms studied in microbiology: bacteria, fungi, microscopic protistans, and viruses. Most of these taxa also have macroscopic representatives. This is especially the case within the fungi. The distinction between a macrofungus and a microfungus is an artificial but convenient one. Unlike microfungi, which are made conspicuous by the diseases or decay they cause, macrofungi are the ones most likely to be observed with the naked eye. Examples of microfungi, which include yeasts and pathogenic species, are illustrated in this activity. These representatives of the fungal kingdom are those that most concern microbiologists.

1. Distinguishing features of Kingdom **Prokaryotae**:

____

____

____

____

____

____

____

____

____

***Spirillum* bacteria**

Staphylococcus

***Anabaena* cyanobacterium**

2. Distinguishing features of Kingdom **Protista** (**Protoctista**):

____

____

____

____

____

____

____

____

Foraminiferan

***Spirogyra* algae**

Diatoms: *Pleurosigma*

3. Distinguishing features of Kingdom **Fungi** (microfungi):

____

____

____

____

____

____

____

____

***Curvularia* sp. conidiophore**

Yeast cells in solution

***Microsporum distortum* (a pathogenic fungus)**

Microorganisms & Biotechnology

Related activities: *Microbial Groups*
Weblinks: *Types of Microbes*

KNOW

The Structure of Viruses

A **virus** is an infectious, highly specialized intracellular parasite. A typical virus (**virion**) contains a single type of nucleic acid (DNA or RNA) encased in a protein coat (**capsid**). Some viruses have an additional membrane, called an envelope, surrounding the capsid. Viruses have no metabolic machinery of their own, and must infect a host cell and use its cellular machinery to replicate. Most viruses are very small, and contain only a small amount of genetic information. However, some viruses (e.g. mimivirus) are quite large (400 nm) and have over 1000 genes. Being non-cellular, viruses do not conform to the existing criteria upon which a five or six kingdom classification system is based. Viruses are distinguished by their structure (see below) and by the nature of their genetic material (single or double stranded DNA or RNA). Viruses can be difficult to study because they must be cultured on a living host (e.g. animal, plant, bacterial culture, or tissue culture) in order to replicate.

Viral Structure

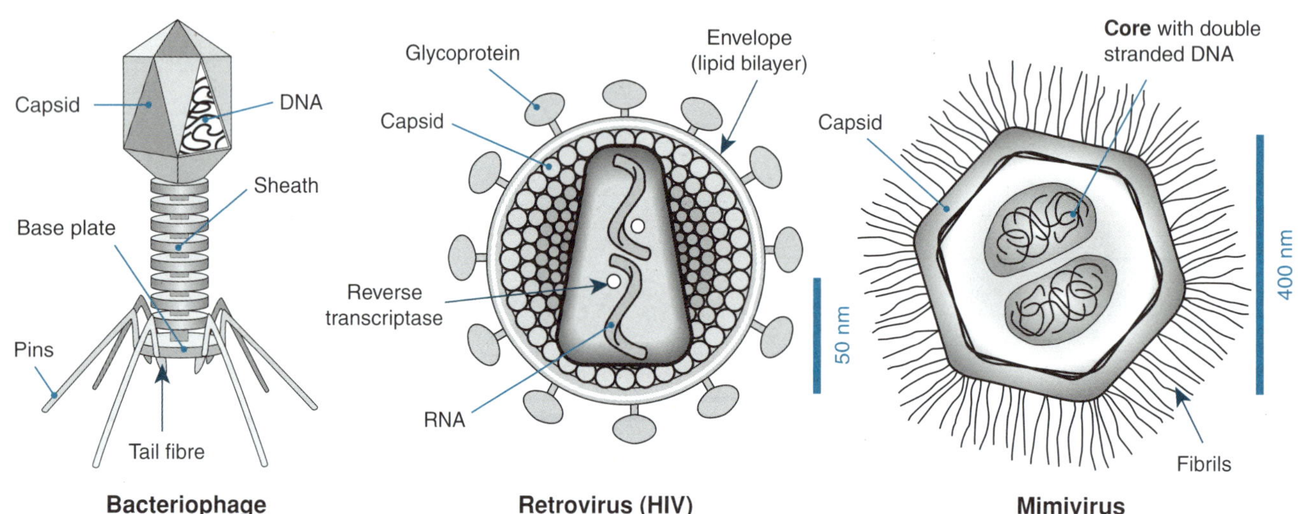

Viral Diversity

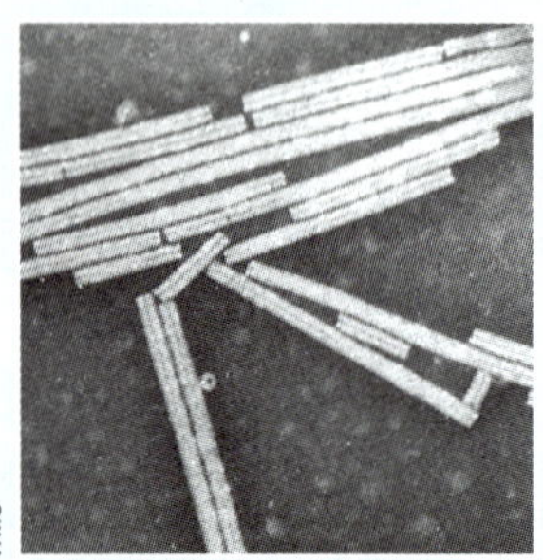

Tobacco Mosaic Virus (TMV): A single stranded RNA plant virus, with a helical capsid.

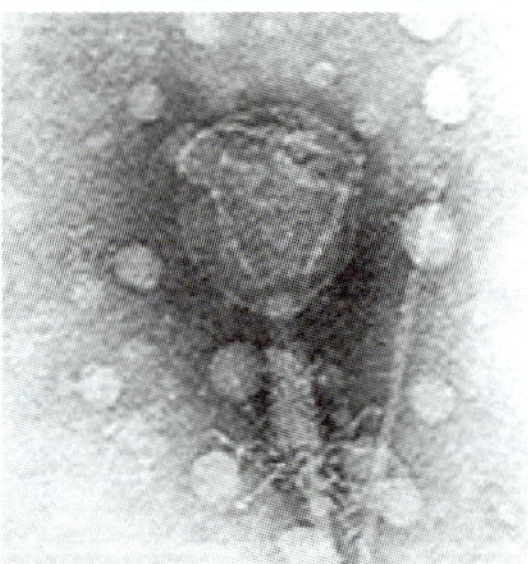

Bacteriophage: A complex virus that uses its contractile tail region to inject DNA into its bacterial host.

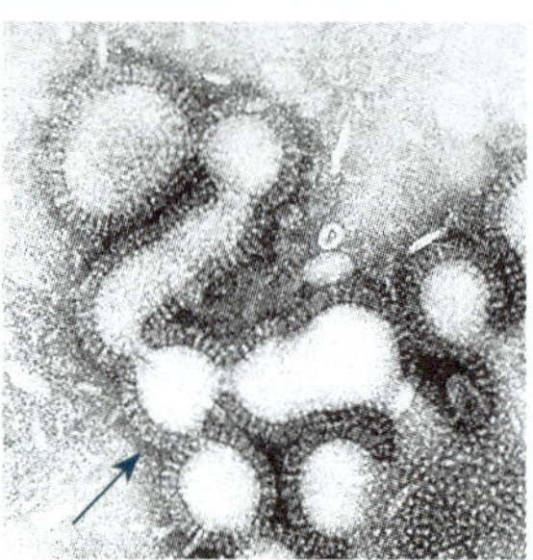

Influenzavirus has a flexible helical capsid and many glycoprotein spikes (arrowed).

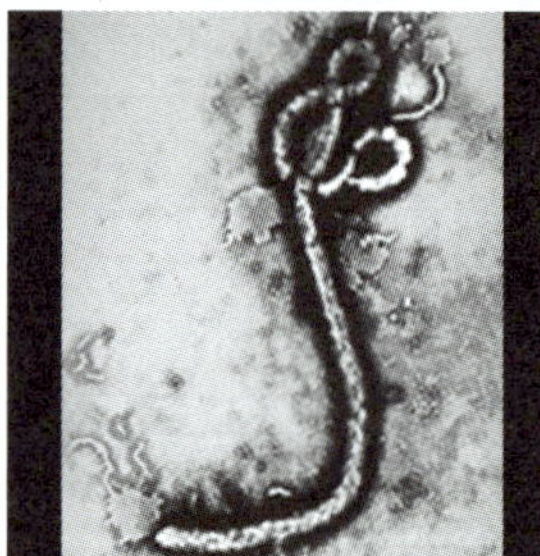

Ebola virus: A helical shaped, RNA filovirus. Ebola causes severe haemorrhagic disease (Ebola).

1. Describe the basic structure of a generalized viral particle (virion): _______________________________________

   ____

   ____

2. Explain why viruses are so difficult to classify using conventional classification systems: _______________

   ____

3. State whether you regard viruses as living or non-living. Give a reason for your answer: _______________

   ____

4. Outline why viruses are classified as obligate intracellular parasites: _______________________________

   ____

5. Explain why viruses are difficult to culture: ____

   ____

© BIOZONE International 2013
ISBN: 978-1-927173-72-5
Photocopying Prohibited

KNOW

Related activities: *Replication in Bacteriophages, Replication in Animal Viruses*
Weblinks: *Types of Microbes*

Replication in Bacteriophages

A **bacteriophage** is a virus that infects a bacterial cell. Sometimes bacteriophage replication does not immediately follow infection. Instead, the virus may enter a **lysogenic cycle**, where its genetic material is inserted into the host's DNA to form a **prophage**. The viral infection is said to be latent in this phase, because although the viral genes are present, they do not disrupt the bacterial cell.

Eventually a trigger causes the prophage to become active, and the **lytic cycle** begins. During the lytic cycle the host's cellular machinery is used to produce new virions. The lytic cycle results in death of the host cell through lysis (breaking) of the cell. Lysis allows the new bacteriophages to escape and infect other bacterial cells.

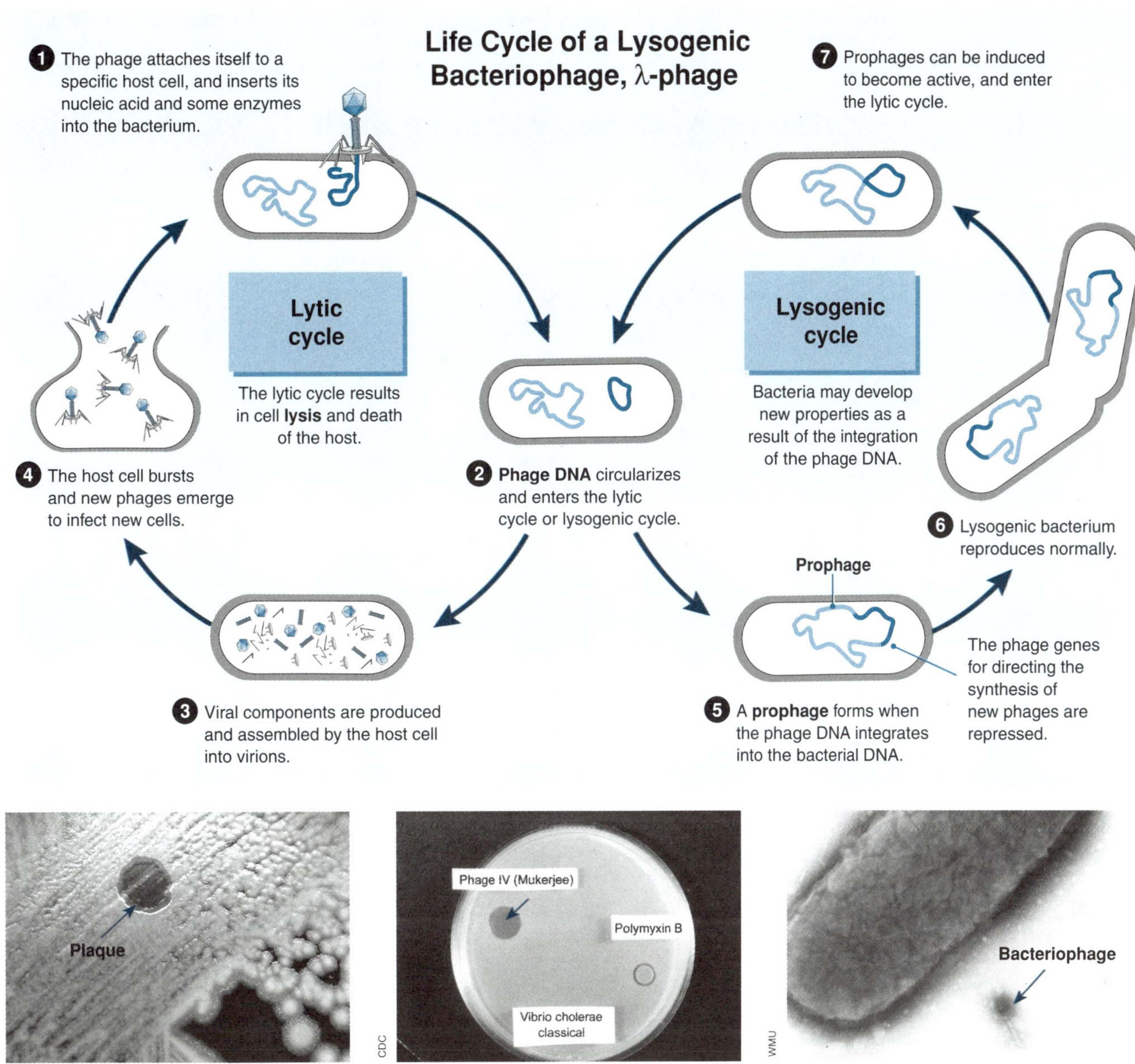

Microorganisms & Biotechnology

Bacteriophages can be used in medicine to diagnosis which bacterial strains are causing a disease. Specific bacteriophages are grown on bacterial cultures. If phage infection occurs, a clearing (plaque) forms (above). This technique is called phage typing. The photos above show a test for *Bacillus anthracis* (above left) and a phage test for *Vibrio cholerae,* the cholera pathogen (above right).

In the photo above, a bacteriophage approaches a rod-shaped bacterium. Pili (not visible) protrude from the bacterium's surface and act as phage receptors.

1. Contrast the lytic and lysogenic cycles of replication in a typical lysogenic bacteriophage (e.g. λ):

2. Identify one possible consequence to a bacterial cell of infection with a lysogenic phage:

3. Explain how bacteriophages can be used to detect the presence of a pathogen:

Related activities: Replication in Animal Viruses
Weblinks: Lytic Cycle, Lysogeny

KNOW

Replication in Animal Viruses

There are some differences between replication in animal viruses and in bacteriophages. Animal viruses differ in their mechanisms for entering a host cell and, once the virus is inside, the way in which the new virions are produced and released is different. This is partly because of differences in host cell structure and metabolism and partly because the structure of animal viruses themselves is highly variable. Enveloped viruses bud out from the host cell, whereas those without an envelope are released by rupture of the cell membrane. Three processes (attachment, penetration, and uncoating) are shared by both DNA- and RNA containing animal viruses but the methods of biosynthesis vary between these two major groups. Generally, DNA viruses replicate their DNA in the nucleus of the host cell using viral enzymes, and synthesize their capsid and other proteins in the cytoplasm using the host cell's enzymes. This is outlined below for a typical enveloped DNA virus. RNA viruses are more variable in their methods of biosynthesis. The example overleaf describes replication in the retrovirus HIV, where the virus uses its own reverse transcriptase to synthesize viral DNA and produce latent proviruses or active, mature retroviruses.

Entry of an Enveloped Virus into a Cell

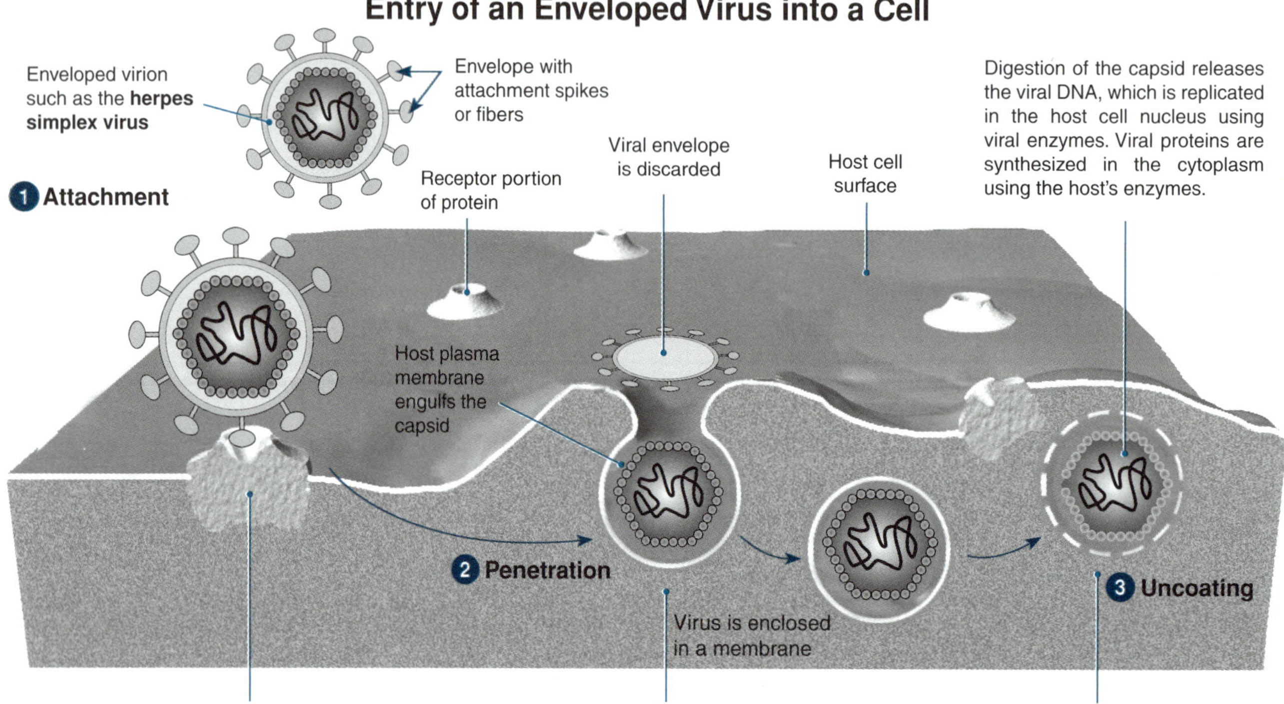

When a viral particle encounters the cell surface, it attaches to the **receptor sites** of proteins on the cell's plasma membrane.

Once the viral particle is attached, the host cell begins to engulf the virus by **endocytosis**. This is the cell's usual response to foreign particles.

The nucleic acid core is uncoated and the **biosynthesis** of new viruses begins. Mature virions are released by budding from the host cell.

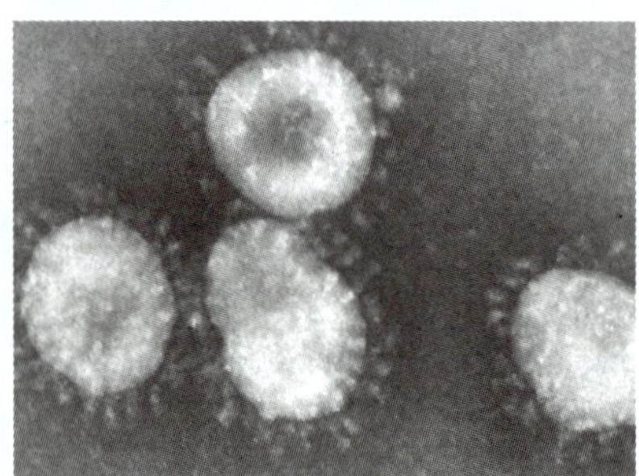

Coronaviruses are irregularly shaped viruses associated with upper respiratory infections and SARS. The envelope bears distinctive projections.

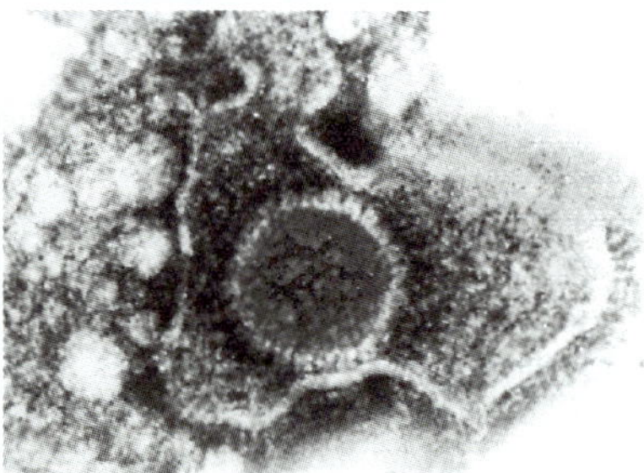

Herpesviruses are medium-sized enveloped viruses that cause various diseases including fever blisters, chickenpox, shingles, and herpes.

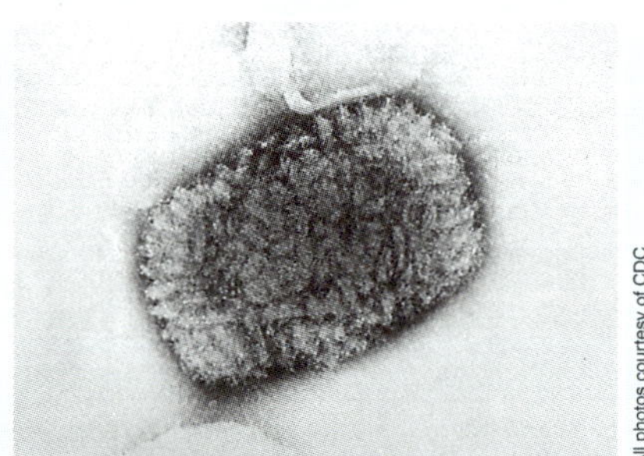

This **Vaccinia** virus belongs to the family of pox viruses; large (200-350 nm), enveloped DNA viruses that cause diseases such as smallpox.

All photos courtesy of CDC

1. Describe the purpose of the glycoprotein spikes found on some enveloped viruses: _______________________

____

2. (a) Explain the significance of endocytosis to the entry of an enveloped virus into an animal cell: _______________

____

____

(b) State where an enveloped virus replicates its viral DNA: ____

(c) State where an enveloped virus synthesizes its proteins: ____

KNOW

Related activities: *Replication in Bacteriophages*
Weblinks: *HIV Life Cycle, Retrovirus Life Cycle*

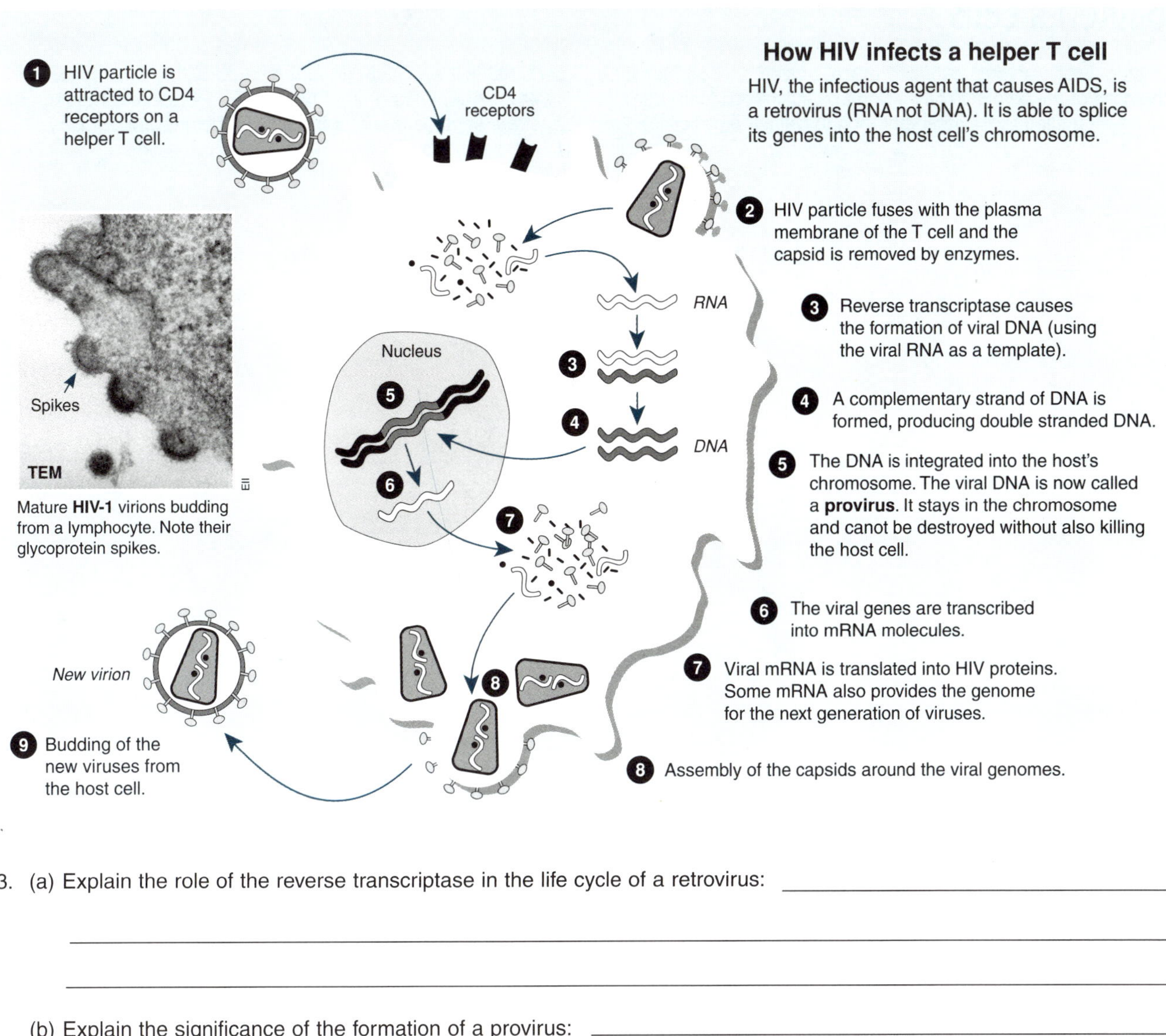

How HIV infects a helper T cell

HIV, the infectious agent that causes AIDS, is a retrovirus (RNA not DNA). It is able to splice its genes into the host cell's chromosome.

Mature **HIV-1** virions budding from a lymphocyte. Note their glycoprotein spikes.

3. (a) Explain the role of the reverse transcriptase in the life cycle of a retrovirus: _______________________

____

____

   (b) Explain the significance of the formation of a provirus: _______________________________

____

____

____

____

4. Complete the following table comparing viral replication in bacteriophage and animal viruses:

Stage	Bacteriophage	Animal viruses
Attachment	Tail fibres attach to cell wall proteins	
Penetration	Viral DNA injected into host cell	
Uncoating	Not required	
Biosynthesis	In cytoplasm of host	In the nucleus and cytoplasm (DNA viruses) or cytoplasm (RNA viruses)
Chronic infection	Lysogeny (virus in lysogenic cycle)	
Release	Host cell is lysed	

Microorganisms & Biotechnology

Bacterial Cells

Bacterial (prokaryotic) cells are much smaller and simpler than the cells of eukaryotes. They lack many eukaryotic features (e.g. a distinct nucleus and membrane-bound cellular organelles). The bacterial cell wall is an important feature. It is a complex, multi-layered structure and often has a role in virulence. These pages illustrate some features of bacterial structure and diversity.

Structure of a Generalized Bacterial Cell

Plasmids: Small, circular DNA molecules (accessory chromosomes) which can reproduce independently of the main chromosome. They can move between cells, and even between species, by **conjugation**. This property accounts for the transmission of antibiotic resistance between bacteria. Plasmids are also used as vectors in recombinant DNA technology.

Cell surface membrane: Similar in composition to eukaryotic membranes, although less rigid.

Cell wall: A complex, semi-rigid structure that gives the cell shape, prevents rupture, and serves as an anchorage point for flagella. The cell wall is composed of a macromolecule called **peptidoglycan**; repeating disaccharides attached by polypeptides to form a lattice. The wall also contains varying amounts of lipopolysaccharides and lipoproteins. The amount of peptidoglycan present in the wall forms the basis of the diagnostic **gram stain**. In many species, the cell wall contributes to their virulence (disease-causing ability).

Fimbriae: Hairlike structures that are shorter, straighter, and thinner than flagella. They are used for attachment, not movement. Pili are similar to fimbriae, but are longer and less numerous. They are involved in bacterial conjugation (below) and as phage receptors.

The cell lacks a nuclear membrane, so there is no distinct nucleus and the chromosome is in direct contact with the cytoplasm. It is possible for free ribosomes to attach to mRNA while the mRNA is still in the process of being transcribed from the DNA.

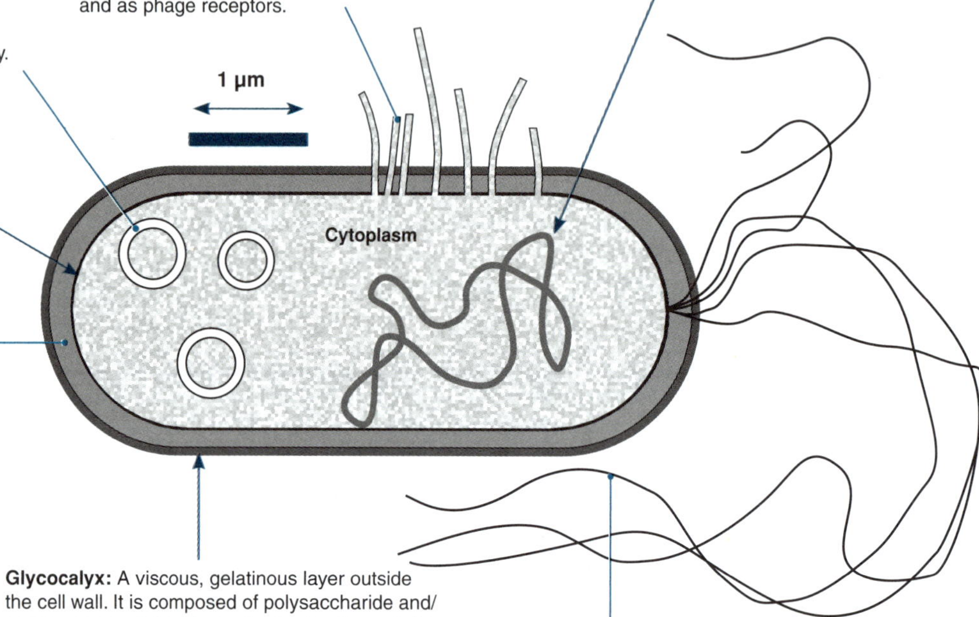

Glycocalyx: A viscous, gelatinous layer outside the cell wall. It is composed of polysaccharide and/or polypeptide. If it is firmly attached to the wall, it is called a **capsule**. If loosely attached, it is called a **slime layer**. Capsules may contribute to virulence in pathogenic species, e.g. by protecting the bacteria from the immune attack. In some species, the glycocalyx allows attachment to substrates.

Flagellum (pl. flagella): Some bacteria have long, filamentous appendages, called flagella, that are used for locomotion. There may be a single polar flagellum (monotrichous), one or more flagella at each end of the cell, or the flagella may be distributed over the entire cell (peritrichous).

Bacterial cell shapes

Most bacterial cells range between 0.20-2.0 µm in diameter and 2-10 µm length. Although they are a very diverse group, much of this diversity is in their metabolism. In terms of gross morphology, there are only a few basic shapes found (illustrated below). The way in which members of each group aggregate after division is often characteristic and is helpful in identifying certain species.

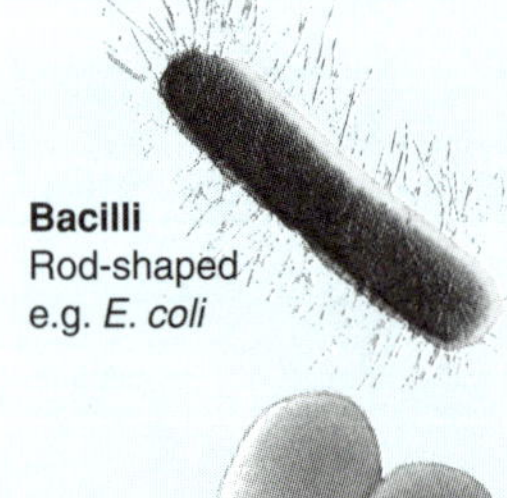

Bacilli
Rod-shaped
e.g. *E. coli*

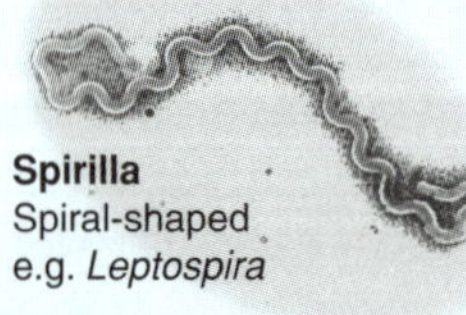

Cocci
Ball-shaped
e.g. *Staphylococcus*

Spirilla
Spiral-shaped
e.g. *Leptospira*

Bacilli: Rod-shaped bacteria that divide only across their short axis. Most occur as single rods, although pairs and chains are also found. The term bacillus can refer (as here) to shape. It may also denote a genus.

Cocci: usually round, but sometimes oval or elongated. When they divide, the cells stay attached to each other and remain in aggregates e.g. pairs (diplococci) or clusters (staphylococci), that are usually a feature of the genus.

Spirilla and vibrio: Bacteria with one or more twists. Spirilla bacteria have a helical (corkscrew) shape which may be rigid or flexible (as in spirochetes). Bacteria that look like curved rods (comma shaped) are called vibrios.

Bacterial conjugation

The two bacteria below are involved in conjugation: a one-way exchange of genetic information from a donor cell to a recipient cell. The plasmid passes through a tube called a **sex pilus** to the other cell. Conjugation is one of the ways in which bacteria can exchange genetic information (e.g. antibiotic resistance). It should not be confused with sexual reproduction, as it does not involve the fusion of gametes or formation of a zygote.

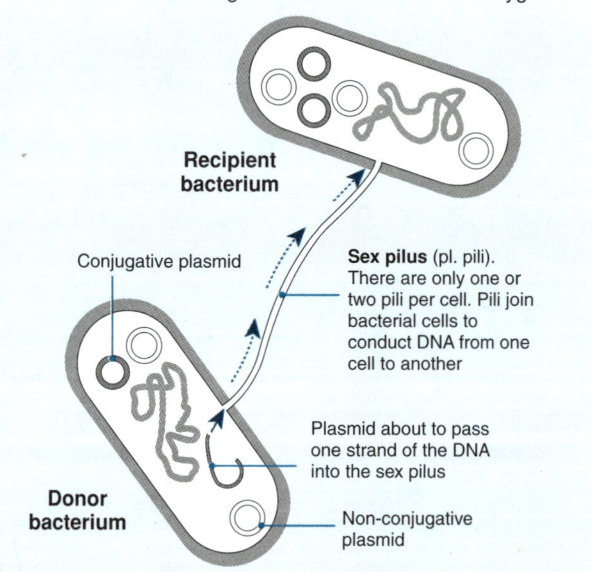

© BIOZONE International 2013
ISBN: 978-1-927173-72-5
Photocopying Prohibited

Related activities: Binary Fission
Weblinks: Bacterial Conjugation Animation

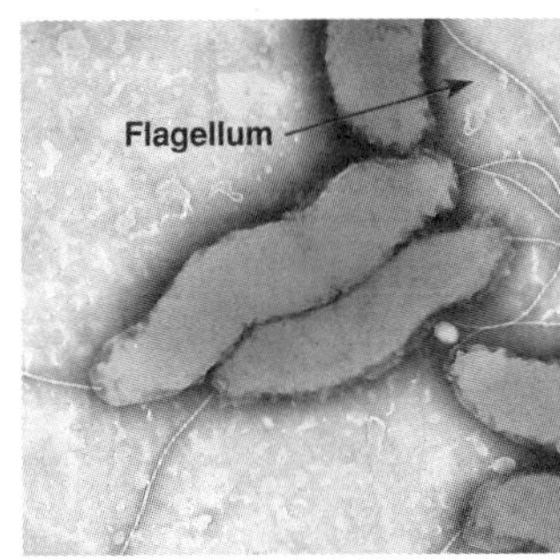

Campylobacter jejuni, a spiral bacterium responsible for foodborne intestinal disease. Note the single flagellum at each end (amphitrichous arrangement).

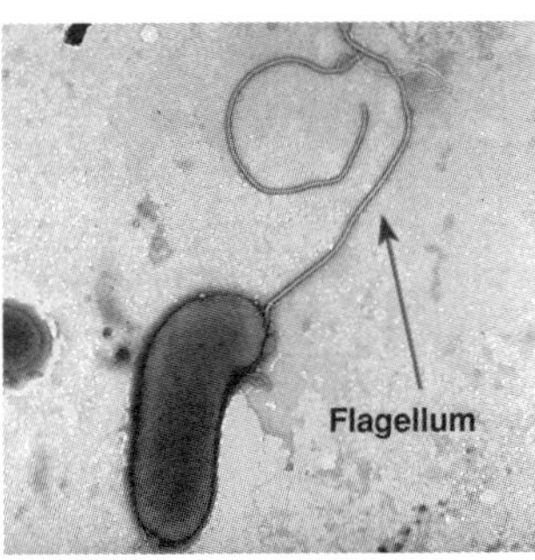

Helicobacter pylori, a comma-shaped vibrio bacterium that causes stomach ulcers in humans. This bacterium moves by means of multiple polar flagella.

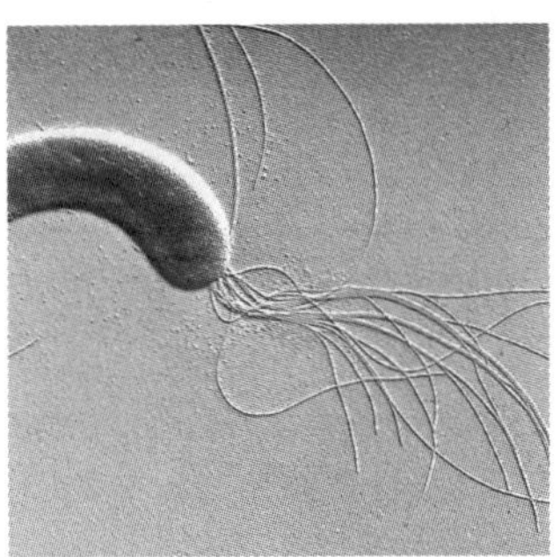

A species of *Spirillum*, a spiral shaped bacterium with a tuft of polar flagella. Most of the species in this genus are harmless aquatic organisms.

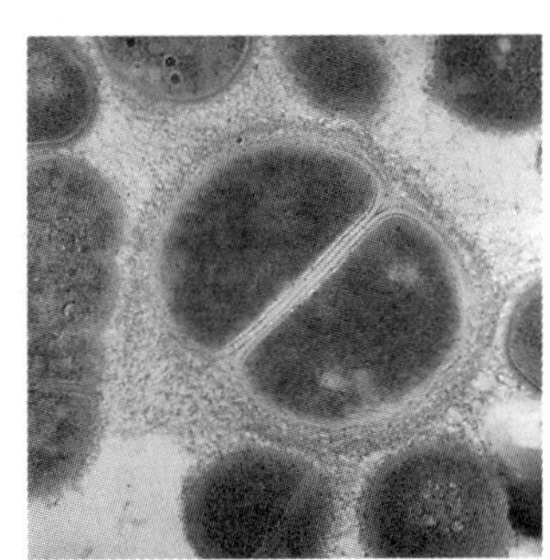

Bacteria usually divide by **binary fission**, a form of asexual reproduction. DNA is copied and the cell splits into two cells (above).

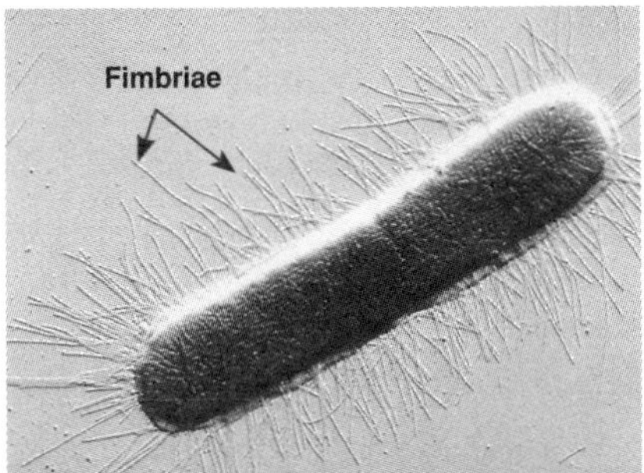

Escherichia coli, a common gut bacterium with **peritrichous** (around the entire cell) **fimbriae**. *E. coli* is a gram negative rod; it does not take up the gram stain but can be counter stained with safranin.

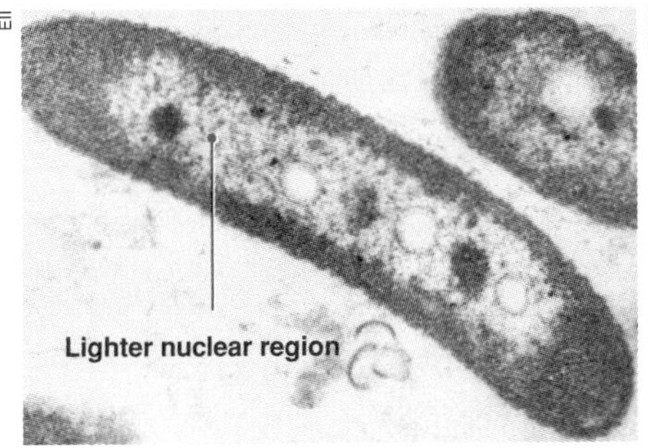

TEM showing *Enterobacter bacteria*, which belong to the family of gut bacteria commonly known as enterics. They are widely distributed in water, sewage, and soil. The family includes motile and non-motile species.

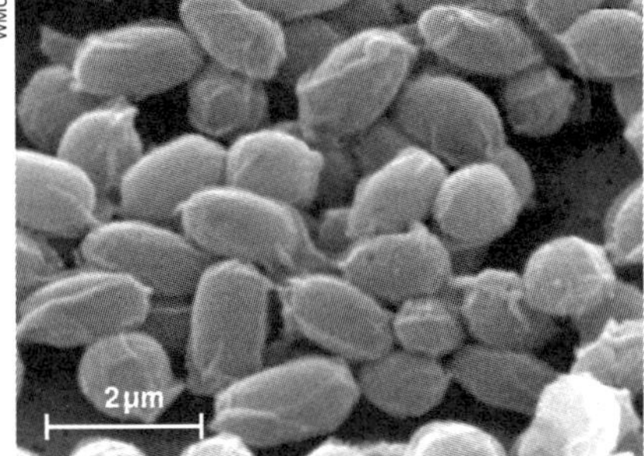

SEM of endospores of ***Bacillus anthracis*** bacteria, which cause the disease anthrax. These heat-resistant spores remain viable for many years and enable the bacteria to survive in a dormant state.

Microorganisms & Biotechnology

1. Describe three distinguishing features of bacterial cells:

   (a) ____

   (b) ____

   (c) ____

2. (a) Describe the function of flagella in bacteria: ____

   ____

   ____

   (b) Explain how fimbriae differ structurally and functionally from flagella: _______________________________________

   ____

   ____

3. From the information provided in this activity, identify the following:

   (a) A bacterium's usual method of reproduction: ____

   (b) A way to survive unfavorable conditions: ____

   (c) A way to transfer genetic information between bacterial cells: ____

   (d) A cell feature important in virulence: ____

   (e) The source of extra chromosomal material: ____

4. (a) Describe the location and general composition of the bacterial cell wall: _______________________________________

   ____

   ____

   (b) Describe how the glycocalyx differs from the cell wall: ____

   ____

   ____

Binary Fission

Binary fission is a form of asexual reproduction carried out by most prokaryotes (bacteria and cyanobacteria), in some eukaryotic organelles, such as mitochondria and chloroplasts, and by some unicellular eukaryotes (although the process is somewhat different in eukaryotic cells). In this process, the parent body divides into two, fairly equal, parts to produce two identical cells. The time required for a bacterial cell to divide, or for a population of bacterial cells to double, is called the **generation time**. Generation times may be quite short (20 minutes) while some species may have a generation time of several days.

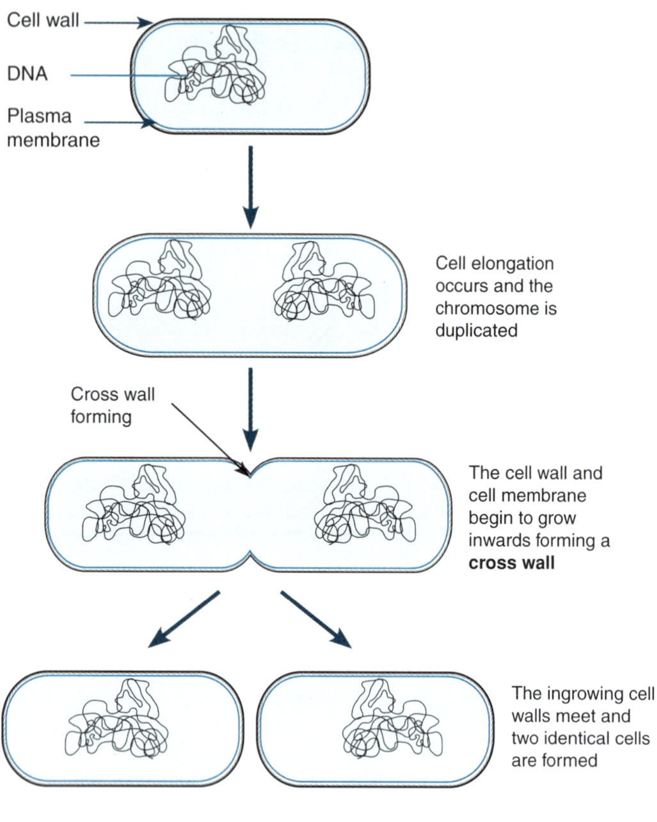

Most bacteria reproduce asexually by binary fission (left). The cell's DNA is replicated and each copy attaches to a different part of the plasma membrane. When the cell begins to pull apart, the replicate and original chromosomes are separated. Binary fission in bacteria does not involve mitosis or cytokinesis.

This gram positive coccus (right) is in the process of binary fission. A cross wall (arrow) has formed.

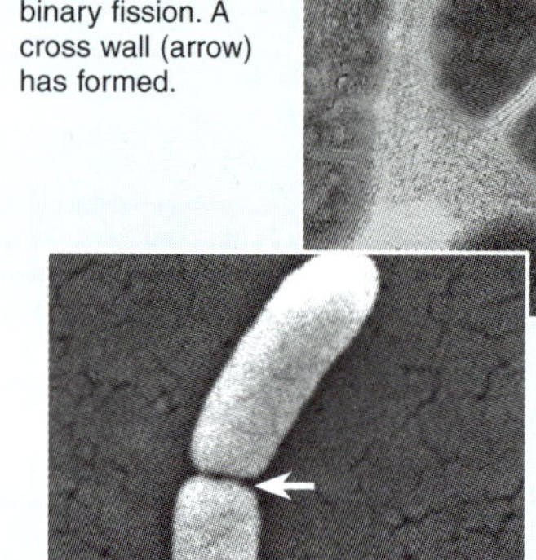

This *Salmonella typhimurium* bacterium (left) has completed cell division. The separation between the two cells can be clearly seen (arrow).

Generation time (minutes)	Population size
0	1
20	2
40	4
60	8
80	
100	
120	
140	
160	
180	
200	
220	
240	
260	
280	
300	
320	
340	
360	

1. What is **binary fission**? _______________________________________

____

____

____

2. Explain why the formation of the **cross wall** is important in binary fission:

____

____

____

3. Explain the term **generation time**: _____________________________

____

____

4. A species of bacteria reproduces every 20 minutes. Complete the table (left) by calculating the number of bacteria present at 20 minute intervals.

5. State how many bacteria were present after:

(a) 1 hour: ____

(b) 3 hours: ____

(c) 6 hours: ____

© BIOZONE International 2013
ISBN: 978-1-927173-72-5
Photocopying Prohibited

DATA

Review of Bacterial Structure

Bacteria are prokaryotes: simple, unicellular organisms lacking a distinct nucleus or membrane-bound organelles. They have several unique features, such as a peptidoglycan cell wall, plasmids, and glycocalyx. There is very little diversity in cell shape. The three main types of cell shape are bacilli (rod shaped), cocci (round), and spiral or vibrio (helical or comma shaped).

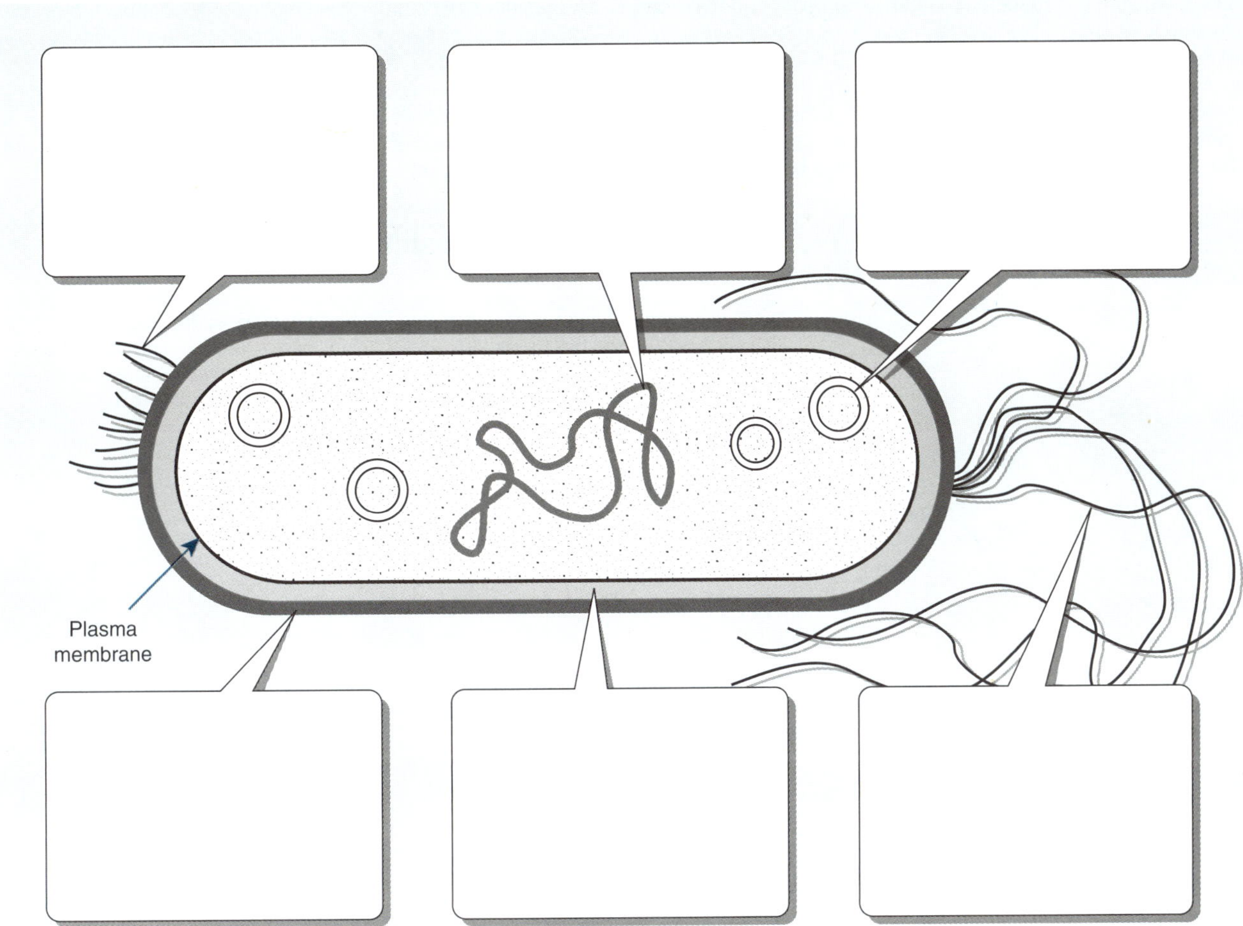

1. Complete the diagram above by labelling the boxes with the organelles or structures they represent and briefly describe the function of each. Use the activity pages about bacterial cells to help you.

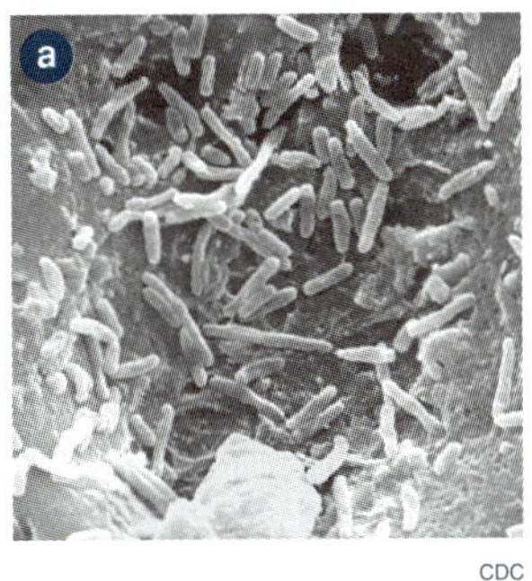

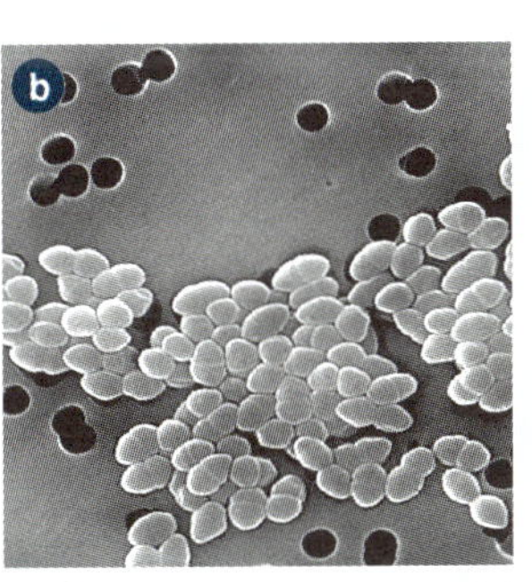

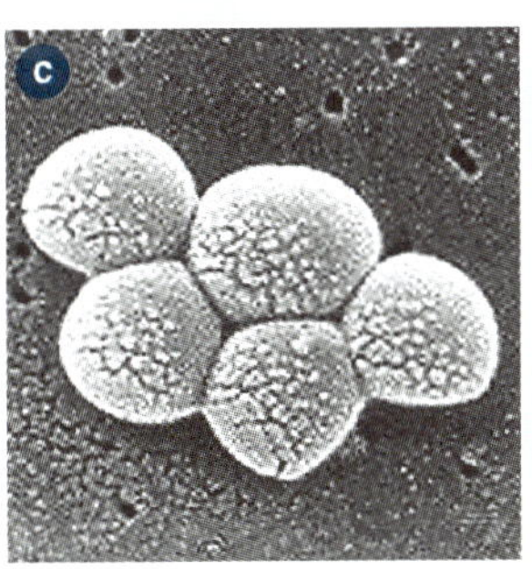

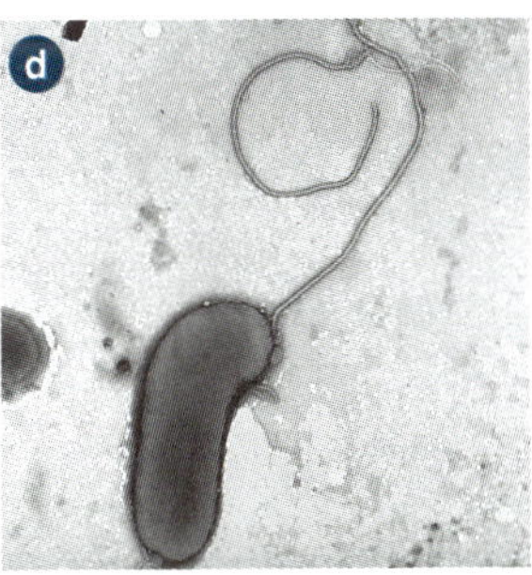

2. Using the correct terminology, identify the bacterial shapes shown in the photos above:

   (a) _______________________________   (c) _______________________________

   (b) _______________________________   (d) _______________________________

3. Briefly describe how variations in the peptidoglycan content of bacterial cell walls can be used to divide bacterial cells into two major groups (gram-positive and gram-negative bacteria):

   ____

   ____

Related activities: Bacterial Cells

KNOW

Antimicrobial Drugs

An **antibiotic** is a chemotherapeutic agent that inhibits or prevents microbial growth. Antibiotics are produced naturally by bacteria and fungi, but some synthetic (manufactured) antimicrobial drugs are also effective against microbial infections. Antimicrobial drugs interfere with the growth of microorganisms (see diagram below) by either killing microbes directly (**bactericidal**) or preventing them from growing (**bacteriostatic**). The ideal antimicrobial drug has **selective toxicity**, killing the pathogen without damaging the host. Some antimicrobial drugs have a narrow **spectrum of activity**, and affect only a limited number of microbial types. Others are **broad-spectrum drugs** and affect a large number of microbial species. When the identity of a pathogen is not known, a broad-spectrum drug may be prescribed in order to save time culturing and identifying it. However, broad spectrum drugs target both the pathogen and the host's normal microflora too. The resident microbial community usually controls the growth of pathogens and other microbes by competing with them. If they are removed, microbes in the community that do not normally cause problems, may flourish and become opportunistic pathogens. Some pathogens have developed **antibiotic resistance**. This means they have developed the ability to survive exposure to an antibiotic. It has serious implications on disease control.

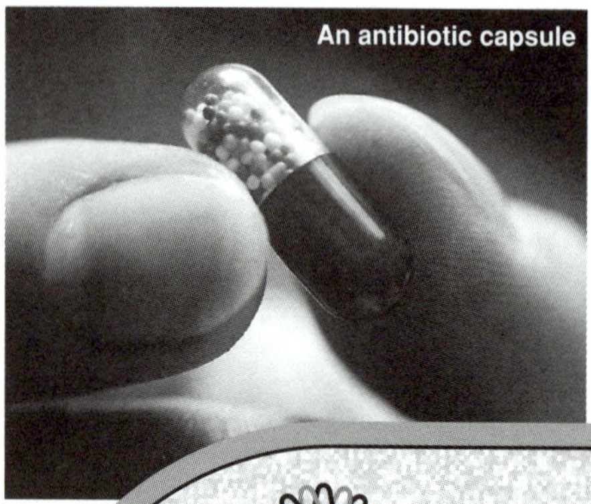

How Antimicrobial Drugs Work

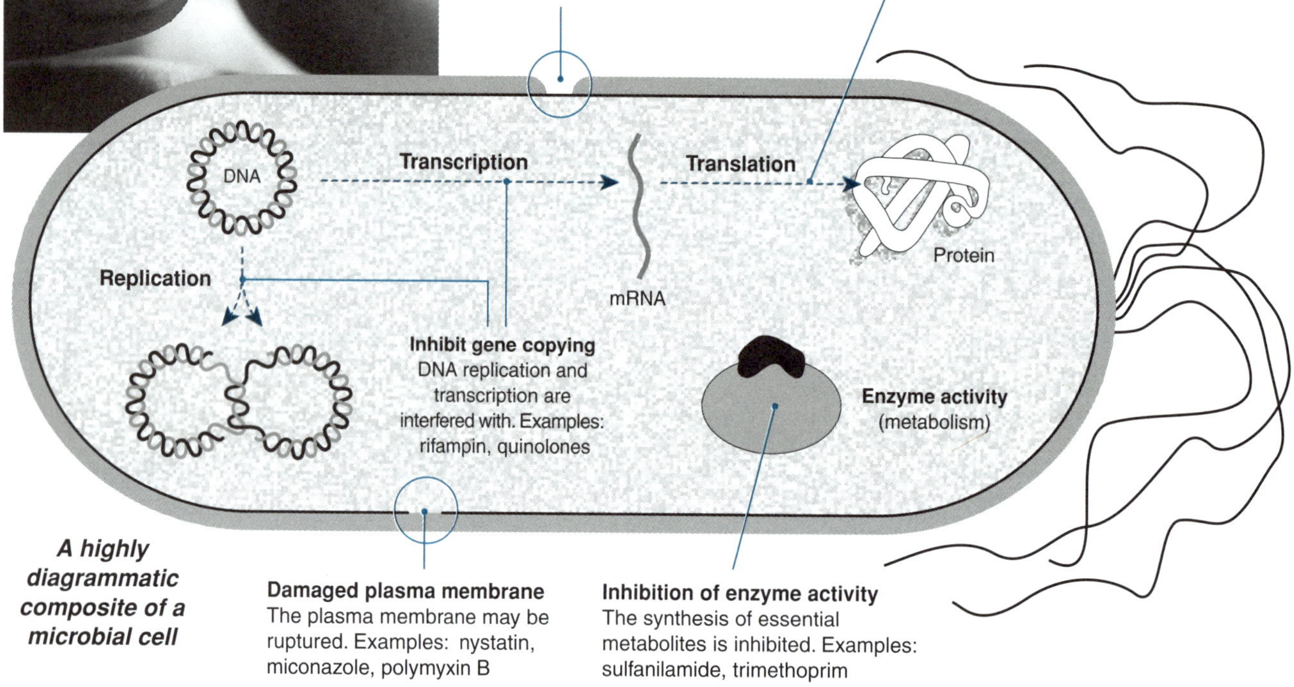

Damaged cell walls
The synthesis of new cell walls during cell division is inhibited. Examples: penicillin, vancomycin, cephalosporins, bacitracin

Inhibited protein synthesis
The process of translation is interfered with. Examples: erythromycin, tetracyclines, chloramphenicol, streptomycin

A highly diagrammatic composite of a microbial cell

Damaged plasma membrane
The plasma membrane may be ruptured. Examples: nystatin, miconazole, polymyxin B

Inhibition of enzyme activity
The synthesis of essential metabolites is inhibited. Examples: sulfanilamide, trimethoprim

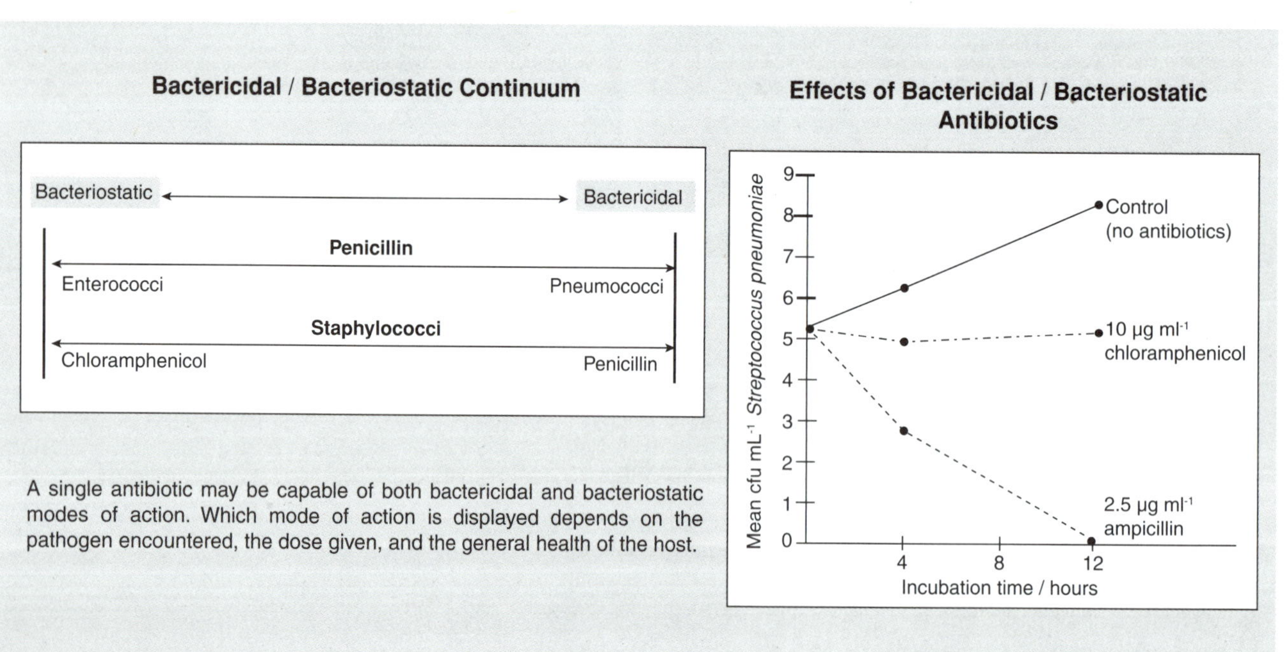

Bactericidal / Bacteriostatic Continuum

A single antibiotic may be capable of both bactericidal and bacteriostatic modes of action. Which mode of action is displayed depends on the pathogen encountered, the dose given, and the general health of the host.

Effects of Bactericidal / Bacteriostatic Antibiotics

© BIOZONE International 2013
ISBN: 978-1-927173-72-5
Photocopying Prohibited

Related activities: Drug Resistance in Pathogens
Weblinks: Penicillin Mode of Action

1. Discuss the requirements of an "ideal" anti-microbial drug, and explain in what way antibiotics satisfy these requirements:

____

____

____

____

2. Some bacteria have ways of tolerating treatment by antibiotics, and are termed 'superbugs'.

   (a) What is **antibiotic resistance**? ____

   ____

   ____

   (b) Why should a course of antibiotics be finished completely, even when the symptoms of infection have gone?

   ____

   ____

3. (a) Explain the difference between bacteriostatic and bactericidal antibiotics and give an account of how each works:

   ____

   ____

   ____

   (b) Using the graph on the previous page, identify the antibiotic with a bacteriostatic action and the antibiotic with a bacteriocidal action. Explain your answer:

   Bacteriostatic: ____

   ____

   Bactericidal: ____

   ____

4. Two students carried out an experiment to determine the effect of antibiotics on bacteria. They placed discs saturated with antibiotic on petri dishes evenly coated with bacterial colonies. Dish 1 contained four different antibiotics labeled A to D and a control labeled CL. Dish 2 contained four different concentrations of a single antibiotic and a control labeled CL.

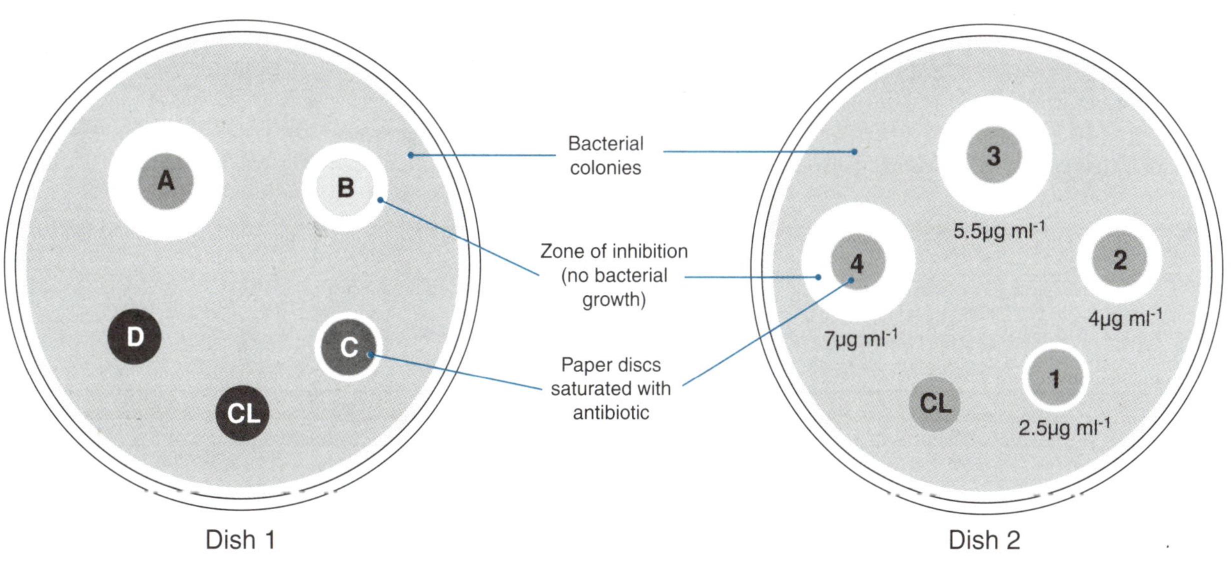

   (a) Which was the most effective antibiotic on Dish 1? _____________________________________

   (b) Which was the most effective concentration on Dish 2? Explain your choice: ________________

   ____

Drug Resistance in Pathogens

Drug resistance occurs when there is a reduction in the effectiveness of a drug. The spread of drug resistance amongst microorganisms is increasing, making it difficult to treat and control diseases such as tuberculosis and malaria. When microorganisms become resistant to most antimicrobial drugs, they are referred to as "superbugs". Examples include methicillin resistant strains of *Staphylococcus aureus* (MRSA), which have acquired genes that provide them with antibiotic resistance to all penicillins. Superbugs are now widespread, and the infections they cause are very difficult to treat. Genes for drug resistance arise through mutation. The high mutation rates and short generation times of microbial pathogens have contributed to the rapid spread of drug resistance. This is well documented for malaria, TB, and HIV/AIDS. Rapid evolution in pathogens is exacerbated by the strong selection pressure created by the wide use and misuse of antimicrobial drugs, the poor quality of available drugs, and poor patient compliance (e.g. not finishing a course of drugs). The most successful treatment for several diseases now appears to be a multi-pronged attack using a cocktail of drugs to target the pathogen at many stages.

Global Spread of Chloroquine Resistance

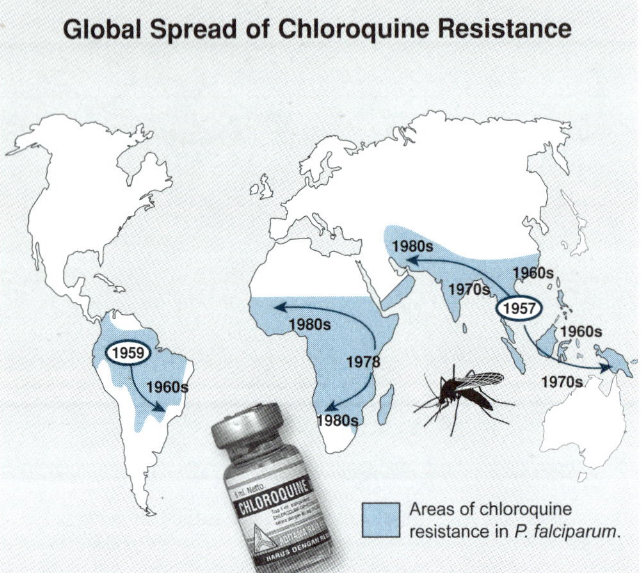

Malaria in humans is caused by several species of *Plasmodium*, a protozoan parasite transmitted by *Anopheles* mosquitoes. The inexpensive antimalarial drug **chloroquine** was used successfully to treat malaria for many years, but its effectiveness has declined since resistance to the drug was first recorded in the 1960s. Chloroquine resistance has spread steadily (above) and now two of the four *Plasmodium* species, *P. falciparum* and *P. vivax* are chloroquine-resistant. *P. falciparum* alone accounts for 80% of all human malarial infections and 90% of the deaths, so this rise in resistance is of global concern. New anti-malarial drugs have been developed, but are expensive and often have serious side effects. Some species of *Plasmodium* are already showing resistance to these new drugs.

Drug Resistance in HIV

Drug-resistant HIV strains arise when the virus mutates during replication. These mutations may alter drug binding capacity or increase viral fitness, or they may be naturally occurring polymorphisms (which occur in untreated patients). Drug resistance is likely to develop in patients who do not follow their treatment schedule closely, as the virus has an opportunity to adapt more readily to a "non-lethal" drug dose. The best practice for managing the HIV virus is to treat it with a cocktail of anti-retroviral drugs with different actions to minimize the number of viruses in the body. This minimizes the replication rate, and also the chance of a drug resistant mutation being produced.

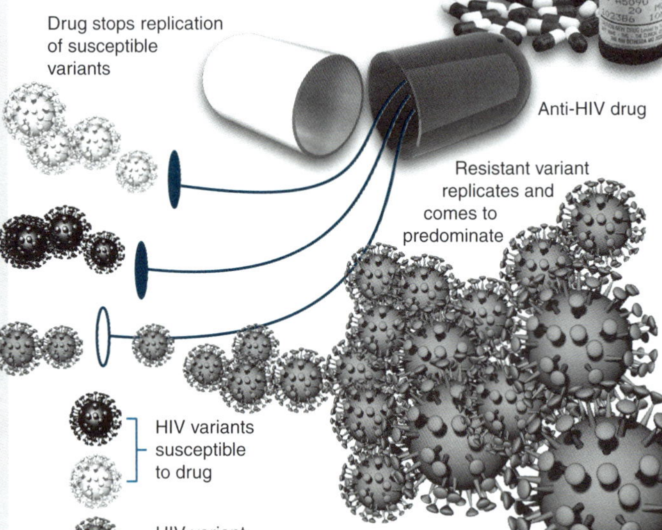

1. Describe how genes for drug resistance arise in a microbial population:

2. Briefly describe three mechanisms by which bacteria achieve drug resistance:

   (a)

   (b)

   (c)

3. Discuss the implications (to humans) of bacteria acquiring several different mechanisms of resistance:

Related activities: Antimicrobial Drugs
Weblinks: The Rise in Antibiotic Resistance, Why Evolution Matters Now

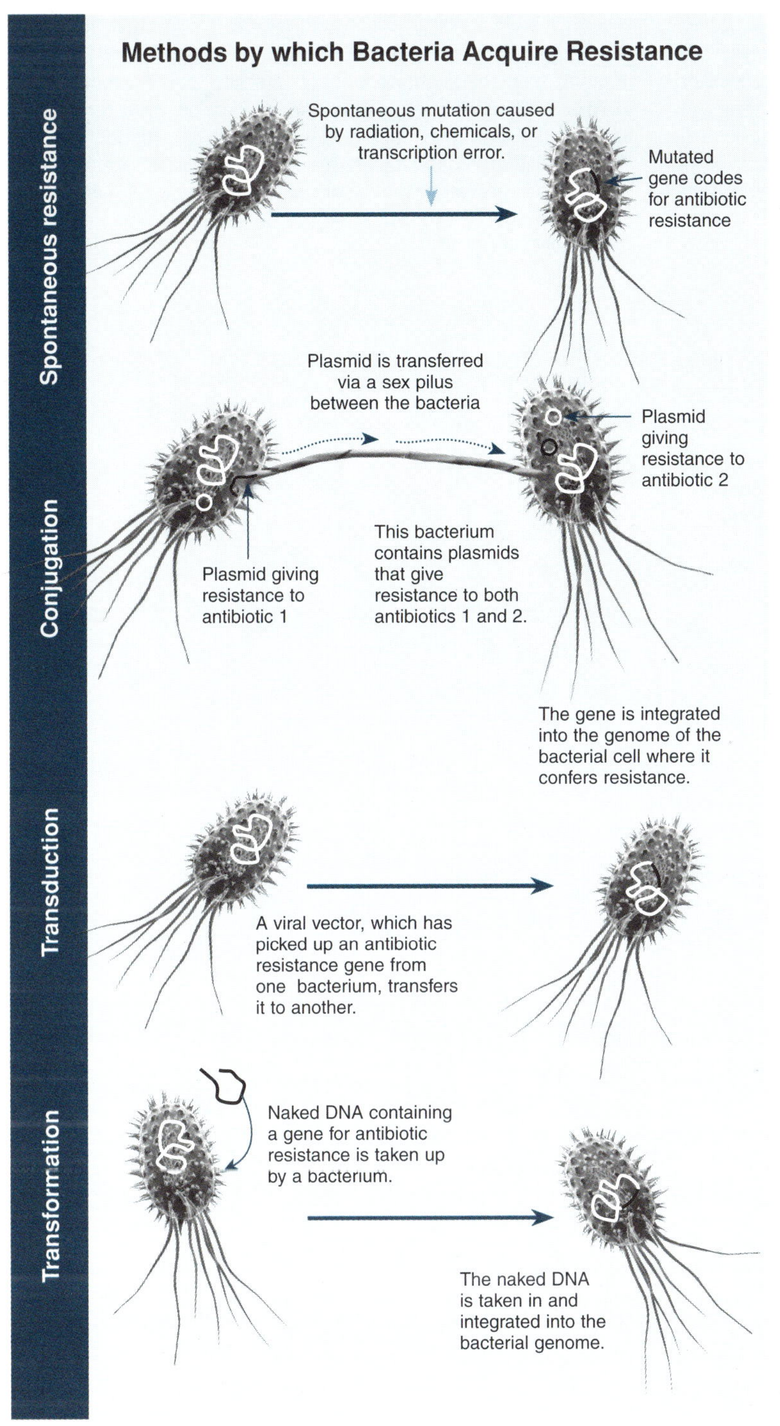

Mechanisms of Resistance

Inactivation

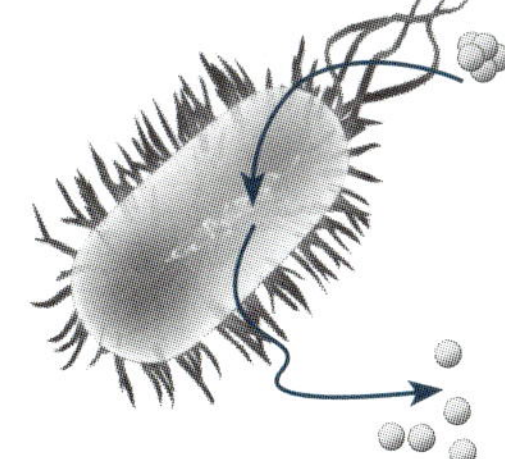

A mutated enzyme produced in the bacterium destroys the antibiotic. Many bacteria resistant to penicillin possess the enzyme penicillinase, which inactivates penicillin by catalyzing the destruction of bonds within the penicillin molecule.

Alteration of target

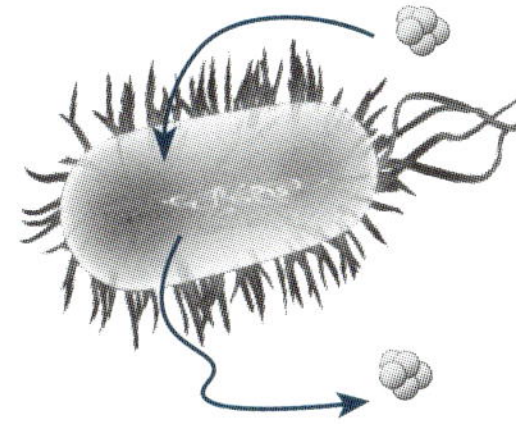

Some antibiotics (e.g. streptomycin) inhibit bacterial protein synthesis. However, if only one amino acid in either of two positions on a ribosome is replaced, a bacterium can develop streptomycin resistance.

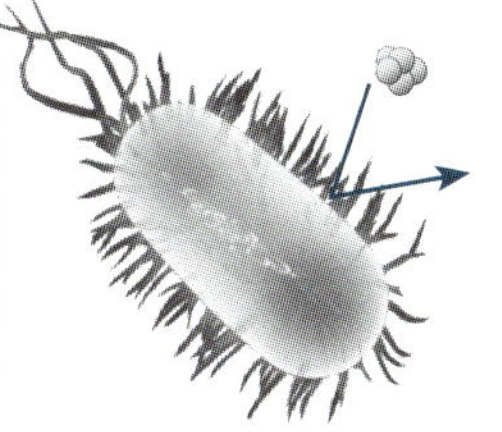

Some antibiotics, such as penicillin, interfere with cell wall synthesis. Therefore mutations to the cell wall proteins can result in resistance.

Alteration of permeability

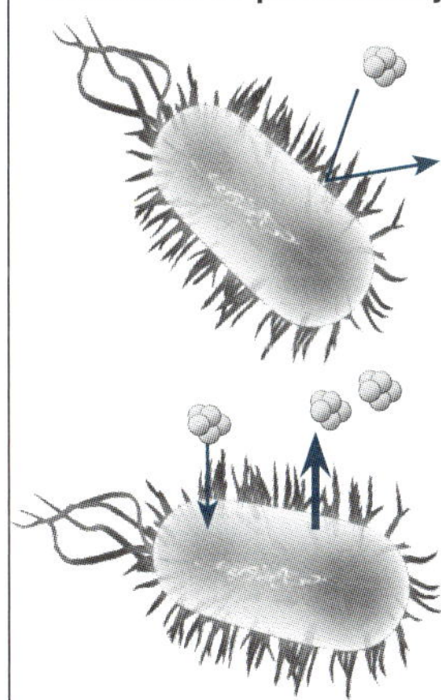

In order to be effective, antibiotics have to get into the bacterial cell and interfere with its cellular processes. Bacterial cells can acquire resistance by excluding the antibiotic or by slowing down its entry enough to render the antibiotic ineffective.

Bacteria can develop proteins that actively pump antibiotics out of their cell faster than the antibiotics can enter.

4. Discuss the factors contributing to the rapid spread of drug resistance in pathogens: _______________________

____

____

____

____

____

____

____

____

Fungi

The fungi are a large, successful group of eukaryotes that includes the yeasts, molds, and fleshy fungi. The study of fungi is called **mycology**. All fungi are chemoheterotrophs: they lack chlorophyll and require organic compounds for a source of energy and carbon. Most fungi are also **saprophytic**, feeding on dead material, although some are parasitic or mutualistic. Fungal nutrition is absorptive and digestion is extracellular (takes place outside the fungal body). Of more than 100,000 fungal species, only about 100 cause harm to humans or other animals. However, many are plant pathogens and virtually every economically important plant species is attacked by one or more fungi. Note that the **lichens** have been reclassified into the fungal kingdom. They are dual organisms, formed by a mutualistic association between a green alga or a cyanobacterium, and a fungus (usually an ascomycete). Features of two fungal groups: yeasts and molds are described below.

Single Celled Fungi: Yeasts

Yeasts are nonfilamentous, unicellular fungi that are typically spherical or oval shaped. Yeasts reproduce asexually by fission or budding. They are facultative anaerobes, a property that is exploited in the brewing, wine making, and bread making industries.

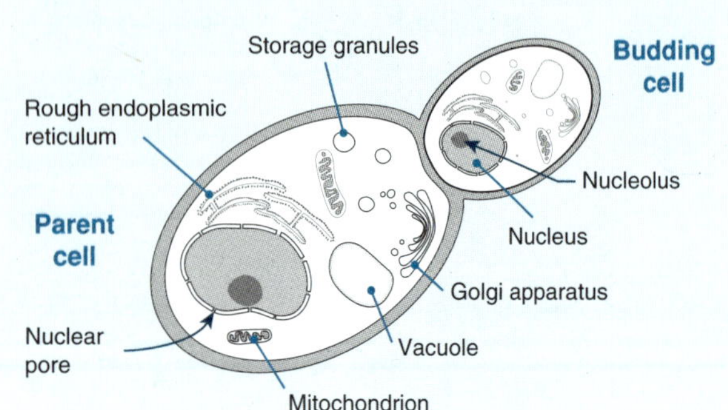

Filamentous Fungi: Molds

Molds are multicellular, filamentous fungi often divided by septa into uni-nucleate, cell-like units. When conditions are favorable, hyphae grow to form a filamentous mass called a **mycelium**.

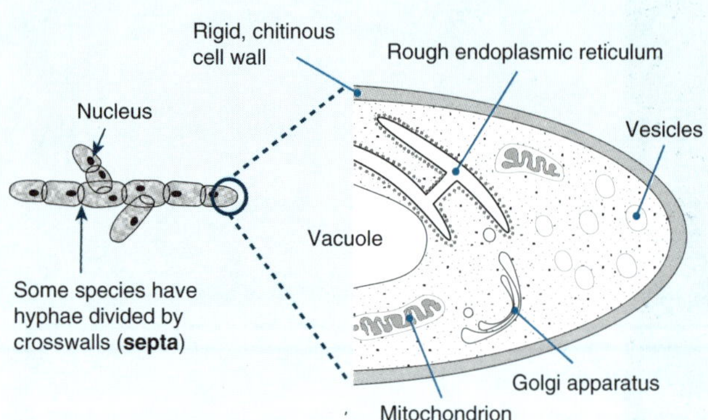

Reproduction in a Filamentous Fungus, *Rhizopus*

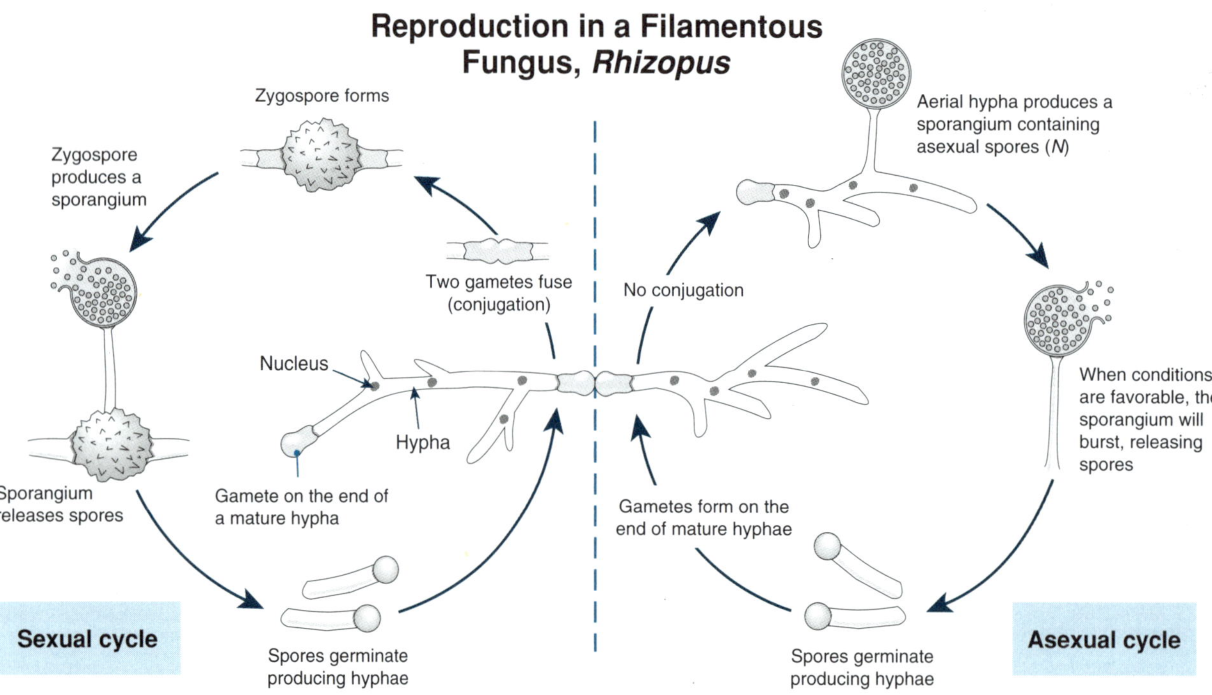

1. Describe three distinguishing features of fungi: ____

   ____

2. Describe the key differences in the reproductive strategies of yeasts and molds: ___________________

   ____

   ____

3. Identify two commonly exploited fungal species and describe how they are used:

   (a) ____

   (b) ____

© BIOZONE International 2013
ISBN: 978-1-927173-72-5
Photocopying Prohibited

KNOW

Related activities: Microbial Groups, Features of Microbial Groups
Weblinks: Types of Microbes-Fungi

Techniques in Microbial Culture

Bacteria and fungi may be cultured in liquid or solid media. These comprise a base of **agar** to which is added the nutrients required for microbial growth. Agar is a gelatinous colloidal extract of red algae, and can be used in solid or liquid form. It is used because of its two unique physical properties. Firstly, it melts at 100°C and remains liquid until cooled to 40°C, at which point it gels. Secondly, few microbes are capable of digesting agar so the medium is not used up during culture. The addition of microbes to an agar plate, or to liquid agar, is called **inoculation** and must be carried out under aseptic conditions. **Aseptic techniques** involve the **sterilization** of equipment and culture media to prevent cross contamination by unwanted microbes. Sterilization is a process by which all organisms and spores are destroyed, either by heat or by chemicals.

Microorganisms & Biotechnology

Conditions for the Culture of Bacteria and Fungi

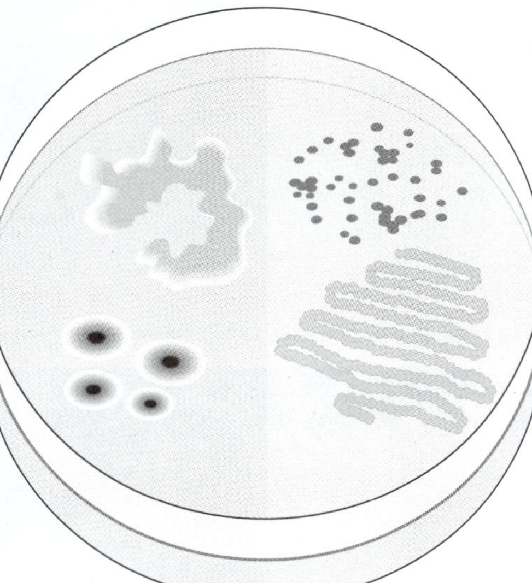

Fungi

Temperature: Most fungi have an optimum temperature for growth of 25°C, but most are adapted to survive between 5 and 35°C.

pH: Fungi prefer a neutral (pH 7) growing environment, although most species can tolerate slightly acidic conditions.

Nutrients: Fungi require a source of carbon and nitrogen to produce protein. They also require trace elements such as potassium, phosphorus and magnesium. Growth factors can be added to increase the rate of fungal growth.

Water potential: Fungi are 85-90% water by mass. Water is constantly lost from the hyphae via evaporation and must be replaced through absorption from the media. To aid water uptake, media have a water potential that is less negative than that of the fungal tissue.

Gaseous environment: The majority of fungi are aerobic and very few species can tolerate anaerobic conditions. This is why fungi always grow on the surface of a culture medium, not inside it.

Bacteria

Temperature: Most bacteria cultured in the school laboratory are classified as **mesophiles**. Mesophiles prefer temperatures between 20 and 40°C.

pH: Most bacteria grow optimally in media with a pH between 6 and 8. Very few bacteria can grow in acidic conditions.

Nutrients: Bacteria need a source of carbon, nitrogen and mineral salts as raw ingredients for cellular growth.

Water potential: All bacteria require water for growth. To prevent cell lysis or dehydration, the water potential of the medium must be such that net water fluxes into and out of the bacterial cell are minimized.

Gaseous environment: Aerobic bacteria will grow only in oxygenated environments, whereas obligate anaerobes (e.g. *Clostridium*) do not tolerate oxygen. Facultative anaerobes grow under aerobic conditions, but are able to metabolize anaerobically when oxygen is unavailable. All bacterial cultures benefit from a low concentration of carbon dioxide.

Inoculating Solid Media

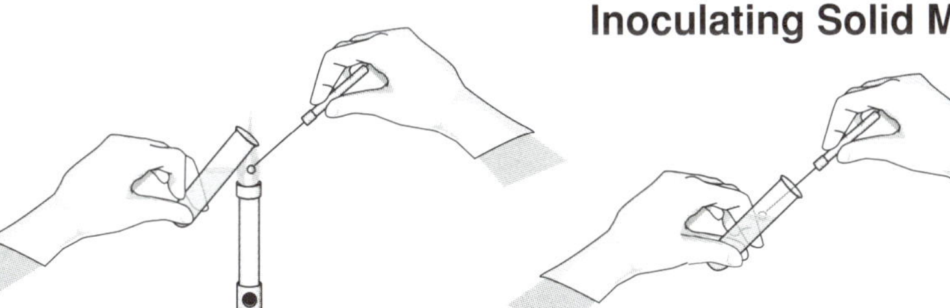

1. Hold the inoculating loop in the flame until it glows red hot. Remove the lid from the culture broth and pass the neck of the bottle through the flame.

2. Dip the cool inoculating loop into the broth. Flame the neck of the bottle again and replace the lid.

3. Raise the lid of the plate just enough to allow the loop to streak the plate. Streak the surface of the media. Seal the plate with tape and incubate upside down.

---

1. Explain why inoculated plates must be stored upside down in an incubator: _______________________________

____

2. Describe the correct procedure for the disposal of microbial plates and cultures: _______________________

____

3. Describe a general method by which you could separate microorganisms through culturing: _______________

____

Related activities: Strain Isolation, Serial Dilution

KNOW

Strain Isolation

In nature, bacteria exist as mixed populations. However, in order to study them in the laboratory they must exist as pure cultures (i.e. cultures in which all organisms are the same species). The most common way of separating bacterial cells on the agar surface is the **streak plate method**. This provides a simple and rapid method of diluting the sample by mechanical means. As the loop is streaked across the agar surface, more and more bacteria are rubbed off until individual separated organisms are deposited on the agar. After incubation, the area at the beginning of the streak pattern will show confluent growth (growth as a continuous sheet), while the area near the end of the pattern should show discrete colonies. Isolated colonies can then be removed from the streak plate using aseptic techniques, and transferred to new sterile medium. After incubation, all organisms in the new culture will be descendants of the same organism (i.e. a pure culture).

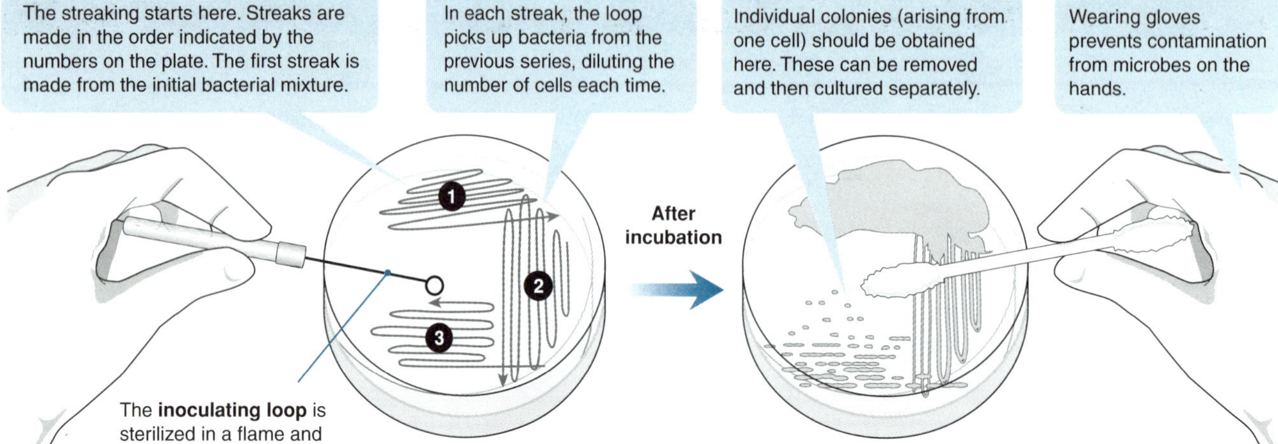

When approximately 10 to 100 million bacterial cells are present, colonies become visible. Note the well-isolated colonies in the photo above. A single colony may be removed for further investigation.

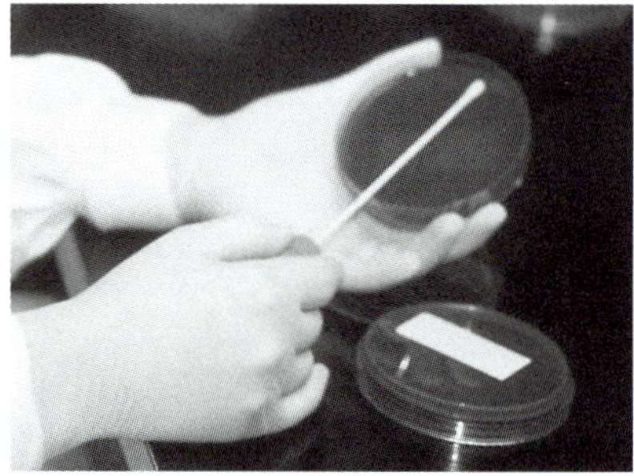

A swab containing a single strain of bacteria is used to inoculate additional nutrient plates to produce pure cultures of bacteria.

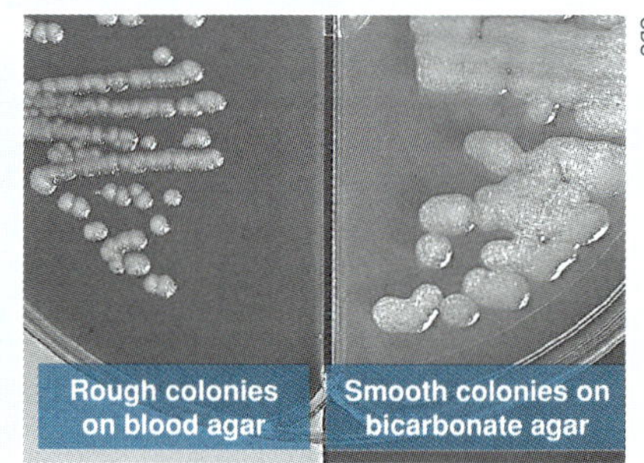

To test purity, a sample of a culture can be grown on a selective medium that promotes the growth of a single species. The photo above shows a positive encapsulation test for *Bacillus anthracis*.

1. Explain the basis by which bacteria are isolated using streak plating: _______________________________________

____

2 Discuss the basic principles of aseptic technique, outlining why each procedure is necessary: ___________________

____

____

____

____

3. Explain the importance of aseptic (sterile) technique in streak plating: ____

____

____

4. State how many bacterial cells must be present on the plate before the colony becomes visible to the naked eye:

____

5. Explain when it might be necessary to use **selective media** to culture bacteria: _________________________________

____

© BIOZONE International 2006-2013
ISBN: 978-1-927173-72-5
Photocopying Prohibited

KNOW

Related activities: Techniques in Microbial Culture, Serial Dilution
Weblinks: How to Streak a Plate

Dilution Plating

The number of microorganisms in a culture can be measured in a number of ways. Some indirect methods measure the dry weight of a culture or measure turbidity, both of which are directly proportional to cell density. Methods that directly count the number of cells in a culture are more commonly used. Microbial populations are often very large, so most counting methods rely on counting a very small sample of the culture. A commonly used indirect method is **serial dilution** followed by plate counts (**dilution plating**). If care is taken with the serial dilution, an accurate estimate of culture density can be obtained.

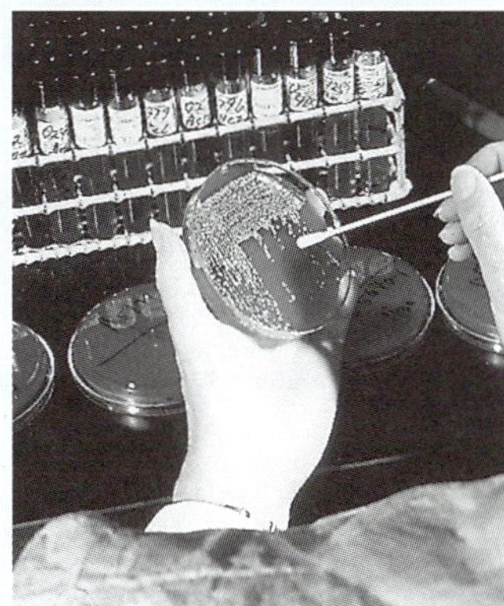

Measuring Microbial Growth Using Dilution Plating

A **serial dilution** is the stepwise dilution of a substance into another solution. By making a series of dilutions and then counting the colonies that arise after plating, the density of the original inoculum (starting culture) can be calculated. To obtain good results, the colonies should be well separated and the number of colonies counted should ideally be between 15-30.

CALCULATION: No. of colonies on plate X reciprocal of sample dilution = no. of bacteria per cm^3.

EXAMPLE: *28 colonies on a plate of 1/1000 dilution, then the original culture contained:*

$28 \times 1000 = 28 \times 10^3\ cm^{-3}$ bacterial cells

Plate counts are widely used in microbiology. It is a useful technique because only the viable colonies are counted, but it requires some incubation time before colonies form. For quality control purposes in some food industries where the food product is perishable (e.g. milk processing) this time delay is unacceptable, and rapid detection methods are used.

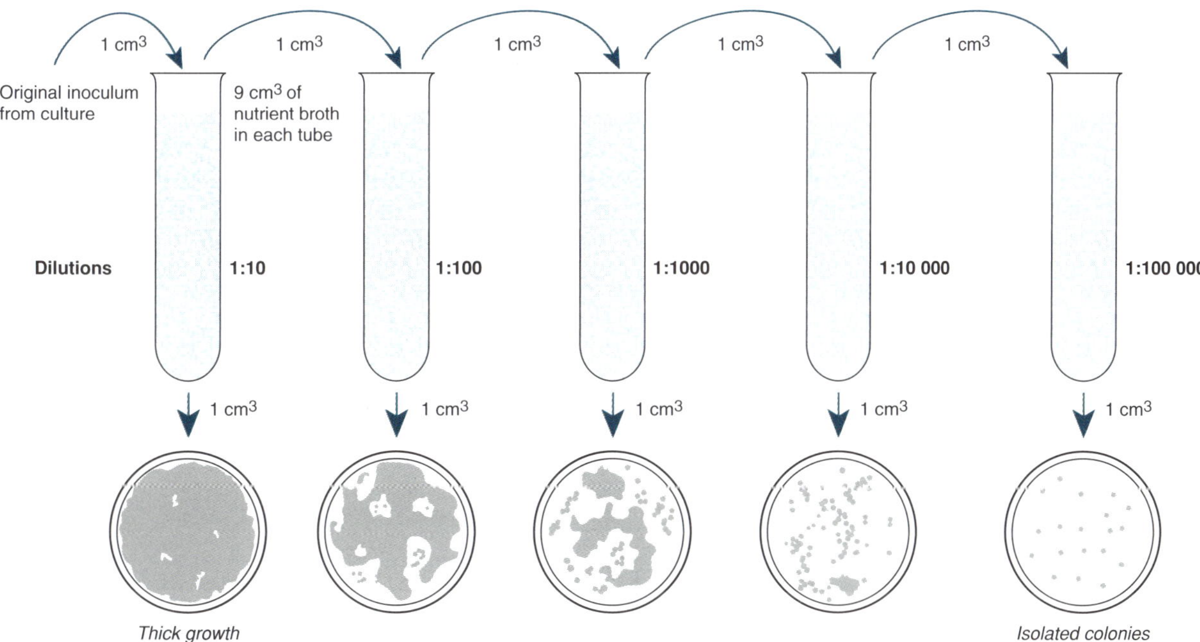

1. In the example of serial dilution above, use the equation provided to calculate the cell concentration in the original culture:

____

2. (a) Explain the term **viable count**: ____

____

(b) Explain why dilution plating is a useful technique for obtaining a viable count: ________________

____

____

(c) Investigate an alternative technique, such as turbidimetry and identify how the technique differs from dilution plating:

____

____

____

____

© BIOZONE International 2013
ISBN: 978-1-927173-72-5
Photocopying Prohibited

Related activities: Techniques in Microbial Culture
Weblinks: Serial Dilution Animation

KNOW

Microorganisms in the Food Industry

Bacteria and fungi are used extensively in many aspects of food technology. Microbes have traditionally been used in the production of fermented foods: alcoholic beverages, bread, and fermented dairy products. The control and efficiency of these uses have been greatly refined in recent times. Genetic engineering has increased the range of microbial products available and has provided alternative sources for products that were once available only through expensive or wasteful means (e.g. production of the enzyme rennin, which is used in cheese making).

Cheese is made by adding cultures of lactic acid bacteria (e.g. *Streptococcus* spp.) and genetically engineered microbial rennin, to milk curd. The microbial activity produce characteristic flavors and textures.

Yoghurt is produced from milk by the action of lactic acid bacteria such as *Lactobacillus bulgaricus* and *Streptococcus thermophilus*. These bacteria break down milk proteins into peptides.

Soy sauce: Filamentous fungi (*Aspergillus soyae* and *A.oryzeae*) digest soy proteins. The culture is fermented in the presence of lactic acid bacteria (*Lactobacillus* spp.) and acid tolerant yeast to develop the flavor.

Bread: The sugars in the bread dough are fermented by the yeast, *Saccharomyces cerevisiae*, producing alcohol and CO_2. The gas causes the dough to rise, while the alcohol is converted to flavor compounds during baking.

Beer and wine: The sugars in fruits or grains are fermented by yeast (e.g. *Saccharomyces carlsbergensis*, *S. cerevisiae*) to alcohol. Beer production first requires a malting process to convert starches in the grain to fermentable sugars.

Sauerkraut production involves the fermentation of cabbage. The initial fermentation involves lactic acid bacteria (*Leuconostoc mesenteroides* and *Enterobacter cloacae*), followed by acid production with *Lactobacillus plantarum*.

Vinegar is produced by the fermentation of alcohol into acetic acid using cultures of acetic acid bacteria (e.g. *Acetobacter* and *Gluconobacter*). When wine is left exposed to oxygen, it is converted into vinegar.

Vitamins and amino acids are dietary supplements produced as by-products of microbial metabolism. Examples include lysine and vitamin B12.

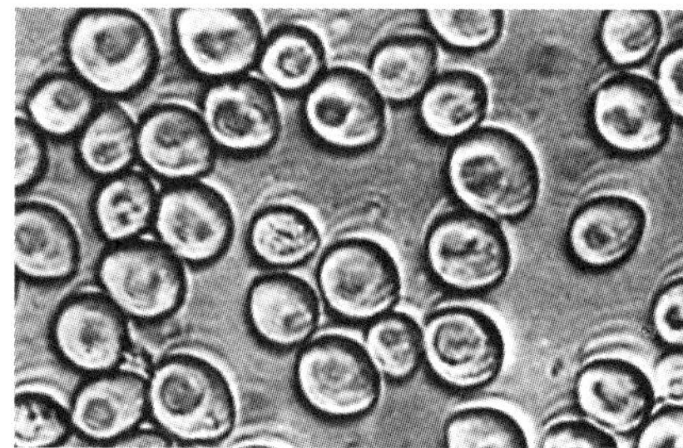

Commercial production of microorganisms: Baker's yeast (*Saccharomyces cerevisiae*, above) is sold for both industrial use and home brewing and baking.

1. Briefly describe two examples of how microorganisms are used in each of the following applications:

    (a) Production of alcoholic beverages: ____

    ____

    ____

    (b) Production of fermented milk products: ____

    ____

    ____

2. Describe one example of how genetic engineering has assisted a traditional biotechnology: _______________________

    ____

Environmental Biotechnology

Environmental biotechnology utilizes microorganisms for a wide variety of environmental applications. Examples include the clean up and treatment of waste water, as biosensors to detect chemical or microbial contaminants, and in bioremediation to clean up oil spills. The mining industry uses microbes to extract metals from low grade ores in a process termed bioleaching. Many metals, including copper, a commercially important metal, are extracted in this way (see below).

Uses of Microorganisms in the Environment

Bioremediation

Bacteria (e.g. *Pseudomonas* spp.) metabolize the hydrocarbons in oil spills, breaking down the oil into its basic constituents. The extremophilic bacterium *Deinococcus radiodurans* has been genetically engineered to digest ionic mercury produced from radioactive nuclear waste.

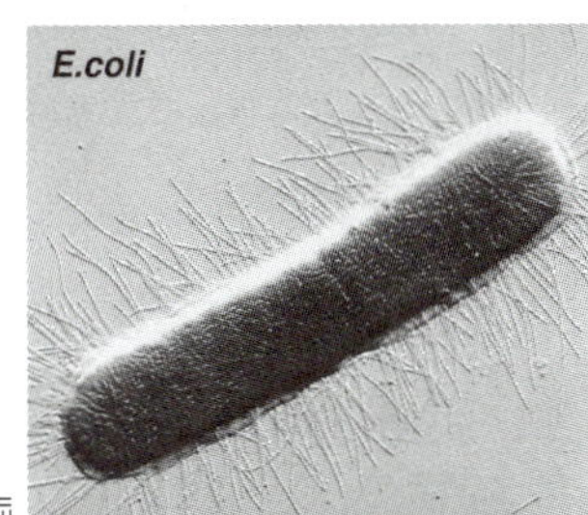

Environmental biosensors

Bacteria (e.g. Lactococcus, *E.coli, Vibrio fischeri, Photobacterium*) can be genetically engineered to detect specific chemical or pathogenic pollutants in the environment. The pollutant may activate a light-emitting compound in the bacterium, which is easily detected.

Treating sewage & wastewater

Microbes (e.g. *Zoogloea* bacteria) are used in sewage and wastewater treatment to reduce the amount of organic material. This is achieved by oxidizing waste to CO_2 and water. Treatment can be anaerobic or aerobic, depending on the treatment phase and type of bacteria used.

Metal mining

Various fungi and bacteria (e.g. *Thiobacillus ferrooxidans*) are used to recover specific metals from otherwise unprofitable grades of ores. Metals such as gold, copper, zinc, nickel, uranium and cobalt can be extracted using microbial action. The process is referred to as bioleaching or biomining.

Microorganisms and Bioleaching

Microbes play an important role in the mining industry where they are used to recover metals from low grade ores which would be unprofitable to mine by conventional methods. A common example is the use of the bacterium *Thiobacillus ferrooxidans* to extract copper. The process is outlined below.

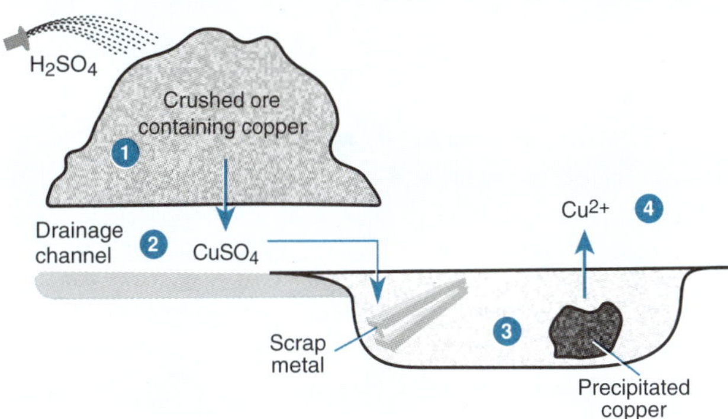

1 Crushed ore is acidified with sulphuric acid to encourage microbial growth. Microbes oxidize the ore releasing Fe (III), which reacts with the copper compound releasing copper ions.

2 The copper ions then form copper sulphate, which is removed from the ore along a drainage channel and into a shallow pond.

3 Scrap metal is placed into the pond. This displaces the copper ion in the copper sulphate, and the copper precipitates out of solution.

4 The precipitated copper is scraped out of the pond and refined electrolytically.

Bioleaching is more cost effective than traditional mining techniques because it is a simpler process. In general, it is also more environmentally friendly as it results in fewer emissions and less damage to the landscape. However, some bioleaching processes produce toxic chemicals, such as sulphuric acid, which could contaminate ground water. Bioleaching takes up a lot of space and is a slower process than smelting. This may also be seen as a disadvantage.

1. Describe two examples of how microorganisms are used in environmental monitoring and clean up:

(a) ____

____

____

(b) ____

____

____

2. Discuss the advantages of using biomining over traditional metal mining techniques: _____________________

____

____

____

Related Activities: Sewage Treatment
Weblinks: Microbes and Activated Sludge

KNOW

Biofuels

Fuels made from biological processes have been used for many years. In many regions of the world dried animal dung is used to fuel fires. More recently there has been a move to produce more commercial quantities of renewable biofuels for use in transport and industry. **Biofuels** include ethanol, **gasohol** (a blend of petrol and ethanol), methanol, and biodiesel made from a blend of plant oils and traditional diesel oil. **Biogas** (methane) is an important renewable gas fuel made by fermenting wastes in a digester.

Gasohol

Gasohol is a blend of finished motor gasoline containing alcohol (generally ethanol but sometimes methanol). In Brazil, gasohol consists of 24% ethanol mixed with petrol.

Advantages

- Cleaner fuel than petrol
- Renewable resource
- Creates many jobs in rural areas

Disadvantages

- Ethanol burns hotter than petrol so petrol engines tend to overheat and they need to be modified
- Fuel tank and pipes need coating to prevent corrosion by ethanol
- Fuel consumption 20% greater compared with petrol

Sources of biomass for ethanol production

- Sugar cane (ethanol is produced in this way in Brazil).
- Corn starch (in the USA).
- Grass, certain waste materials (paper, cardboard), and from wood. Fast-growing hardwood trees can be treated to release cellulose. Once released, it may be converted to simple glucose by hydrolytic enzymes and then fermented to produce ethanol.

Biogas

Methane gas is produced by anaerobic fermentation of organic wastes such as sewage sludge at sewage waste treatment stations, animal dung, agricultural wastes, or by the rotting contents of landfill sites.

Stages in methane production

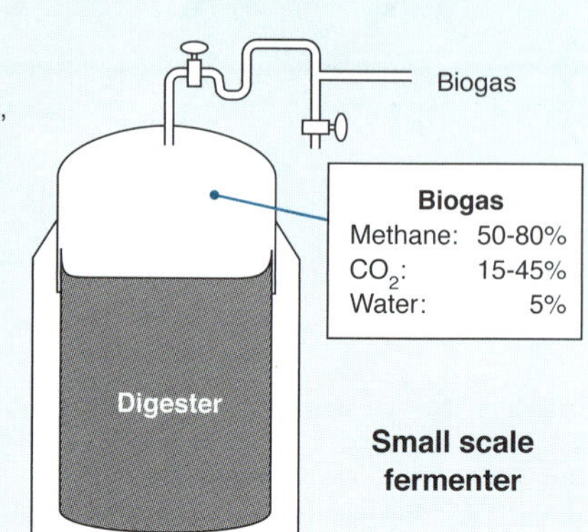

Saprophytic bacteria (facultative anaerobes) break down fats, proteins, and polysaccharides.

↓

Acid-forming bacteria break down these monomers to short-chain organic acids.

↓

Methanogen bacteria (strict anaerobes) produce methane gas.

Corn Ethanol: The Promise That Failed

Corn harvest

Ethanol plant

At the beginning of this millennium, ethanol was heavily promoted as a carbon neutral, high energy liquid fuel and the best alternative to petrol. In 2010, the U.S. government provided US$5.68 billion in subsidies to meet its mandate that biofuels make up 10% of the fuel for the U.S. passenger vehicle fleet. As a result, corn ethanol production increased to 49 billion liters and consumed 40% of all corn grown internally. The corn ethanol industry, which required 13 million hectares of land, competed directly with the food and livestock feed industries and resulted in a rise in food prices. The Congressional Research Service reported that even if the entire U.S. corn crop was used to produce ethanol for transport, it would only provide 18% of that country's transport fuel needs.

The carbon neutrality of corn ethanol is also disputed. It requires large amounts of fuel to grow, harvest, transport, and distill the crop. Ethanol also contains only two thirds the energy of the equivalent volume of gasoline.

As an alternative, corn waste after harvest could provide up to 1.4 billion tons of useful waste and produce 30% of the U.S. transport fuel needs. However, this would use the organic material that is normally plowed back into the field as fertilizer. This would reduce soil fertility and increase dependence on synthetic fertilizers, which themselves are costly to produce and create problems of water contamination.

1. Explain the nature of the following renewable fuels:

   (a) Biogas: ____

   ____

   (b) Gasohol: ____

   ____

2. Suggest how a small biogas fermenter could be used on a farm to reduce waste and provide a fuel source:

   ____

   ____

   ____

© BIOZONE International 2013
ISBN: 978-1-927173-72-5
Photocopying Prohibited

Sewage Treatment

Once water has been used by household or industry, it becomes sewage. Sewage includes toilet wastes and all household water, but excludes storm water, which is usually diverted directly into waterways. In some cities, the sewerage and stormwater systems may be partly combined, and sewage can overflow into surface water during high rainfall. When sewage reaches a treatment plant, it can undergo up to three levels of processing (purification). Primary treatment is little more than a mechanical screening process, followed by settling of the solids into a sludge. Secondary sewage treatment is primarily a biological process in which aerobic and anaerobic microorganisms are used to remove the organic wastes. Advanced secondary treatment targets specific pollutants, particularly nitrates, phosphates, and heavy metals. Before water is discharged after treatment, it is always disinfected (usually by chlorination) to kill bacteria and other potential pathogens.

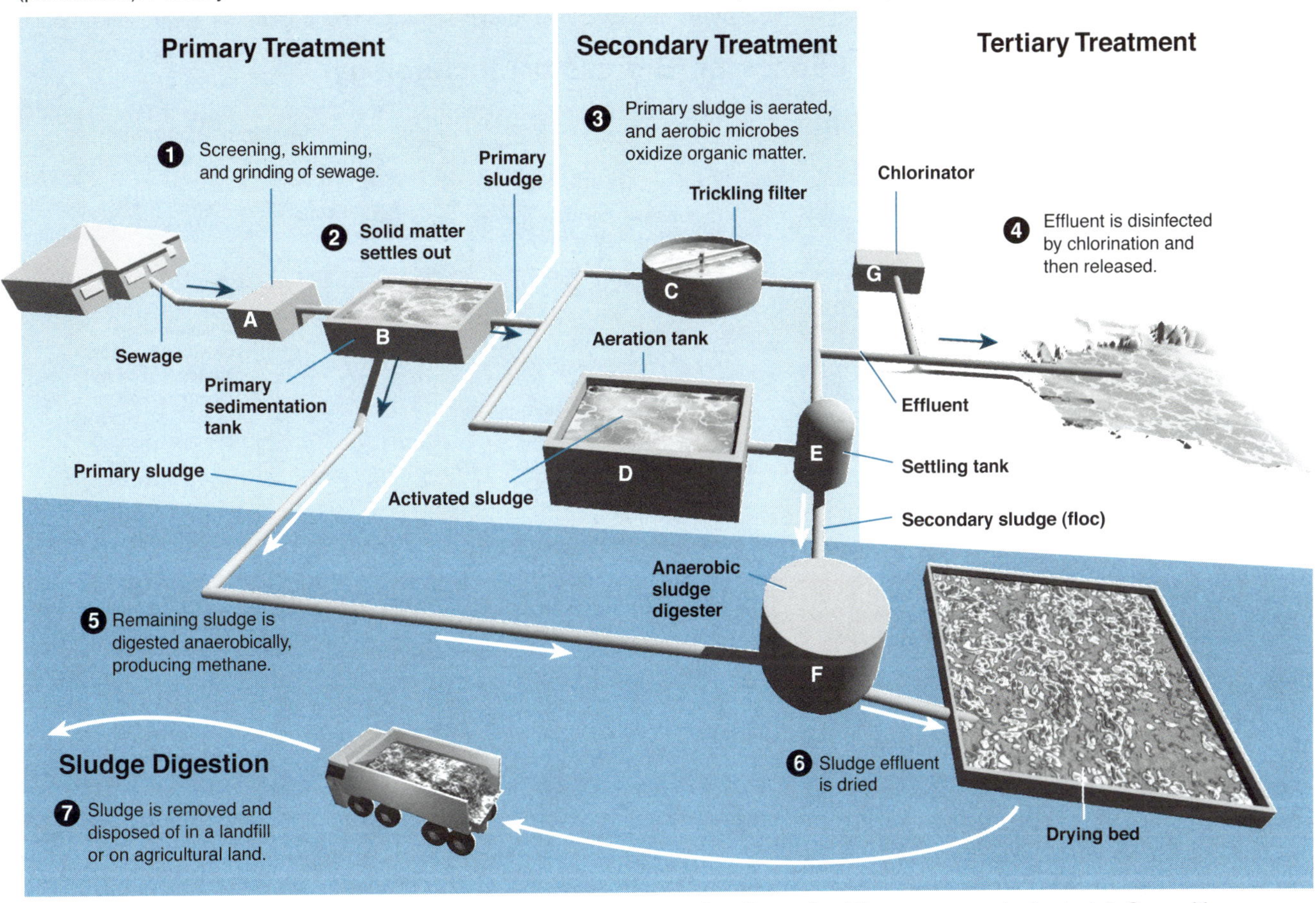

1. Using the information provided in the diagram and text above, classify each of the processes indicated A-G as either mechanical, biological, or chemical. If you wish, color code these on the diagram for easy reference:

   A: _______________________   D: _______________________   G: _______________________

   B: _______________________   E: _______________________

   C: _______________________   F: _______________________

2. Using the diagram above for reference, investigate the sewage treatment process in your own town or city, identifying the specific techniques and problems of waste water management in your area. Make a note of the main points to cover in the space provided below, and develop your discussion as a separate report. Identify:

   (a) Your urban area and treatment station: _______________________

   (b) The volume of sewage processed: _______________________

   (c) The degree of purification: _______________________

   (d) The treatment processes used (list): _______________________

   (e) The discharge point(s): _______________________

   (f) Problems of waste water management: _______________________

   ____

   (g) Future options or plans: _______________________

   ____

Related activities: Environmental Biotechnology
Weblinks: Microbes and Activated Sludge

KNOW

Industrial Microbiology

Industrial production of microbial products involves large scale culture of fungi and bacteria to produce commercially valuable substances. Many pharmaceuticals and food ingredients (flavorings, thickeners, stabilizers, and enzymes) are produced using these microbial fermentations. The microbes are first **isolated** and then cultured in an appropriate environment. The desired product is then extracted from the cells themselves (e.g. enzymes) or from the culture medium (e.g. antibiotics). While it is relatively easy to grow microbes on a small scale, **scaling up** these procedures for use on an industrial scale creates problems. **Bioreactors**, designed for either **batch culture** or **continuous culture**, optimize the conditions for microbial growth and production of the desired product. This requires constant monitoring and adjustment of growth conditions. Many of the microbes used in industry produce valuable commodities as by-products of their normal metabolism. Others are natural mutants with faulty metabolic pathways, and some are genetically engineered to express a particular gene as its protein product.

Industrial Fermenter (Bioreactor) Technology

PHOTO: Bioengineering AG (Switzerland)

The photograph above shows an industrial scale bioreactor used for the production of diphtheria and pertussis vaccine. The types of microorganisms that are well suited to use in industry show certain properties: they have simple nutritional requirements, temperature and pH optima for maximum growth, amenability to culture in large scale fermenters, and a high growth rate (therefore high productivity).

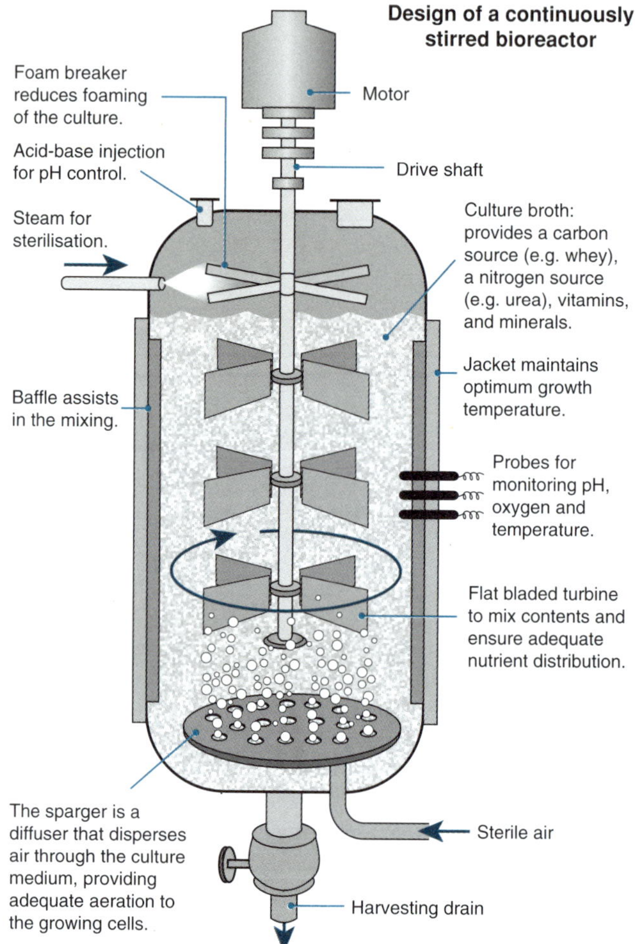

The Problems Associated With Scaling Up

A number of problems must be solved in order to scale up relatively simple laboratory procedures to full sized industrial biofermenters:

- All undesirable organisms must be prevented from entering the fermenter. The absence of undesirable microbes within a biotechnology process is called **asepsis**. Contamination can result in spoiled or low quality product, low product yield, and increased expense because of lost production time and extra clean-up costs.

- Aerobic microbes must be given an adequate supply of oxygen.

- Powerful motors are needed to mix the culture which has a porridge like consistency.

- Optimum nutrient levels must be maintained.

- The heat generated by microbial activity needs to dissipated. The entire culture must be keep at a constant temperature.

- Waste products need to be constantly removed.

- The build up of foam due to the production of carbon dioxide must be monitored and controlled.

- Rigorous testing using scale models (left) helps to ensure that the problems associated with scaling up have been eliminated.

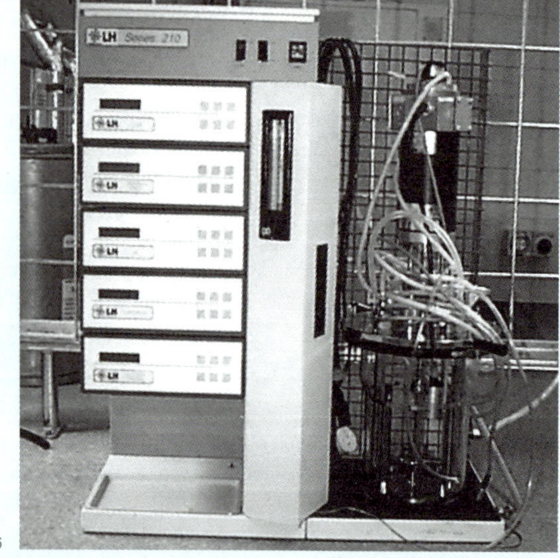

CF

© BIOZONE International 2013
ISBN: 978-1-927173-72-5
Photocopying Prohibited

Continuous Culture

Continuous culturing involves constant addition of fresh culture medium into the bioreactor and removal of material out of the bioreactor. The desired components are harvested from the material removed from the bioreactor. Nutrient addition and product removal occurs at an equal rate to maintain a constant volume. Continuous culturing is often used when a young culture of actively producing cells is required (e.g. some antibiotics are only produced during active growth).

Advantages

- Continuous growth over long periods.
- Population can be kept in exponential growth for extended periods.
- Equipment is in constant use, so there is less down time.
- Nutrients are added and inhibitory metabolites are constantly removed to maintain optimum growth.

Disadvantages

- It can be difficult to maintain optimum culture conditions.
- Contamination is more likely to occur.
- Product consistency can be difficult to control.

Batch Culture

Batch culturing involves adding cells to a fixed volume of culture medium. The culture medium is harvested as a batch at the end of the process. The process is halted when all of the nutrients are used, or a threshold level of toxic metabolites is reached and further growth of the culture is inhibited. Most large scale production is carried out by batch cultures.

Advantages

- Bioreactor conditions are easier to manipulate.
- There is less risk of contamination.
- Product quality is easier to control.

Disadvantages

- More down time as equipment must be cleaned between each batch.
- Product output is determined by the limited nutrient supply, and build up of inhibitory metabolites.

1. Describe the primary difference between a continuous and batch culture system: _______________

____

____

2. Explain why continuous culture is often used when the harvested product is biomass (cells) or a primary metabolite:

____

____

____

3. Explain when batch culture (with final harvest of the end-product) would be used in preference to continuous culture:

____

____

____

4. Explain the importance of asepsis in industrial processes involving microbial cultures: _______________

____

____

5. Outline how industrial biofermenters overcome the following problems associated with scaling up:

(a) Heat generated by microbial activity: _______________

____

(b) Microbial demand for oxygen: _______________

____

(c) Nutrient demand: _______________

____

Microbial Growth and Metabolites

Microbial growth follows a well established pattern comprising several phases (below). During their growth, microbes produce intermediate and end products as part of their normal metabolism. Such products are termed **metabolites** and fall into two categories. **Primary metabolites** are compounds that are essential for the continuation of the microbes metabolic activity. They are usually produced in small quantities and may be utilized by the organism. **Secondary metabolites** are not required for microbial metabolism, but may be useful for the microbe (e.g. in inhibiting competitors). They frequently accumulate in large quantities during the stationary phase of growth. Examples of secondary metabolites that are produced commercially for human use include penicillin, quinine, and codeine. Bioreactor conditions can be manipulated to promote the production of specific metabolites, although it is generally more difficult to control the production and harvest of primary (as opposed to secondary) metabolites.

Microbial Growth in a Closed Culture

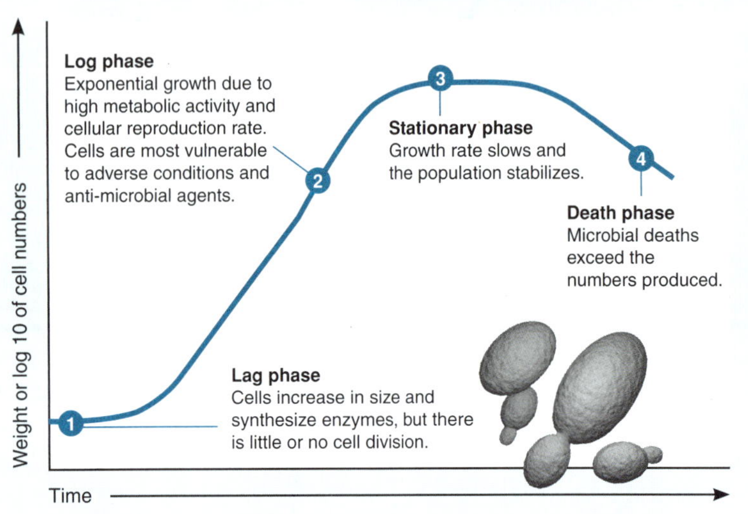

1. **Lag phase:** Cell numbers are relatively constant as the organisms adjust to the conditions and prepare for growth.

2. **Log phase:** The phase of **exponential growth**. In conditions optimal for microbial growth, the cells begin multiplying at an exponential rate, quickly increasing cell numbers. For yeast, the generation time is approximately 1 hour, but the doubling time of some bacteria can be as little as 15 minutes.

3. **Stationary phase:** In a closed culture system no new nutrients are added and waste products are not removed. Microbial growth slows as the nutrients become depleted and waste products build up. The growth rate equals the death rate, so there is no net growth in the microbial population, and numbers stabilize.

4. **Death phase:** Microbial numbers decrease as the death rate exceeds growth rate; a result of a lack of nutrients and build of toxic metabolites.

The graph above illustrates the growth curve for a yeast culture grown within a closed culture system. Bacteria show a similar growth curve. Growth curves of microbial cell numbers against time typically show these four phases.

Production of Primary Metabolites

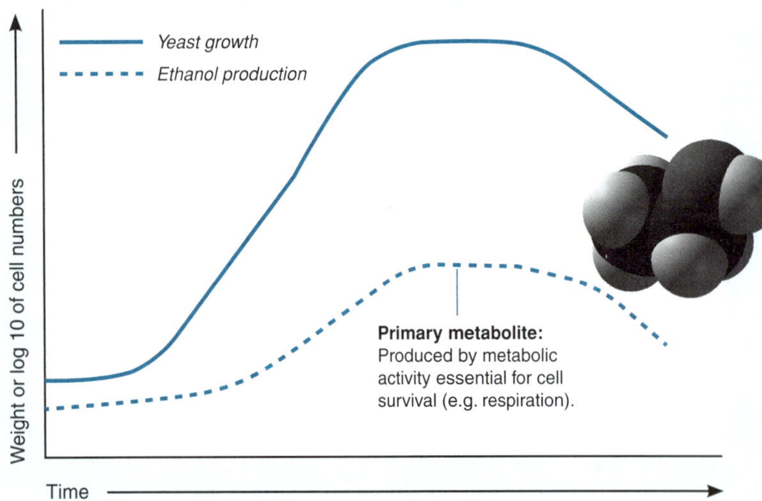

During the log phase of microbial growth (in culture), many intermediate metabolic products are produced, which are further required for growth or for energy-yielding catabolism. These **primary metabolites** are produced in excess of requirements and accumulate in the culture, from which they can be extracted and purified.

Primary metabolites form at the same time as the cells grow, so their production curves are very similar to the organism's growth curve. Microbial production of primary metabolites contributes significantly in modern biotechnology. Through fermentation, microorganisms growing on inexpensive carbon sources can produce valuable products such as amino acids, nucleotides, organic acids, and vitamins.

The graph (left) compares the production curve of the primary metabolite ethanol, with the growth curve for yeast.

Amino acids, nucleotides, proteins, carbohydrates, lipids, and vitamins are primary metabolites needed for culture growth. Acetone, ethanol, butanol, and organic acids are required for deriving energy. The quantity of some of these metabolites exceeds the requirements of the producers and accumulates in the culture.

© BIOZONE International 2013
ISBN: 978-1-927173-72-5
Photocopying Prohibited

Production of Secondary Metabolites

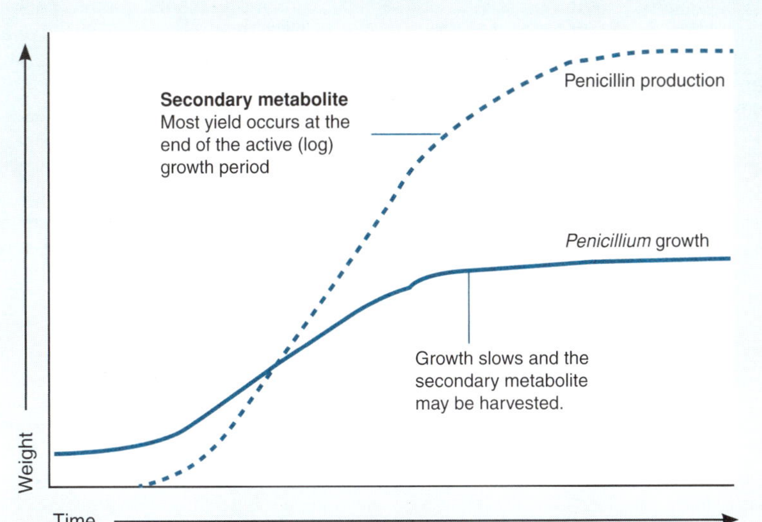

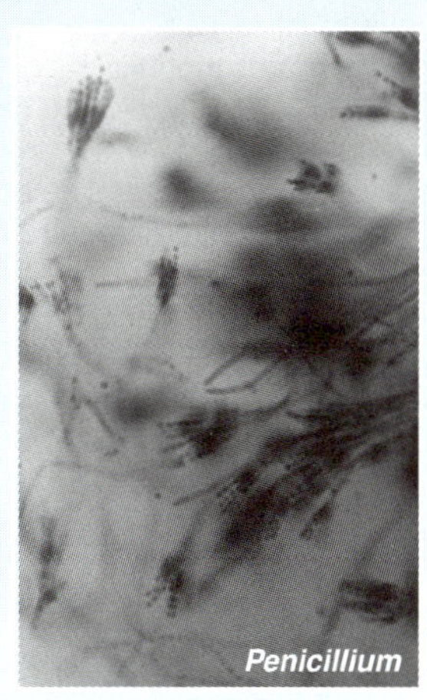

Secondary metabolites are organic compounds which are not immediately essential to microbial survival or reproduction. Secondary metabolites are often produced as defense mechanisms or to allow the organism to compete against other species.

The graph (above) illustrates the production of penicillin, a secondary metabolite produced by species of the fungus, _Penicillium_. Penicillin is produced once the microbe has largely completed its growth and has entered the stationary phase. Many important antibiotics are produced as secondary metabolites by bacteria and fungi.

Secondary metabolites are produced by a limited number of microorganisms, when one or more nutrients in the culture medium are depleted.

Many secondary metabolites (including some from genetically engineered microorganisms) have beneficial uses to humans as pharmaceuticals. Examples include atropine, erythromycin, morphine, and penicillin.

1. (a) Explain why there is an initial lag in the growth of a microorganism placed into a new culture:

(b) Suggest how this time lag could be reduced when starting new culture:

2. Describe the effect on the microbial growth curve of adding fresh nutrients and removing toxic by-products:

3. (a) Explain why the curve for a primary metabolite production closely resembles that of the organism's growth curve:

(b) Explain why this is not the case for production of a secondary metabolite:

4. Explain the differences between a primary and secondary metabolite in microbial culture:

5. Explain why a secondary metabolite might be produced after a microbe had completed most of its growth phase:

Industrial Production of Enzymes

Humans have used enzymes for thousands of years in food and beverage production, but the use of enzymes in industry is a comparatively recent development. Many industries now rely on the large scale production of microbial enzymes to catalyze a range of reactions. In the absence of enzymes, these reactions sometimes require high temperatures or pressures to proceed. Industrial enzymes must be relatively robust against denaturation and capable of maintaining activity over a wide temperature and pH range. Enzyme technology involves the production, isolation, purification, and application of useful enzymes. Commercial enzymes are produced from three main sources: plants, animals, and microorganisms (mainly bacteria and fungi). Most enzymes used in industrial processes today are microbial in origin and are produced in industrial-scale microbial fermentations using liquid or semi-solid growth media. Note that the term **fermentation**, when used in reference to industrial microbiology, applies to both aerobic and anaerobic microbial growth in **bioreactors**. Generalised plans for the industrial production of both extracellular and intracellular enzymes are illustrated below. Note that the isolation of intracellular enzymes (below, right) is more complex because the cells must first be disrupted to release the enzymes within.

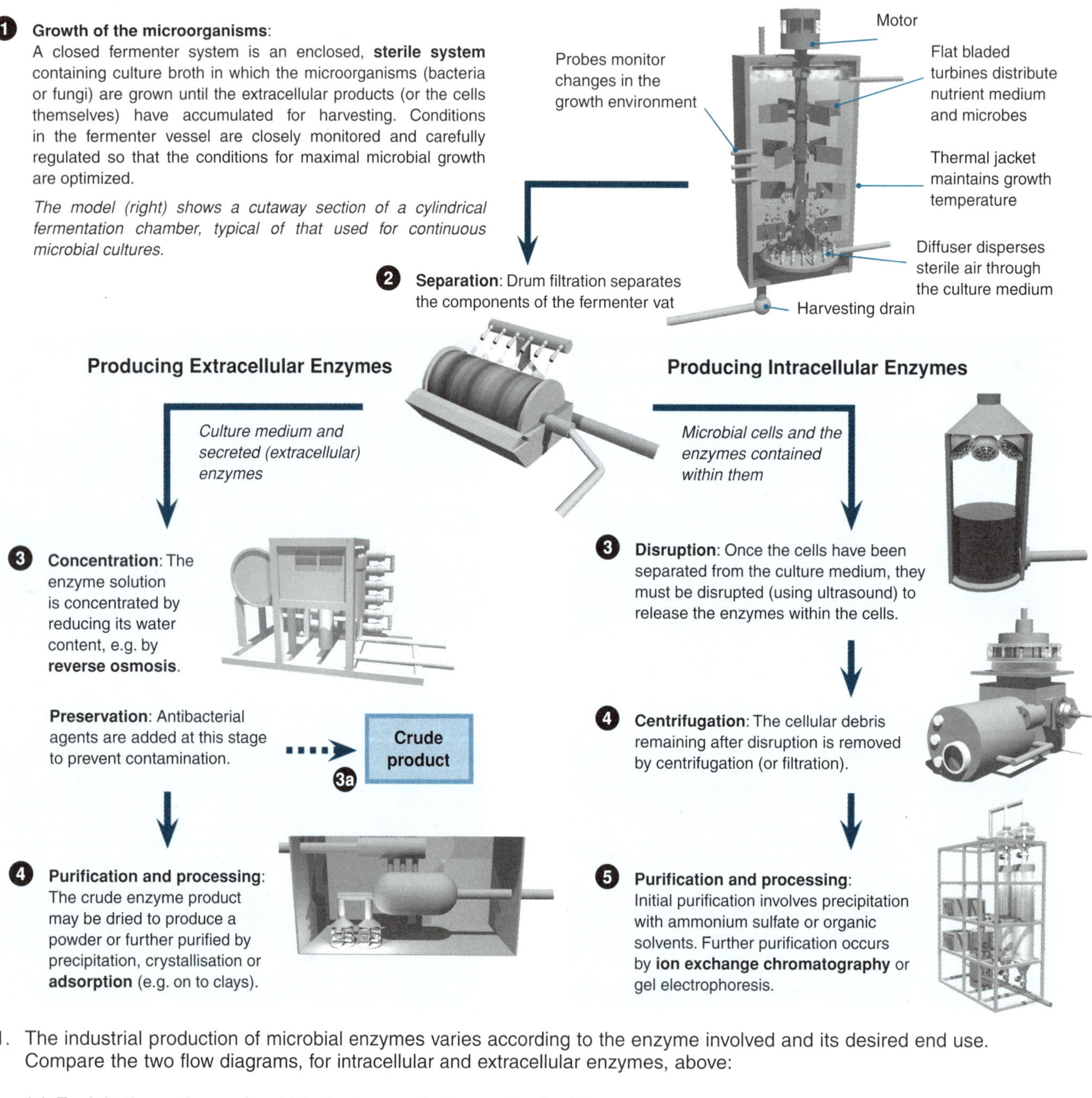

1. The industrial production of microbial enzymes varies according to the enzyme involved and its desired end use. Compare the two flow diagrams, for intracellular and extracellular enzymes, above:

   (a) Explain the main way in which the two production methods differ: _______________________________________

   ____

   (b) Suggest the reason for this difference: ____

   ____

2. Enzyme solutions can be packaged and used as crude extracts without further purification (3a). State one benefit of this:

   ____

© BIOZONE International 2013
ISBN: 978-1-927173-72-5
Photocopying Prohibited

KNOW

Related activities: Putting Enzymes to Use, Applications of Enzymes
Weblinks: Enzyme Technology

Putting Enzymes to Use

Depending on the way in which the desired end-product is produced, enzymes may be used as crude whole cell preparations or as cell-free enzyme extracts. Whole cell preparations are cost effective, and appropriate when the processes involved in production of the end product are complex, as in waste treatment and the production of semi-synthetic antibiotics. Cell free enzyme extracts are more expensive to produce, but can be a more efficient option overall. To reduce costs and improve the efficiency of product production, enzymes are sometimes immobilised within a matrix of some kind and the reactants are passed over them. The various methods by which enzymes are put to work are compared in the diagram below.

Industrial enzymes

	Advantages	**Disadvantages**	**Methods of Enzyme Immobilization**
Cell free enzyme extract Enzyme is used in solution	There is generally a high level of enzyme activity when the enzymes are free in solution.	The enzyme may be washed away after use. The end-product is not enzyme free and may require purification.	**Micro-encapsulation** The enzyme is held within a membrane, or within alginate or polyacrylamide capsules.
Immobilized enzyme Enzyme is held in an inert material	The enzymes can be used repeatedly and recovered easily (this reduces costs). The enzyme-free end-product is easily harvested. The enzymes are more stable due to the protection of a matrix. The life of some enzymes, e.g. proteases, is extended by immobilization.	The entrapment process may reduce the enzyme activity (more enzyme will be needed). Some methods offering high stability (e.g. covalent bonding) are harder to achieve. Immobilization can be costly.	**Lattice entrapment** Enzyme is trapped in a gel lattice, e.g. silica gel. The substrate and reaction products diffuse in and out of the matrix. **Covalent attachment** Enzyme is covalently bonded to a solid surface e.g. collagen or a synthetic polymer.
Whole cell preparation Whole cells may be immobilized	Useful for enzymes that are unstable or inactivated when outside the cell. Useful for complex processes utilising more than one intracellular enzyme.	Less expensive and more rapid than first producing a pure enzyme extract. Some of the substrate is used for microbial growth, so the process is less efficient overall.	**Direct cross-linking** Glutaraldehyde is used to cross-link the enzymes. They then precipitate out and are immobilized without support.

Microorganisms & Biotechnology

1. (a) Explain one benefit of using a cell free enzyme extract to produce a high-value end-product:

____

(b) Identify one factor that might be important when deciding *not* to use a cell free extract: _______________

____

2. (a) Describe two benefits of using immobilized enzymes (rather than enzymes in solution) for industrial processes:

____

____

(b) Describe a disadvantage associated with the use of immobilized enzymes: _______________

____

(c) Describe a factor that would affect the rate of end-product harvest from immobilized enzymes:

____

3. The useful life of protease enzymes is extended when they are immobilized (as opposed to being in solution). Using what you know of enzyme structure, explain why immobilization has this effect in this case:

____

____

4. Suggest why immobilization would reduce the activity of certain enzymes: _______________

____

____

Related activities: Applications of Enzymes
Weblinks: Enzyme Technology

KNOW

Applications of Enzymes

Microbes are ideal organisms for the industrial production of enzymes because of their high productivity, ease of culture in industrial fermenters, and the ease with which they can be genetically modified to produce particular products. In addition, because there is an enormous diversity in microbial metabolism, the variety of enzymes available for exploitation is very large. Some of the microorganisms involved in industrial fermentations, and their enzymes and their applications are described below.

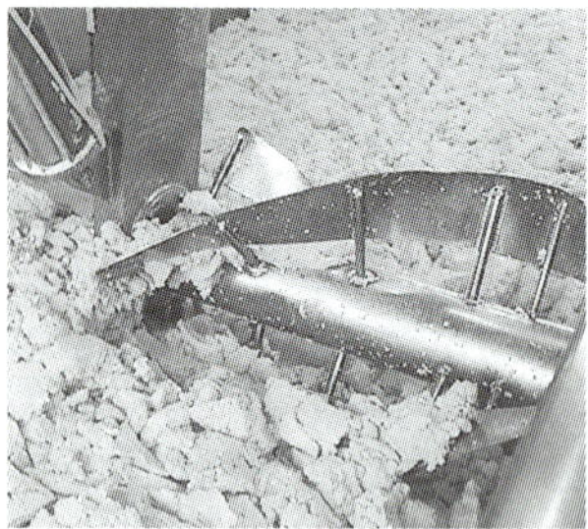

Enzymes are used in various stages of **cheese production**, e.g. chymosin from GE microbes now replaces the rennin previously obtained from calves.

In **beer brewing,** proteases (from bacteria) are added to prevent cloudiness. Amyloglucosidases are used to produce low calorie beers.

Citric acid is used in **jam production** and is synthesized by a mutant strain of the fungus *Aspergillus niger,* which produces the enzyme citrate synthase.

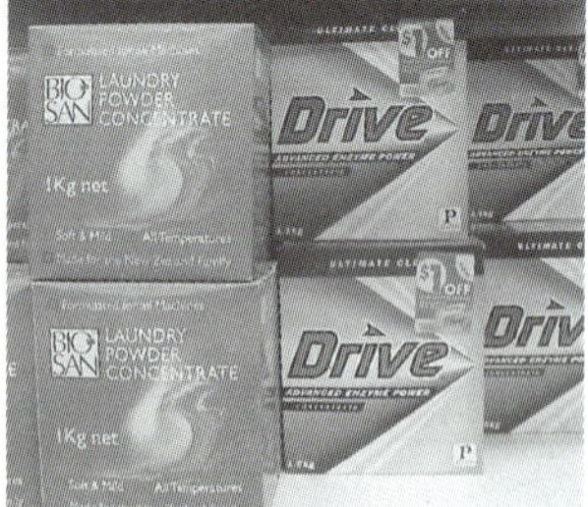

Biological detergents use proteases, lipases, and amylases extracted from fungi and thermophilic bacteria to break down organic material in stains.

Fungal ligninases are used in **pulp and paper industries** to remove lignin from wood pulp and treat wood waste.

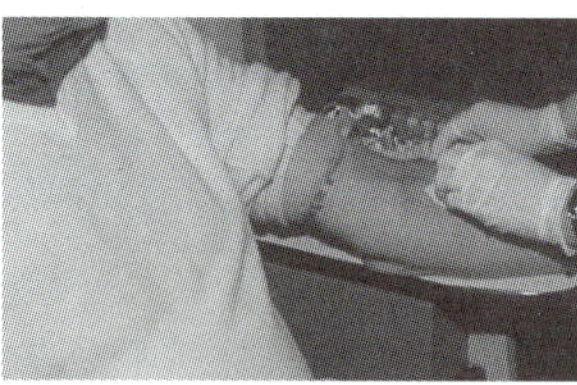

Medical treatment of blood clots employs protease enzymes such as streptokinase from *Streptomyces* spp.

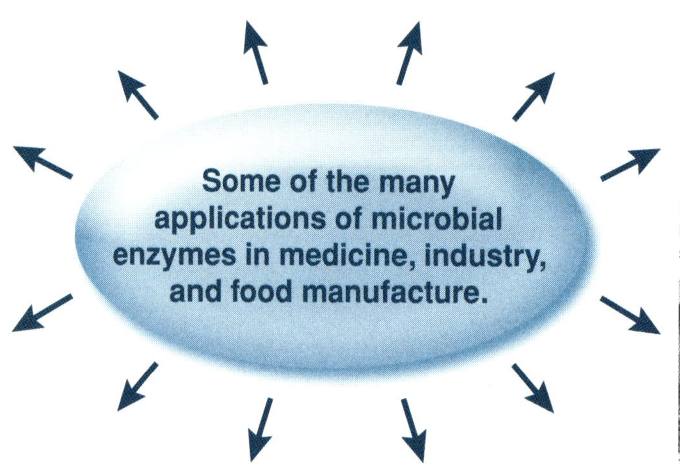

In **soft centered chocolates,** invertase from yeast breaks down the solid filling to produce the soft center.

Bacterial proteases are used to break down the wheat protein (gluten) in flour, to produce low gluten breads.

Cellulases and pectinases are used in the manufacture of packaged (as opposed to fresh) fruit juices to speed juice extraction and prevent cloudiness.

The silver residues from old photographs can be reclaimed for reuse when proteases are used to digest the gelatin of old films.

The lactase from bacteria is used to convert lactose to glucose and galactose in the production of low-lactose and lactose free milk products.

Tanning industries now use proteases from *Bacillus subtilis* instead of toxic chemicals, such as sulfide pastes, to remove hairs and soften hides.

The enzyme, **glucose oxidase**, from *Aspergillus niger*, is immobilized in a semi-conducting silicon chip. It catalyzes the conversion of glucose (from the blood sample) to gluconic acid.

Hydrogen ions from the gluconic acid cause a movement of electrons in the silicon, which is detected by a transducer. The strength of the electric current is directly proportional to the blood glucose concentration.

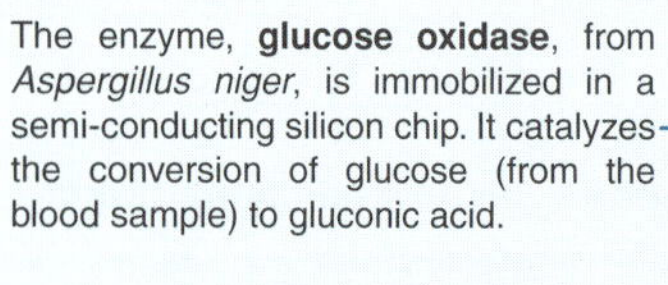

Biosensors are electronic monitoring devices that use biological material to detect the presence or concentration of a particular substance. Enzymes are ideally suited for use in biosensors because of their specificity and sensitivity. This example illustrates how **glucose oxidase** from the fungus *Aspergillus niger* is used in a biosensor to measure blood glucose level in diabetics.

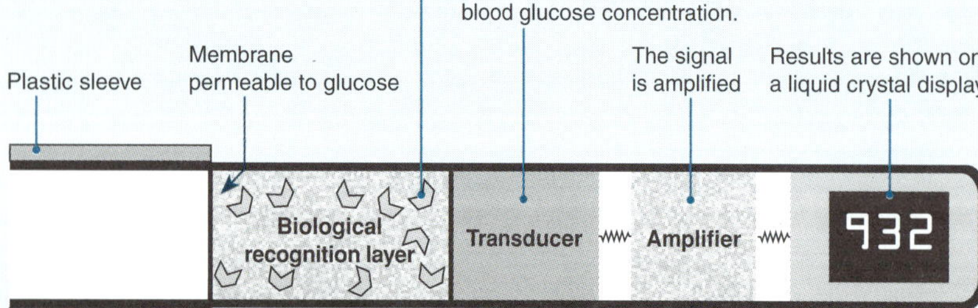

KNOW

Related activities*: Putting Enzymes to Use*
Weblinks*: Enzyme Technology*

1. Identify two probable consequences of the absence of enzymes from a chemical reaction that normally uses them:

   (a) ____

   (b) ____

2. Identify three properties of microbial enzymes that make them highly suitable as industrial catalysts. For each, explain why the property is important:

   (a) ____

   ____

   (b) ____

   ____

   (c) ____

   ____

3. Choose one example from those described in the diagram opposite and, in more detail, identify:

   (a) The enzyme and its specific microbial source: _______________________________

   ____

   (b) The application of the enzyme in industry and the specific reaction it catalyzes: _______________

   ____

   ____

   ____

4. (a) Outline the basic principle of enzyme-based biosensors: _______________________

   ____

   (b) Suggest how a biosensor could be used to monitor blood alcohol level: _______________

   ____

   ____

   ____

5. For each of the examples described below, suggest how the use of microbial enzymes has improved the efficiency, cost effectiveness, and/or safety of processing compared with traditional methods:

   (a) Use of microbial proteases to treat hides in the tanning industry: _______________

   ____

   ____

   ____

   (b) Use of microbial chymosin in cheese production: _______________________________

   ____

   ____

   ____

   (c) Use of fungal ligninases to treat wood waste: _______________________________

   ____

   ____

   ____

Microorganisms & Biotechnology

White Wine Production

Yeasts are involved in producing almost all alcoholic beverages: wines, beers, and distilled spirits such as rum and whisky. The alcohol produced in the manufacture of these beverages is a metabolic by-product of **fermentation** by the yeast. Wines are made from grapes, which contain sugars that are directly available to the yeast for fermentation. There are literally hundreds of different variations on the wine making process. The color of wine is not determined by the juice of the grape, which is usually clear, but by the presence or absence of the grape skin during fermentation. White wine can be made from any color of grape as the skins are separated from the juice. The steps in the manufacturing white wine are illustrated below.

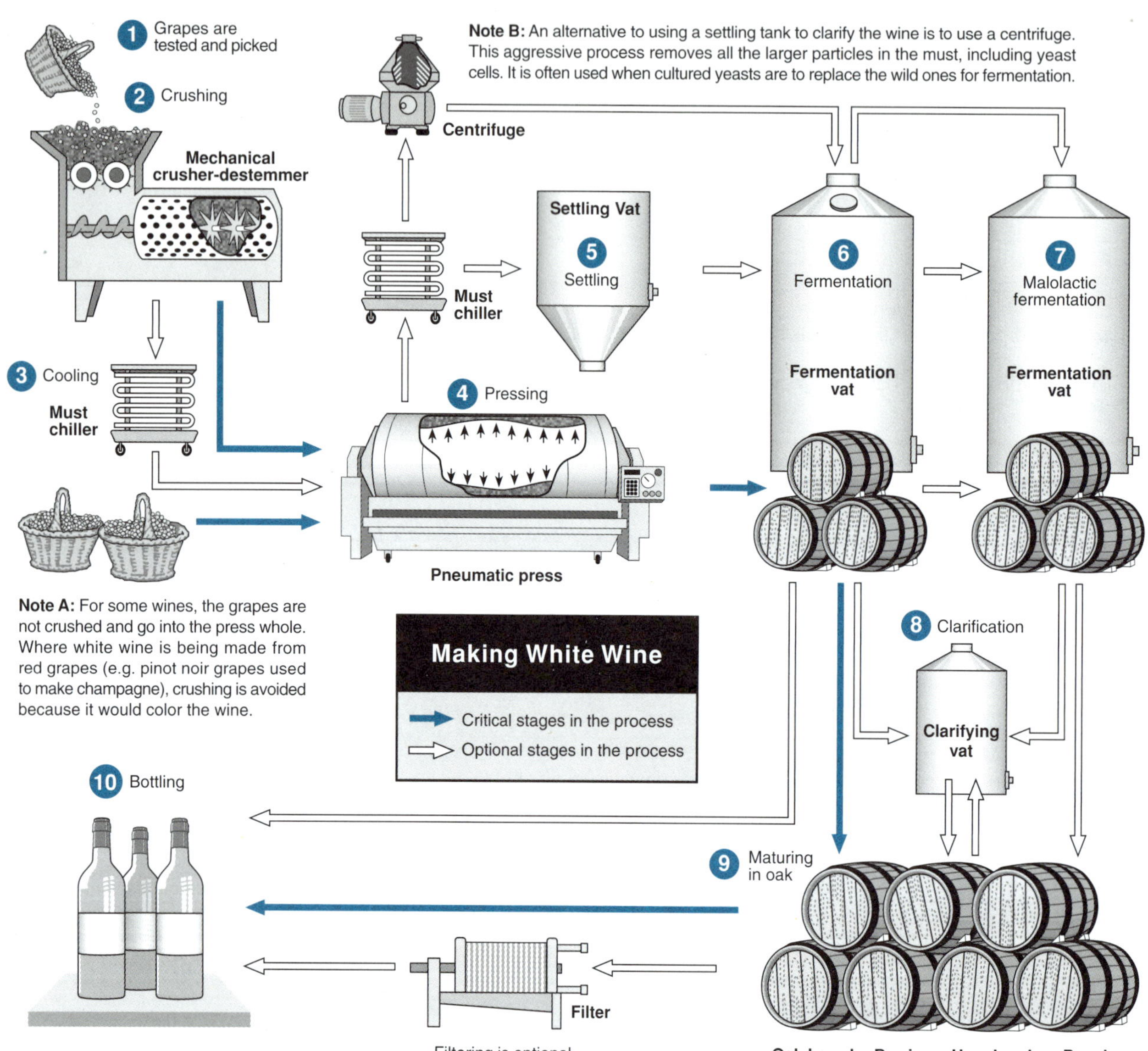

1. Grapes are tested for acidity and sugar levels before picking.

2. Before crushing, the grapes are separated from the leaves and stems. Crushing produces 'must'; a mix of skins and juice. Sulfite may be added at this stage. This dissipates before the fermentation stage (see Note A above).

3. If warm weather makes the temperature of the must too high, the juice is cooled by pumping it through 'must chillers'. Delaying fermentation until after pressing is essential.

4. White wine grapes are always pressed. Modern pneumatic presses (illustrated above) prevent pips and stems breaking; something that could add bitter flavors to the wine (important to avoid in white wine).

5. The juice is drained into settling vats where the pip, stem and skin fragments settle to the bottom of the vat. The clean juice is racked into separate vats ready for fermentation (see Note B above).

6. The traditional oak casks used for fermentation are being increasingly replaced by stainless steel vats which enable better control of yeast activity through temperature regulation. Most often, a cultured yeast *Saccharomyces cerevisiae* is added, although some winemakers choose to use the wild yeasts present on the skin of the grapes. The yeast ferments the sugars present in the grape juice.

7. A second, malolactic fermentation may occur naturally or may be induced to soften acidic flavors and add complexity to the wine. This fermentation, carried out by bacteria and not yeast, converts the harsher malic acid into softer lactic ones.

8. After fermentation of the juice, the wine is stabilized by filtration, centrifuging, or fining in a clarification vat with a small amount of a bentonite clay (which collects remaining yeasts, proteins and grape particles, and precipitates them to the bottom of the vat). If not removed, protein can cause cloudiness in the finished wine. Bitartrates are removed by chilling the wine. If left in the wine, they cause crystal formation when it is chilled, although they are harmless and tasteless.

9. Some wines are bottled after chilling, but wines requiring further development undergo maturation in oak barrels (e.g. chardonnay).

10. Because wines are susceptible to air and bacteria, the bottles are sterilized and filled in the absence of air. Bottled wines requiring further maturation are cellared before commercial release.

© BIOZONE International 2013
ISBN: 978-1-927173-72-5
Photocopying Prohibited

Related activities: Microorganisms in the Food Industry, Red Wine Production
Weblinks: White Wine Production

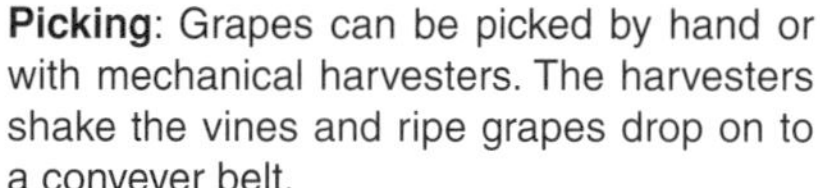

Picking: Grapes can be picked by hand or with mechanical harvesters. The harvesters shake the vines and ripe grapes drop on to a conveyer belt.

Pressing: The wine is pressed to remove the solids and separate the wine. It is then clarified in a series of settling vats.

Fermentation: After the addition of the yeast *Saccharomyces cerevisae*, fermentation occurs in stainless steel tanks, grouped into 'tank farms'.

Photos: VMW

1. Using the information above and on the previous page for guidance, investigate the wine making process for a named white wine. Note that in the generalized diagram shown on the previous page, obligatory processes in the production are indicated by black arrows and white arrows indicate alternative or additional stages. Summarize the important points in the process in the spaces provided below:

   (a) Name of white wine and winemaker (if relevant): ____

   (b) Steps in production (i.e. picking, pressing, settling, fermenting, fining, bottling), including the reasons for these:

   (c) Special features of the process for this example: ____

Red Wine Production

Red wine is made from red (or black) grapes, but its red color is bestowed by the skin being left in contact with the juice during fermentation. The grape varieties used for red wines vary tremendously in their characteristics, most importantly color, flavor, and tannins. Many of the basic steps in red wine production are similar to those outlined for making white wines (see the previous activity), but there are important differences related to the extent of crushing, pressing (grapes are always pressed in white wine production), maceration, and alternative fermentation processes.

Harvest: The condition of the grapes at the time of harvest is crucial to wine quality. Overripe or underripe grapes have too much or too little sugar and this affects alcohol content and wine quality.

Vine trimming: This is done to improve the light penetration to the grapes. It can carried out at various stages during the growing season and may be done by hand or using machines.

Destemming: is a mechanical process that occurs immediately prior to crushing. Although it is not always necessary, destemming prevents excessive tannins in the wine.

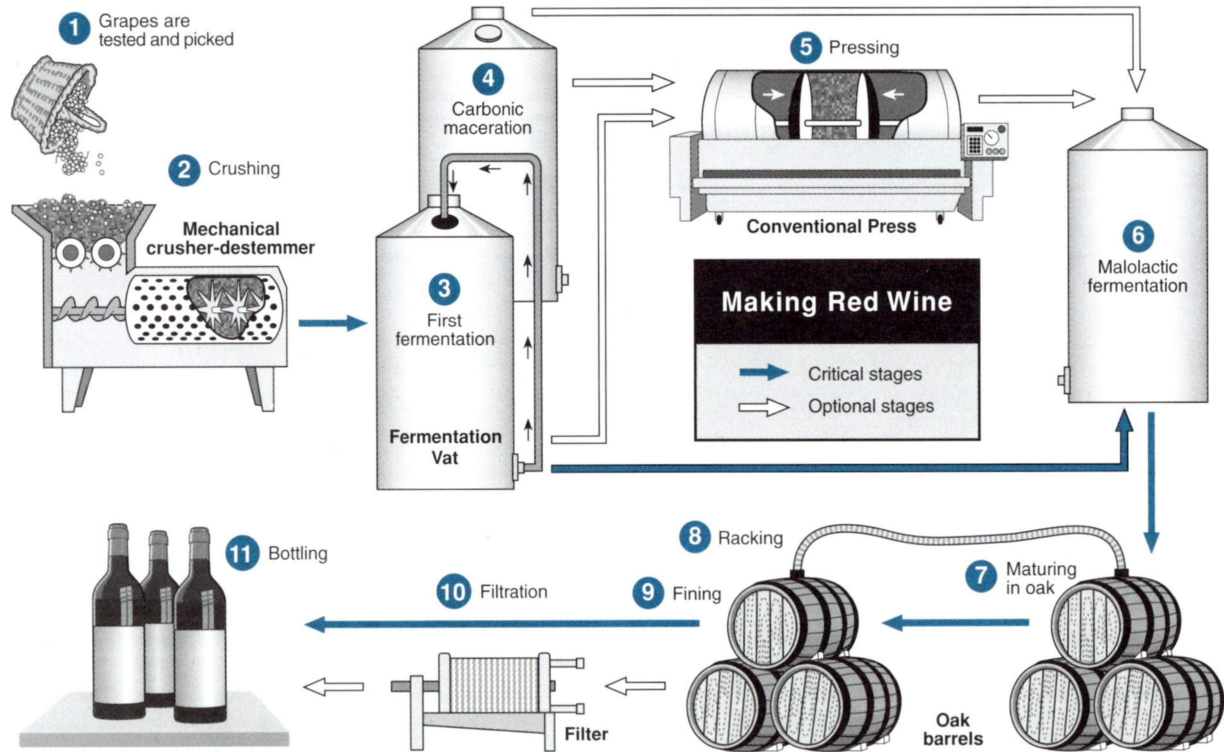

1. Grapes are tested and picked as for white wine production.

2. The grapes are crushed and destemmed. Destemming is not always necessary and bunches may be crushed whole. Stems are removed if the winemaker wishes to avoid high levels of tannin in the wine.

3. While many red wines are still fermented in vats made of oak, stainless steel vats are increasingly popular as they are easy to cool and so offer better control over the fermentation temperature. High temperatures reduce the fruit flavors in the wine. Maceration is the period during which the grapes skins are left in contact with the juice. Usually lasting 5-7 days, the length of time given to maceration determines the depth of color and tannin of the wine.

4. Carbonic maceration is an alternative fermentation process in which the fruit is allowed to ferment spontaneously under a protective layer of CO_2. The weight of the grapes is sufficient to crush the fruit and release the juice without mechanical pressure. These wines are soft and for drinking without ageing (e.g. Beaujolais Nouveau).

5. Pressing the grape mass (called pomace) is carried out after the 'free run' juice has been removed from the fermentation vat.

6. Malolactic fermentation is almost always encouraged in red winemaking. This secondary (bacterial) fermentation softens the acidity, while adding complexity and stability to the wine.

7. High quality red wines are almost always matured in oak barrels. Maturing in oak contributes wood tannin and vanilla flavors.

8. The wine is racked every few months by transferring it to a clean, sterile barrel, gently aerating it and leaving any sediment in the old barrel.

9. The wine is clarified (a process called fining) by pouring egg white or bentonite clay on to the surface.

10. A fine filter may be used to ensure stability and 'brightness' of the wine. Some winemakers believe this strips the wine of its character.

11. Because wines are susceptible to air and bacteria, the bottles are sterilized and filled in the absence of air.

KNOW

Related activities: Microorganisms in the Food Industry, White Wine Production
Weblinks: Red Wine Production

Ageing: The wine is aged in oak barrels, where changes in the aroma and flavors occur. The extent and type of barrel ageing varies depending on wine type and quality.

Monitoring the wine: The wine is regularly tested in the barrel as it ages to check sugar and alcohol content. Here, a **hydrometer** is used to measure the specific gravity of the wine.

Bottling: Quality control and sterile conditions during the bottling process are very important. Bottle ageing before release is still important for some red wines but is becoming less common.

1. Using the information above and on the previous page for guidance, investigate the wine making process for a named red wine. Note that in the diagram shown on the previous page, obligatory processes in the production are indicated by black arrows and white arrows indicate alternative or additional stages. Summarise the important points in the process in the spaces provided below:

(a) Name of red wine and winemaker (if relevant): ____

(b) Steps in production, including any special processes and the reasons for these: _______________________

(c) Special features of the process for this example: ____

Beer Brewing

Brewing is one of the oldest forms of traditional biotechnology. 5000 years ago, the ancient Sumerians and Babylonians used yeast (without knowing what it was) to brew beer, which they flavored with cinnamon. Today, most beers are made from barley and hops. Brewing is divisible into seven stages, with finishing being an important final part of the whole process. At this stage, bacterial proteases are added to break down the yeast and prevent cloudiness. Amyloglucosidases are used to break down sugars in the production of low calorie beers. Traditional beers are stored in barrels and allowed to condition to develop their characteristic qualities. Modern beers are pasteurized, and standardized for color and flavor before bottling.

The Commercial Production of Beer

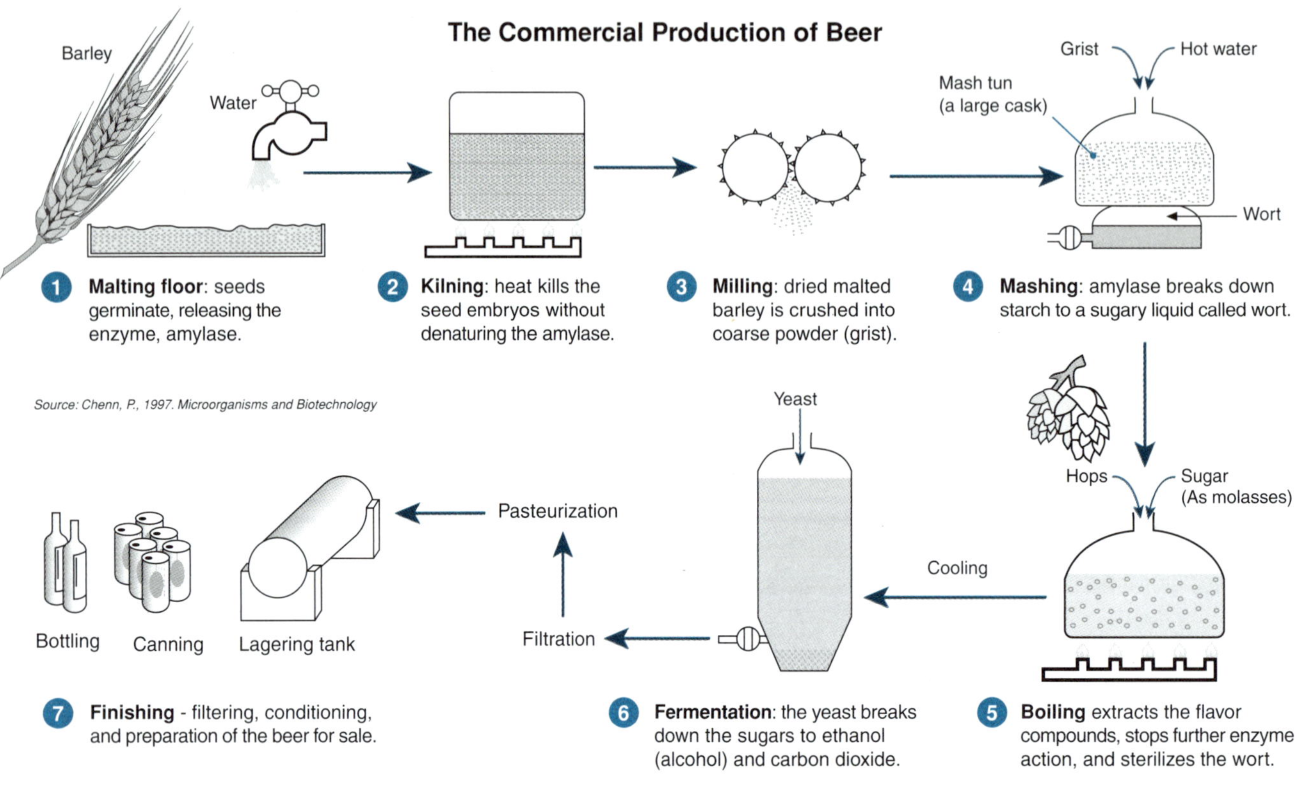

Source: Chenn, P., 1997. Microorganisms and Biotechnology

Investigate the production of beer (brewing). Discuss the key processes involved in each of the seven steps illustrated:

1. **Malting:** ____

2. **Kilning:** ____

3. **Milling:** ____

4. **Mashing:** ____

5. **Boiling:** ____

6. **Fermentation:** ____

7. **Finishing:** ____

KNOW

Related activities: *Microorganisms in the Food Industry*
Weblinks: *How It's Made: Beer*

Bread Making

Using yeast to make foods and drinks is probably the oldest form of biotechnology. Modern methods of bread making use varieties of the yeast *Saccharomyces*. When the raw ingredients are mixed, the proteins in the flour (called gluten) are hydrated and they coalesce to form a sticky, elastic dough. Enzymes, having survived the milling process when grains are made into flour, act on the starch in the dough to make a mixture of sugars. During the leavening or proving process, yeast uses the sugars (anaerobically) and produces ethanol and carbon dioxide gas which causes the bread to rise. *Lactobacilli* may grow during the early stages of proving, producing lactic acid which contributes to the final flavor and inhibits growth of other organisms. Baking inactivates the yeast, evaporates the ethanol, and stops the enzymatic reactions as it cooks the flour. Bakeries may add other ingredients such as vitamin C, whiteners, raising agents, stabilizers, and flavorings.

The Commercial Production of Bread

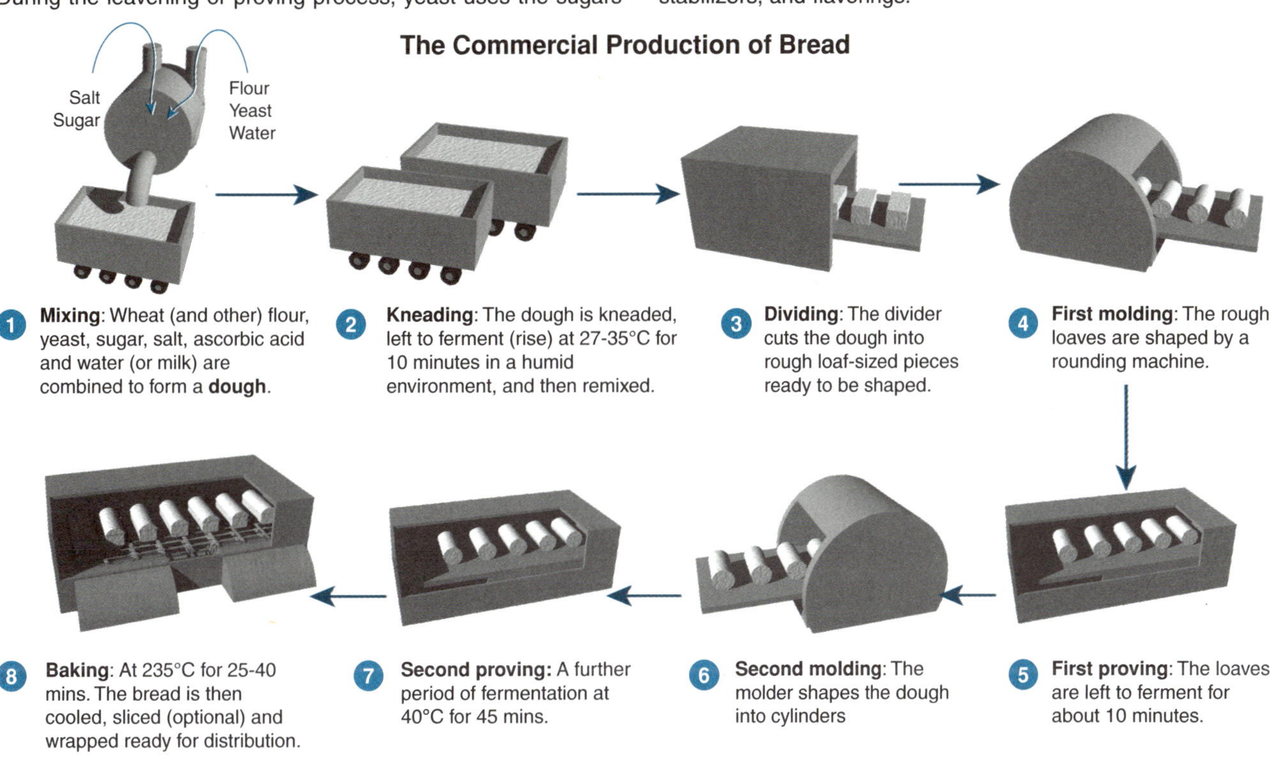

1 Mixing: Wheat (and other) flour, yeast, sugar, salt, ascorbic acid and water (or milk) are combined to form a **dough**.

2 Kneading: The dough is kneaded, left to ferment (rise) at 27-35°C for 10 minutes in a humid environment, and then remixed.

3 Dividing: The divider cuts the dough into rough loaf-sized pieces ready to be shaped.

4 First molding: The rough loaves are shaped by a rounding machine.

8 Baking: At 235°C for 25-40 mins. The bread is then cooled, sliced (optional) and wrapped ready for distribution.

7 Second proving: A further period of fermentation at 40°C for 45 mins.

6 Second molding: The molder shapes the dough into cylinders

5 First proving: The loaves are left to ferment for about 10 minutes.

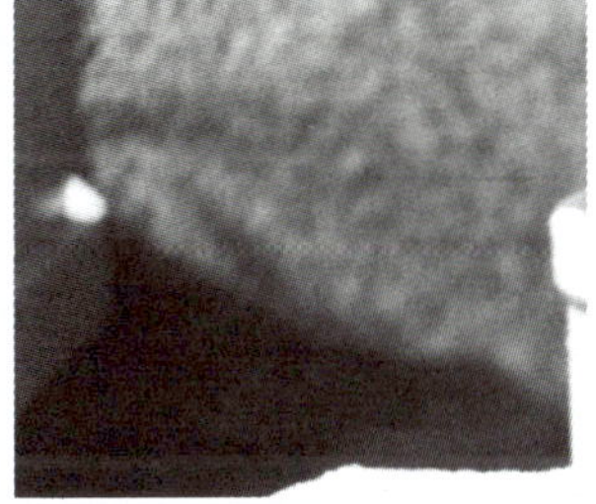

Bread making is one of the oldest and simplest of biotechnologies, involving mixing of wheat flour, water, and yeast to form a dough.

Kneading results in the physical and chemical changes in the gluten (flour proteins) which give the dough its elastic and resilient texture.

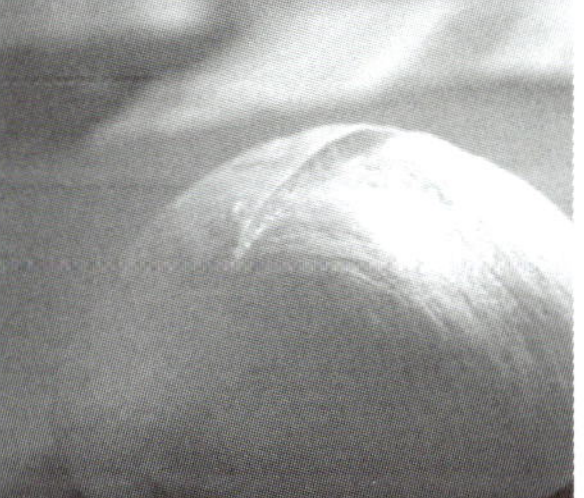

During proving, the dough is left to ferment and the yeast metabolizes sugars to produce ethanol and CO_2. The CO_2 causes the dough to rise.

Baking kills the yeast, evaporates the ethanol, and cooks the flour. Modern bakeries can produce about 10 000 loaves per hour.

1. Explain the role of each of the following in the bread-making process:

   (a) Sugar: ____

   (b) Yeast: ____

   (c) Water (or milk): ____

2. (a) Explain what happens to the dough during the fermentation (or proving) stages: _______________________

   ____

   (b) Suggest why the dough goes through two fermentations: ____

   ____

3. Suggest why gluten free bread is flat and dense: ____

   ____

Related activities: Microorganisms in the Food Industry

Weblinks: How It's Made: Bread

KNOW

Cheese Making

Milk is composed of approximately 4% fat, 3% protein (mostly casein) and 5% lactose (milk sugar). The rest is mainly water. All cheese production requires the formation of a solid curd which, in ripened cheeses, is formed by the action of an enzyme, rennin (chymosin). Curds formed by the addition of acid are used to make fresh cheeses like cottage and cream cheese. The diagram below outlines the processes involved in creating different varieties of ripened cheeses. Most share the same basic steps.

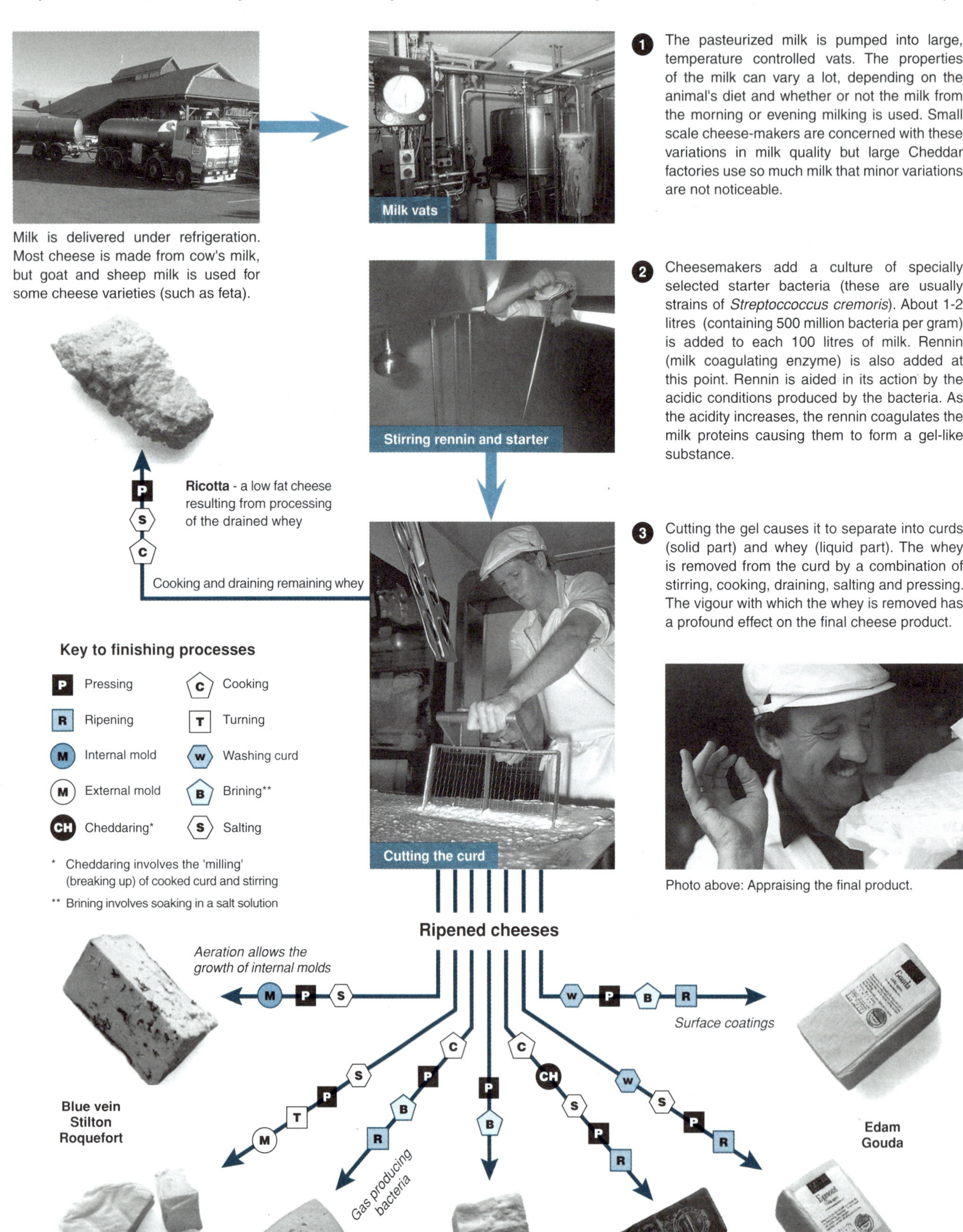

Milk is delivered under refrigeration. Most cheese is made from cow's milk, but goat and sheep milk is used for some cheese varieties (such as feta).

Ricotta - a low fat cheese resulting from processing of the drained whey

Cooking and draining remaining whey

1 The pasteurized milk is pumped into large, temperature controlled vats. The properties of the milk can vary a lot, depending on the animal's diet and whether or not the milk from the morning or evening milking is used. Small scale cheese-makers are concerned with these variations in milk quality but large Cheddar factories use so much milk that minor variations are not noticeable.

2 Cheesemakers add a culture of specially selected starter bacteria (these are usually strains of *Streptoccoccus cremoris*). About 1-2 litres (containing 500 million bacteria per gram) is added to each 100 litres of milk. Rennin (milk coagulating enzyme) is also added at this point. Rennin is aided in its action by the acidic conditions produced by the bacteria. As the acidity increases, the rennin coagulates the milk proteins causing them to form a gel-like substance.

3 Cutting the gel causes it to separate into curds (solid part) and whey (liquid part). The whey is removed from the curd by a combination of stirring, cooking, draining, salting and pressing. The vigour with which the whey is removed has a profound effect on the final cheese product.

Photo above: Appraising the final product.

All photos kindly supplied by Kapiti Cheeses Ltd

Key to finishing processes

P Pressing		**C** Cooking	
R Ripening		**T** Turning	
M Internal mold		**W** Washing curd	
M External mold		**B** Brining**	
CH Cheddaring*		**S** Salting	

* Cheddaring involves the 'milling' (breaking up) of cooked curd and stirring

** Brining involves soaking in a salt solution

© BIOZONE International 2013
ISBN: 978-1-927173-72-5
Photocopying Prohibited

KNOW

Related activities: *Microorganisms in the Food Industry*

Weblinks: *How It's Made: Cheese*

Various starter cultures is used in cheese making. *Streptococcus cremoris* strains are used for most cheeses cultured at 30°C and 38°C. Thermophilic bacteria, which grow best at 42°C, are used for cheeses requiring higher cooking temperatures (swiss and parmesan cheeses). Additional microorganisms are used to give specific characteristics to cheeses. *Propionibacterium shermanii* produces the carbon dioxide gas that produces the holes in swiss cheese and creates the typical sweet nutty flavor. Blue-green molds (*Penicillium* spp.) produce the veining on blue cheese. The texture of the cheese is loose enough that adequate oxygen can reach the aerobic molds. Fungi contribute to these cheeses by using the lactic acids produced during the cheese making process and releasing odorous by-products. These give the cheeses their characteristic smells.

In making Brie and Camembert cheeses, the curds are poured into round molds. These are then pressed and ripened (see next photograph).

The characteristic rinds of Camembert and Brie are produced by white molds. Here a paint brush applies a coating for smear ripening the cheese.

Some cheeses are waxed while they mature. They are marketed with this coating in place. Here cheddar is being waxed by dipping into a hot tub.

1. In the production of most cheese types, the bacterium *Streptococcus cremoris* is used. Explain why thermophilic bacterial varieties are used for producing cheeses requiring higher cooking temperatures:

2. Explain why the loose texture of a blue cheese is important for the development of the internal mould:

3. The texture of a cheddar is dry and somewhat crumbly. Explain how cheddaring contributes to these qualities:

4. Cheese makers take great care not to introduce foreign mold spores into the area when desirable molds are being introduced. Explain why they are careful in this respect:

5. Using the information provided for guidance, investigate the cheese making process for a named cheese. Summarize the important points in the process in the spaces provided below. If required, develop this summary as a separate report:

   (a) Name of the cheese and cheesemaker (if relevant):

   (b) Microorganisms involved:

   (c) Steps in production, including the reasons for these (list):

   (d) Special features of the process for this example (list or briefly describe):

Yoghurt Making

The biochemistry of yoghurt production is similar to that of cheese: suitable lactic acid **bacteria** are inoculated into milk and the **lactic acid** they produce coagulates the milk proteins and thickens the yoghurt. The starter culture for yoghurt contains roughly equal amounts of two **symbiotic** bacteria, *Lactobacillus bulgaricus* and *Streptococcus thermophilus*. *L. bulgaricus* metabolizes lactose in the milk anaerobically to produce the lactic acid responsible for the formation of the yoghurt. *L. bulgaricus* also produces peptidases, which break down the milk proteins into peptides and amino acids. These stimulate the growth of the *Streptococcus* in the culture. *S. thermophilus* produces carbon dioxide and methanoic acid, which together lower the pH and, in turn, stimulate the growth and metabolism of the *Lactobacillus*. Natural yoghurt's characteristic flavor comes from the **lactic acid** and from **ethanal**, a metabolic by-product released by both bacteria. Traditional yoghurt was much thinner and more acidic than the commercially available yoghurt today. The addition of flavoring, coloring and fruit pulp have been developed to cater for modern tastes and recently so-called 'bio' yoghurts produce a milder tasting, sweeter, creamier yoghurt. 'Bio' yoghurts use *L. acidophilus* and *Bifidobacterium bifidum* incubated at a lower temperature for a longer period of time.

The Commercial Production of Yoghurt

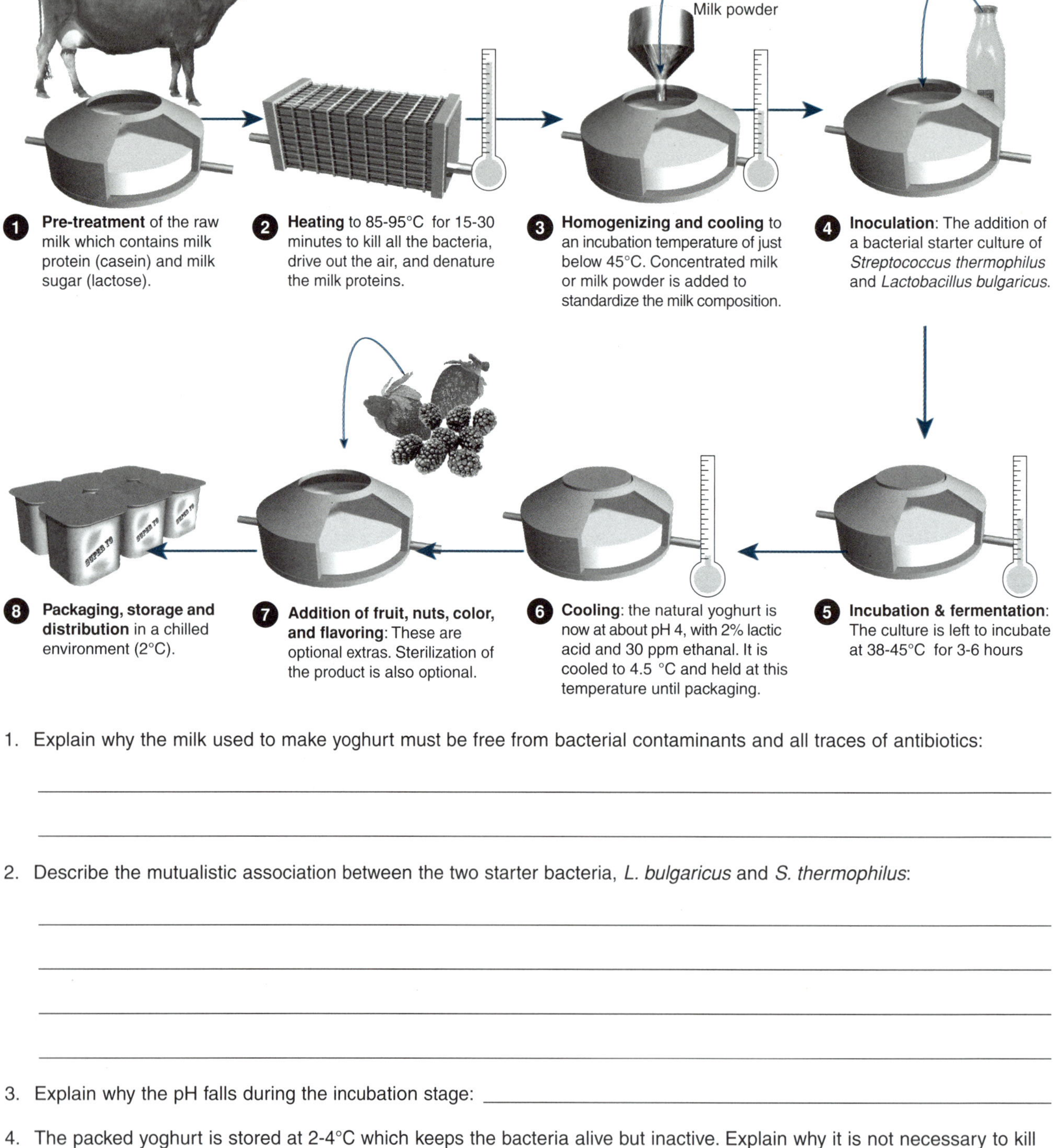

1 **Pre-treatment** of the raw milk which contains milk protein (casein) and milk sugar (lactose).

2 **Heating** to 85-95°C for 15-30 minutes to kill all the bacteria, drive out the air, and denature the milk proteins.

3 **Homogenizing and cooling** to an incubation temperature of just below 45°C. Concentrated milk or milk powder is added to standardize the milk composition.

4 **Inoculation**: The addition of a bacterial starter culture of *Streptococcus thermophilus* and *Lactobacillus bulgaricus*.

8 **Packaging, storage and distribution** in a chilled environment (2°C).

7 **Addition of fruit, nuts, color, and flavoring**: These are optional extras. Sterilization of the product is also optional.

6 **Cooling**: the natural yoghurt is now at about pH 4, with 2% lactic acid and 30 ppm ethanal. It is cooled to 4.5 °C and held at this temperature until packaging.

5 **Incubation & fermentation**: The culture is left to incubate at 38-45°C for 3-6 hours

1. Explain why the milk used to make yoghurt must be free from bacterial contaminants and all traces of antibiotics:

2. Describe the mutualistic association between the two starter bacteria, *L. bulgaricus* and *S. thermophilus*:

3. Explain why the pH falls during the incubation stage:

4. The packed yoghurt is stored at 2-4°C which keeps the bacteria alive but inactive. Explain why it is not necessary to kill the bacteria before eating the yoghurt:

© BIOZONE International 2013
ISBN: 978-1-927173-72-5
Photocopying Prohibited

KNOW

Related activities: *Microorganisms in the Food Industry*
Weblinks: *How It's Made: Yoghurt*

Soy Sauce Production

Soy sauce manufacture originated in China 2500 years ago. The traditional fermentation process takes months to complete, and conditions during fermentation are carefully monitored to ensure the final product has the correct flavor characteristics. There are three main steps in the traditional **soy sauce fermentation** process: **Koji-making**, **brine fermentation**, and **refinement**. During Koji-making, a soy and wheat mixture is cooked, cooled, and inoculated with a fungus, usually ***Aspergillus oryzae*** or ***Aspergillus sojae***. Enzymes produced by the mold break down the starch and proteins to simple sugars and peptides. These are used as fuel by the microorganisms in the brine fermentation stage. In this stage, which can take up to 11 months, lactic acid

bacteria ferment the sugars to lactic acid which lowers the pH. Yeasts also produce alcohols, which contribute to the flavor of soy sauce. Salt provides flavor and establishes a favorable chemical environment for the lactic acid bacteria and yeast. Salt also helps to protect the finished product from spoilage. The final stage of refinement involves separating the liquid from the more solid by-product, and pasteurization to kill microorganisms. Some modern manufacturing techniques use a **chemical hydrolysis method** (rather than fermentation) to produce soy sauce in a matter of days rather than months. Soy sauce produced by these chemical methods are considered inferior to the traditional fermented product and may contain potentially harmful residues.

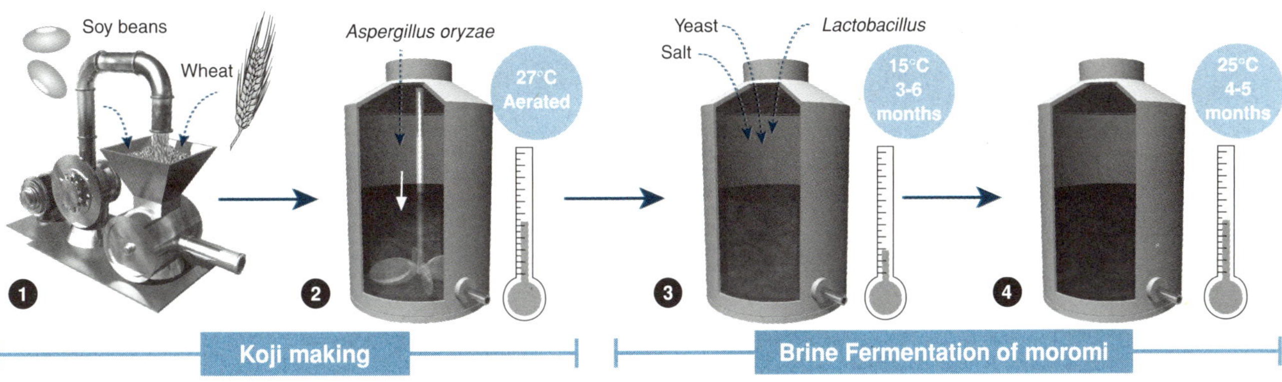

Koji making

In the first stage of the koji-making process, soy beans and wheat are crushed and mixed together with water to produce a mash.

The mash is cooked, cooled to 27°C, **inoculated** with the fungi ***Aspergillus*** and matured in large aerated vats for three days. The mash is now called **koji**.

Brine Fermentation of moromi

The koji is fermented with salt in deep tanks. ***Lactobacillus*** and **yeast** enhance fermentation. The mixture is now called **moromi**. This fermentation takes 3-6 months at 15°C.

A second fermentation at 25°C for 4-5 months ages the soy sauce. Brine fermentation utilizes the sugars and peptides produced during the koji making stage.

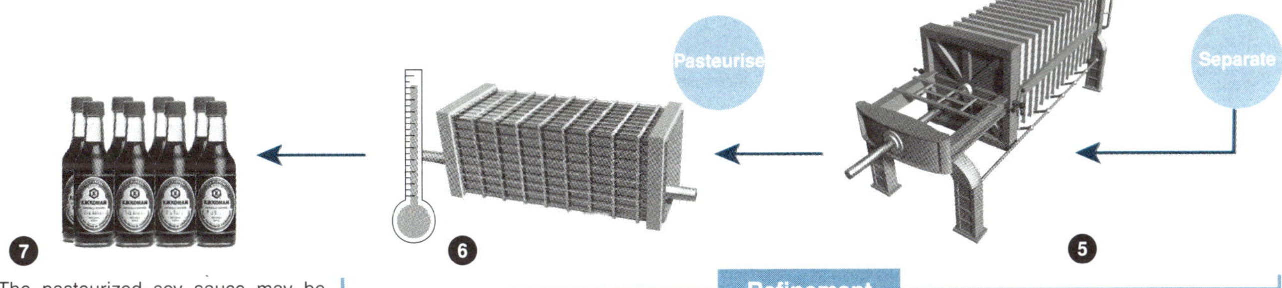

Refinement

The pasteurized soy sauce may be filtered a second time to improve clarity. Alcohol, sodium benzoate or benzoic acid may be added as preservatives before the soy is bottled.

The liquid is pasteurized to kill any microorganisms and enhance the flavor profile of the soy sauce.

The mixture is now a thick paste. The liquid soy sauce is **separated** from solid material using a filter press. A hydraulic press pushes the liquid through layers of cloth filters.

1. How would crushing the soy beans and wheat before inoculation enhance the Koji-making process:

____

2. Explain the contribution of each of the following microorganisms to the production of fermented soy sauce:

(a) Fungus (*Aspergillus* spp.) ____

(b) Lactic acid bacteria: ____

(c) Yeasts: ____

3. (a) Suggest why the soy sauce produced using chemical hydrolysis is regarded as inferior to the fermented product:

____

____

(b) Suggest why commercial producers might choose to use this method anyway: _______________________________

____

Related activities: Microorganisms in the Food Industry
Weblinks: How It's Made: Soy Sauce

KNOW

Food Preservation

Without intervention, **food spoilage** begins as soon as an item is picked, slaughtered, or manufactured. While many food spoilage factors (bruising, oxidation, humidity) alter the nutritional quality and appearance (texture, color, flavor) of food, other spoilage factors can have more serious consequences. The consumption of food spoiled by the presence of microbes or their toxins, could cause illness, or even death, from **food poisoning**. For this reason, it is vital that perishable foods be preserved to prevent microbial growth and extend their shelf life. **Food preservation** describes any process that prevents or slows food spoilage. Basic storage and handling techniques often safeguard the flavor and appearance of food, but more advanced techniques (below) are required to ensure that food stored for a prolonged period remains safe for human consumption.

Preparing Korean kimchi (pickled vegetables)

Pickling preserves food by lowering the pH to below 4.6 and killing the microbes that cannot survive the acidic environment. There are two pickling methods. The first involves **adding salt** and allowing an anaerobic fermentation by the native bacteria (e.g. *Lactobacillus*). This fermentation produces lactic acid, which lowers the pH and inhibits the growth of harmful microbes. The second method involves storing the food in a prepared **acid solution**, often vinegar (acetic acid) to achieve the lower pH.

HTST Equipment for pasteurizing

Heat treatments are used with liquid food products such as milk and fruit juice to logarithmically reduce (but not eliminate) the numbers of microorganisms present. High temperature short time (HTST) treatments involve heating the product to 71.7°C for 15-20 seconds. The more extreme ultra-heat treatment (UHT) process, which also kills bacterial spores, requires heating to 135°C for 1-2 seconds before packaging into sterile containers. UHT products have a shelf life of 6-9 months, compared with up to two weeks for a HTST treated product.

Preserving food in a **sugar syrup** produces a high osmotic pressure environment. Microbial cells have a lower osmotic pressure than the medium, so water leaves their cells causing cell dehydration and death. Fruits are commonly preserved in this manner.

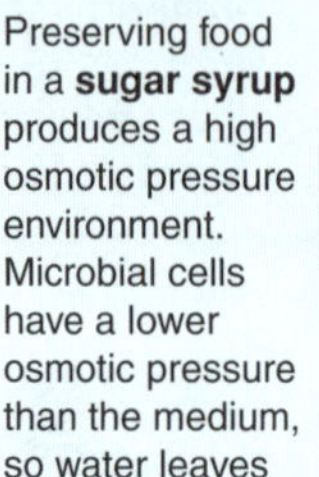

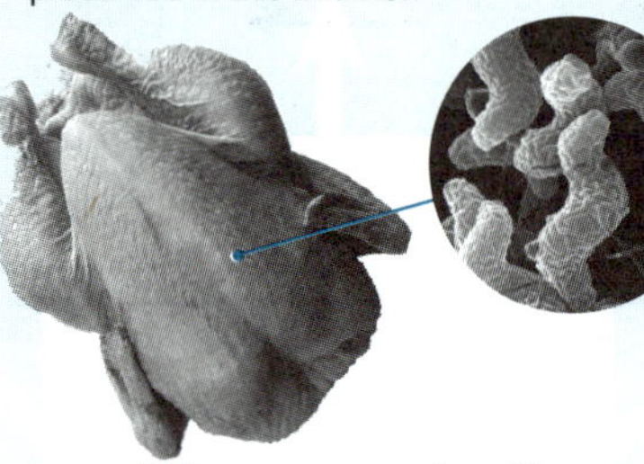

Why preserve food?

Food may harbour pathogenic organisms such as *Salmonella* and *Campylobacter* (above). Food preservation techniques aim to reduce or destroy the number of harmful microbes, increasing the food's shelf life and lowering the risk of food poisoning on consumption.

Food irradiation uses ionizing radiation (electron beams, X-rays, or gamma rays) to destroy microbes on food. Irradiation kills microorganisms by damaging their DNA, but it does not destroy prions or toxins. Irradiation is commonly used to preserve fruit, vegetables, and spices but this must be clearly indicated (above).

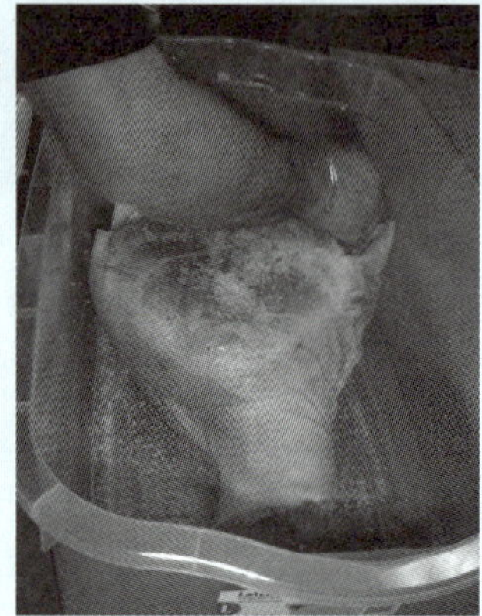

Curing ham by adding salt

Adding **salt** to food draws moisture out from the food by osmosis. The food environment becomes drier, reducing the available water and thereby inhibiting microbial growth. Salt concentrations of up to 20% are required for effective preservation. Meat, such as pork products (above), are often preserved in this way.

Freezing turns the water contained within food into ice, reducing its water activity. With no available water present, microbial growth is inhibited. Freezing is not a method of sterilization, and does not necessarily kill microbes, but the very low temperature (-18°C) slows down most chemical reactions, prolonging the shelf life of frozen food to several months. Fruit, vegetables (above), meat, fish, and shellfish are commonly frozen.

1. Describe a benefit and a disadvantage of using heat treatments to prolong the shelf life of a food product:

   (a) Benefit: ____

   (b) Disadvantage: ____

2. Explain how high salt and sugar act to prolong the shelf life of perishable foods: _______________

   ____

   ____

   ____

KEY TERMS: Mix and Match

INSTRUCTIONS: Test your vocabulary by matching each term to its correct definition, as identified by its preceding letter code.

antibiotic

antibiotic resistance

Archaea

aseptic technique

bacterium (pl. bacteria)

binary fission

biofuel

bioremediation

continuous culture

food preservation

fungus (pl. fungi)

Gram stain

lag phase

log (exponential) growth

microbe (=microorganism)

plasmid

primary metabolite

protist

secondary metabolite

sewage treatment

strain isolation

virus

A Culture of microorganisms in a medium that is receiving a steady supply of nutrients. The end product is constantly harvested at a rate which equals nutrient addition so a constant volume is maintained.

B A non-cellular obligate intracellular parasite, requiring a living host to reproduce.

C A compound produced by a microorganism and not required for its own metabolism, but often beneficial to it (e.g. by inhibiting competitor growth).

D An organism that can be seen only by using a microscope (bacteria, protozoans, viruses, and some algae and fungi).

E Fuel that is formed from renewable organic compounds, often in the form of waste material such as animal dung or wood pulp.

F A domain of prokaryotes more primitive than Bacteria, typically found in harsh environments.

G The process of removing contaminants from wastewater and household sewage.

H A compound produced by a microorganism that is essential to its own metabolic activity (e.g. normal growth, development, and reproduction).

I Technique carried out under sterile conditions to minimize microbial contamination.

J A compound produced by microorganisms that is used to inhibit or destroy potential competitors or pathogens.

K An acquired ability to survive exposure to an antibiotic.

L A member of the domain of prokaryotes comprising the true bacteria, which are distinct structurally and metabolically from the more ancient Archaea.

M A term encompassing the techniques and processes that prevent or slow down food spoilage.

N Microbiology technique designed to isolate pure bacterial strains.

O Growth that occurs in multiples based on earlier populations. An accelerating growth rate.

P The use of microorganisms to remove pollutants and contaminants from an environment.

Q The first phase of growth in a closed microbial culture, in which there is no appreciable increase in numbers. Cell numbers are relatively constant.

R A small circular piece of DNA commonly found in bacteria.

S A member of the kingdom Protista: a unicellular or simple multicellular organism, e.g. algae.

T A type of asexual reproduction carried out by most bacteria where the parent cell splits into two identical cells.

U A terrestrial heterotrophic organism, with rigid cell walls of chitin.

W A staining technique used to classify bacteria into two categories, based on the chemical composition of the cell wall.

VOCAB

Chapter 2

Cloning and Cell Culture

Key concepts

▶ Cloning is the process of producing genetically identical individuals. It can occur naturally or assisted by human intervention.

▶ Cloning technology has many applications, including in the rapid production of transgenics.

▶ A clone can be produced from a somatic cell using a technique called somatic cell nuclear transfer (SCNT).

▶ Stem cell technology offers a way to provide immune-compatible tissues for medicine.

Key terms

adult stem cells

clone

embryo splitting

embryonic stem cells (ESC)

micropropagation

multipotent

pluripotent

potency

self renewal

somatic cell nuclear transfer (SCNT)

therapeutic cloning

tissue engineering

totipotent

Learning Objectives

☐ 1. Use the **KEY TERMS** to compile a glossary for this topic.

☐ 2. Explain what is meant by a **clone**. Identify the current and potential uses of cloning technology. Distinguish between cloned organisms and cloning of stem cell lines.

Plant Tissue Culture

pages 53-54

☐ 3. Describe how plants are cloned by **micropropagation** (tissue culture), including reference to: growth media, aseptic technique, and use of plant growth regulators. Discuss, in a balanced way, the benefits and drawbacks of plant tissue culture.

☐ 4. Discuss the applications of micropropagation in modern horticulture, including as a way in which to rapidly propagate transgenic plants and as a way of speeding up the selection process.

Cloning in Animals

pages 55-57

☐ 5. Appreciate that cloning has traditionally been achieved through **embryo splitting**. Explain the principles involved in this technology and identify its disadvantages.

☐ 6. Describe the use of somatic cell nuclear transfer to produce cloned animals (e.g. Dolly the sheep). Compare SCNT with cloning by embryo splitting. Describe the advantages and disadvantages of SCNT.

☐ 7. Describe the benefits, disadvantages, and potential consequences of cloning as a general technique. Include reference to its effects on genetic diversity.

Stem Cells and Tissue Engineering

pages 58-59

☐ 8. Describe the properties of **stem cells**, including **self-renewal** and **potency**. Describe the usual role of stem cells in multicellular organisms.

☐ 9. Distinguish between **totipotent** and **pluripotent** cells. Distinguish between **embryonic stem cells** (ESC) and **adult stem cells** with respect to potency.

☐ 10. Describe the advantages of using ESC in **therapeutic cloning**. Explain how these ESC are produced using **somatic cell nuclear transfer** (SCNT). Discuss how stem cell technology meets, or could meet, human needs and demands.

☐ 11. Identify technical and ethical difficulties associated with stem cell technology and tissues engineering.

Weblinks:
www.thebiozone.com/
weblink/MnB-3725/

Plant Tissue Culture

Plant tissue culture, or **micropropagation**, is a method used for **cloning** plants. It is used widely for the rapid multiplication of commercially important plant species with superior genotypes, as well as in the recovery programmes for endangered plant species. Plant productivity and quality may be rapidly improved, and resistance to disease, pollutants, and insects increased. Continued culture of a limited number of cloned varieties leads to a change in the genetic composition of the population (genetic variation is reduced). New genetic stock may be introduced into cloned lines periodically to prevent this reduction in genetic diversity. Micropropagation is possible because differentiated plant cells have the potential to give rise to all the cells of an adult plant. It has considerable advantages over traditional methods of plant propagation (see table below), but it is very labor intensive. In addition, the optimal conditions for growth and regeneration must be determined and plants propagated in this way may be genetically unstable or infertile, with chromosomes structurally altered or in unusual numbers. The success of tissue culture is affected by factors such as selection of **explant** material, the composition of the culturing media, plant hormone levels, lighting, and temperature.

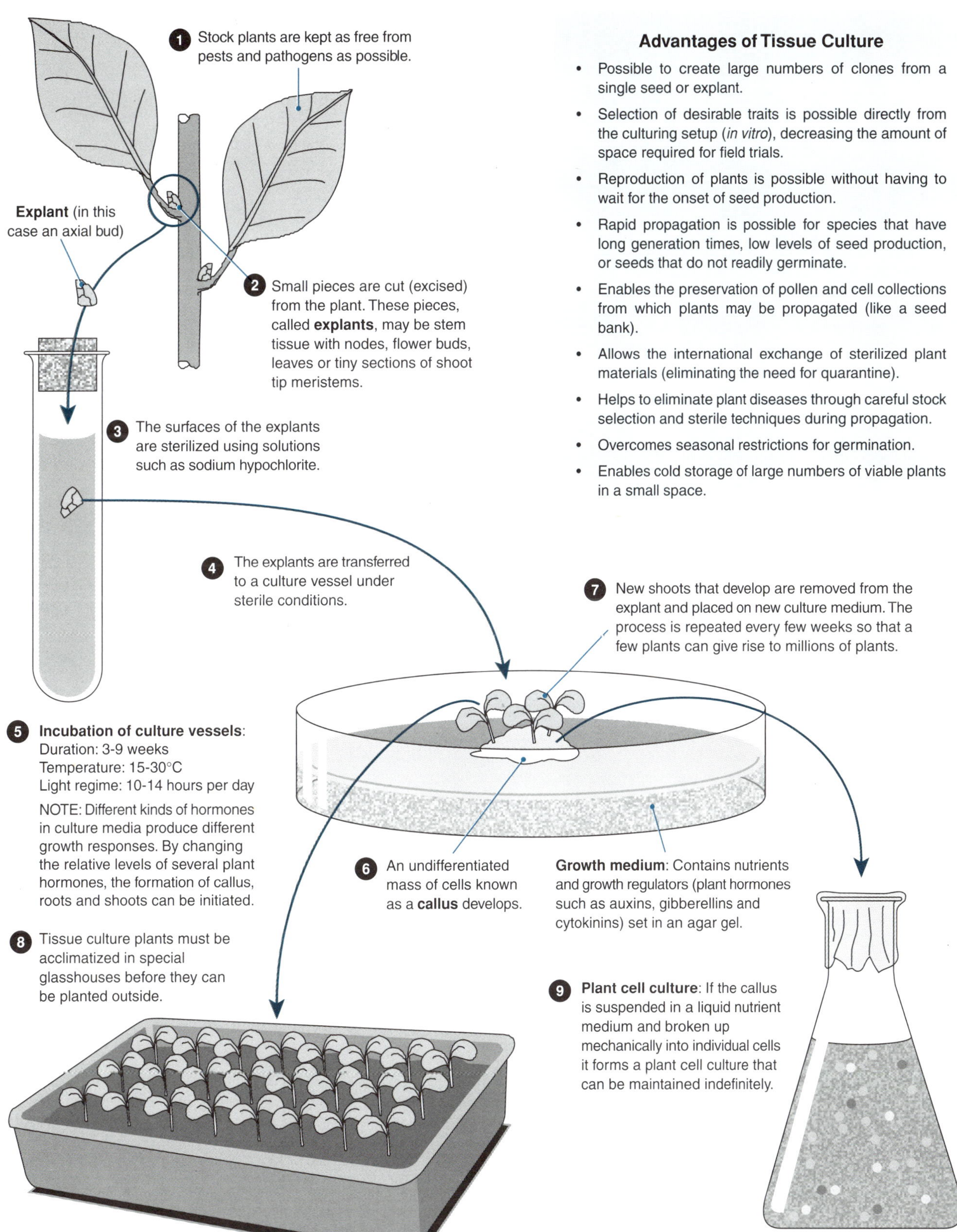

Advantages of Tissue Culture

- Possible to create large numbers of clones from a single seed or explant.
- Selection of desirable traits is possible directly from the culturing setup (*in vitro*), decreasing the amount of space required for field trials.
- Reproduction of plants is possible without having to wait for the onset of seed production.
- Rapid propagation is possible for species that have long generation times, low levels of seed production, or seeds that do not readily germinate.
- Enables the preservation of pollen and cell collections from which plants may be propagated (like a seed bank).
- Allows the international exchange of sterilized plant materials (eliminating the need for quarantine).
- Helps to eliminate plant diseases through careful stock selection and sterile techniques during propagation.
- Overcomes seasonal restrictions for germination.
- Enables cold storage of large numbers of viable plants in a small space.

Cloning and Cell Culture

KNOW

Micropropagation of the Tasmanian blackwood tree *(Acacia melanoxylon)*

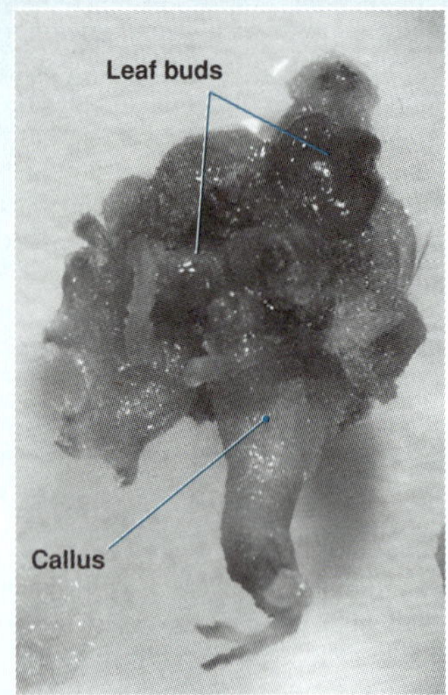

Greening and formation of leaf buds on a callus growing on culturing medium.

Shoots with juvenile leaves growing from a callus on media. They appear identical to those produced directly from seeds.

Seedling with juvenile foliage 6 months after transfer to greenhouse.

Micropropagation is increasingly used in conjunction with genetic engineering to propagate transgenic plants. Genetic engineering and micropropagation achieve similar results to conventional selective breeding but more precisely, quickly, and independently of growing season. The **Tasmanian blackwood** (above) is well suited to this type of manipulation. It is a versatile hardwood tree now being extensively trialed in some countries as a replacement for tropical hardwoods. The timber is of high quality, but genetic variations between individual trees lead to differences in timber quality and color. Tissue culture allows the multiple propagation of trees with desirable traits (e.g. uniform timber color). Tissue culture could also help to find solutions to problems that cannot be easily solved by forestry management. When combined with genetic engineering (introduction of new genes into the plant) problems of pest and herbicide susceptibility may be resolved. Genetic engineering may also be used to introduce a gene for male sterility, thereby stopping pollen production. This would improve the efficiency of conventional breeding programmes by preventing self-pollination of flowers (the manual removal of stamens is difficult and very labor intensive).

Information courtesy of Raewyn Poole, University of Waikato (unpublished MSc thesis)

1. Explain the general purpose of plant **micropropagation**: _______________________________________

____

2. (a) Explain what a **callus** is: ____

____

   (b) Explain how a callus may be stimulated to initiate root and shoot formation: _______________________

____

3. Discuss the advantages and disadvantages of **micropropagation** compared with traditional propagation methods:

____

____

____

____

____

____

____

____

____

4. Describe a potential problem with micropropagation in terms of long term ability to adapt to environmental changes:

____

____

Cloning by Embryo Splitting

Clones are genetically identical individuals produced from one parent. Livestock breeds frequently produce only one or two individuals per pregnancy and all individuals in a herd will have different traits. Cloning makes it possible to produce high value herds with identical traits more quickly. Embryo splitting, or artificial twinning, is the simplest way to create a clone as it simply replicates the natural twinning process. A fertilized egg is grown into eight cells before being split into four individual embryos, each consisting of just two cells. The four genetically identical embryos are then implanted into surrogate mothers.

While this technique produces multiple clones, the clones are derived from an embryo whose physical characteristics are not completely known until the animal matures. This represents a serious limitation for practical applications when the purpose of the procedure is to produce high value livestock quickly. In 2000, a rhesus macaque was cloned in this manner, with the goal of producing identical individuals that could be used to perfect new therapies for human disease. Cloning technology can also be used to produce early embryos from which undifferentiated stem cells can be isolated for use in tissue and cell engineering.

Livestock are selected for cloning on the basis of desirable qualities such as wool, meat, or milk productivity.

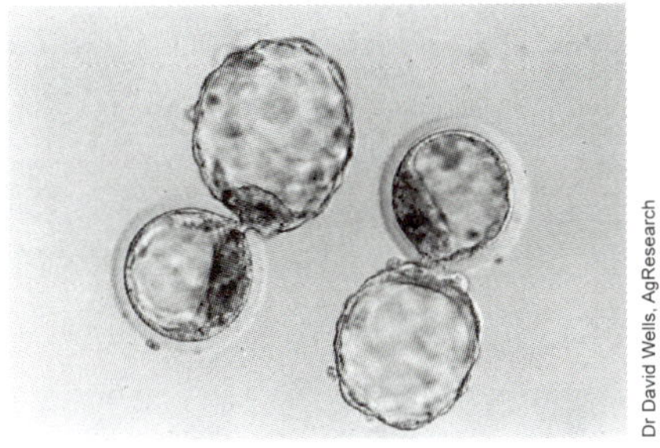

Cloned embryos immediately prior to implantation into a surrogate. These are at the blastocyst stage (a mass of cells that have begun to differentiate).

The individuals produced by embryo splitting have the same characteristics as the parents.

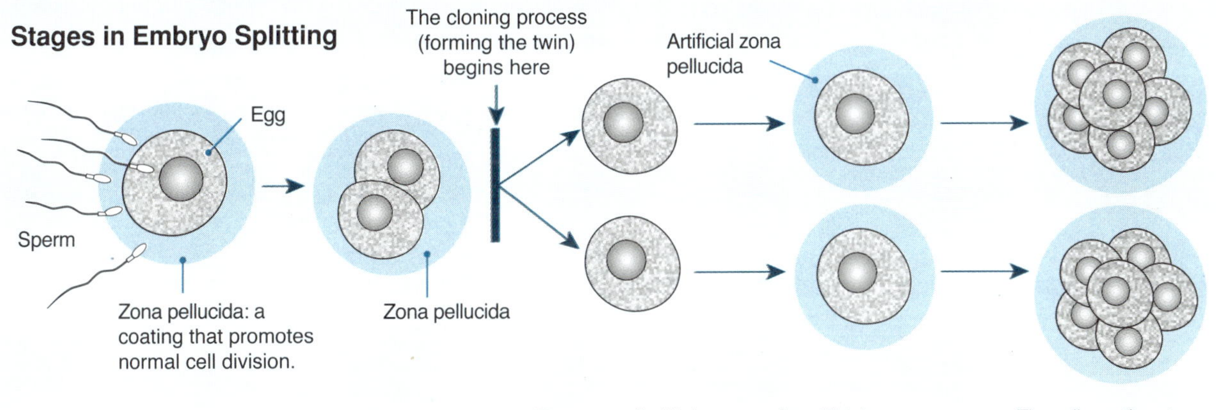

1. With respect to animals, explain the term **cloning**: ____

____

2. Briefly list the possible benefits to be gained from cloning the following:

   (a) Stem cells for medical use: ____

   ____

   ____

   ____

   (b) High milk yielding cows: ____

   ____

   ____

   ____

3. Suggest one reason why it would undesirable to produce all livestock using embryo splitting: ____________

____

Related activities: Cloning by Nuclear Transfer

KNOW

Cloning and Cell Culture

Cloning by Somatic Cell Nuclear Transfer

The Issue

Clones produced in using traditional embryo-splitting must mature before their phenotype is known. Scientists wanted to speed up the selection process and produce clones directly from a proven phenotype.

The technique developed to do this is called **somatic cell nuclear transfer**. It involves returning a somatic cell (from an individual of known phenotype) to a dormant state and then fusing it with an egg cell in which the nucleus is removed. Embryonic development is triggered and the resulting embryo is implanted into a surrogate mother.

The primary focus of the new cloning technologies is to provide an economically viable way to rapidly produce transgenic animals with very precise genetic modifications.

Concept 1

Somatic cells can be made to return to a dormant or embryonic state so that their genes will not be expressed.

Concept 2

The nucleus of a cell can be removed and replaced with the nucleus of an unrelated cell. Cells can be made to fuse together.

Concept 3

Fertilized egg cells produce embryos. Egg cells that contain the nucleus of a donor cell will produce embryos with DNA identical to the donor cell.

Concept 4

Embryos can be implanted into surrogate mothers and develop to full term with seemingly no ill effects.

Somatic Cell Nuclear Transfer (SCNT)

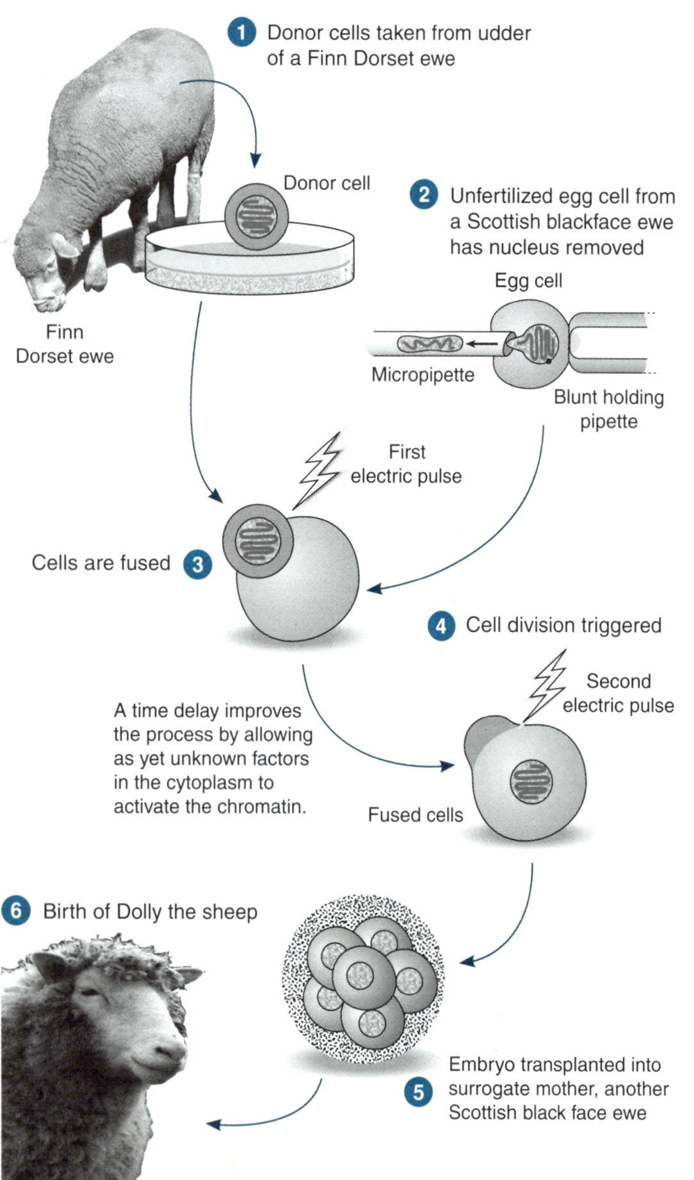

Techniques

Donor cells from the udder of a Finn Dorset ewe are taken and cultured in a low nutrient media for a week. The nutrient deprived cells stop dividing and become **dormant**.

An **unfertilized egg** from a Scottish blackface ewe has the nucleus removed using a micropipette. The rest of the cell contents are left intact.

The dormant udder cell and the recipient denucleated egg cell are fused using a mild electric pulse.

A second electric pulse triggers cellular activity and cell division, jump starting the cell into development. This can also be triggered by chemical means.

After six days the embryo is transplanted into a surrogate mother, another Scottish blackface ewe.

After a 148 day gestation 'Dolly' is born. DNA profiling shows she is genetically identical to the original Finn Dorset cell donor.

Outcomes

Dolly, a Finn Dorset lamb, was born at the Roslin Institute (near Edinburgh) in July 1996. She was the first mammal to be cloned from **non-embryonic** cells, i.e. cells that had already differentiated into their final form. Dolly's birth showed that the process leading to cell specialization is not irreversible and that cells can be 'reprogrammed' into an embryonic state. Although cloning seems relatively easy there are many problems that occur. Of the hundreds of eggs that were reconstructed only 29 formed embryos and only Dolly survived to birth.

Further Applications

In animal reproductive technology, cloning has facilitated the rapid production of genetically superior stock. These animals may then be dispersed among commercial herds. The **primary focus** of the new cloning technologies is to provide an economically viable way to rapidly produce transgenic animals with very precise genetic modifications.

Related activities: Cloning by Embryo Splitting

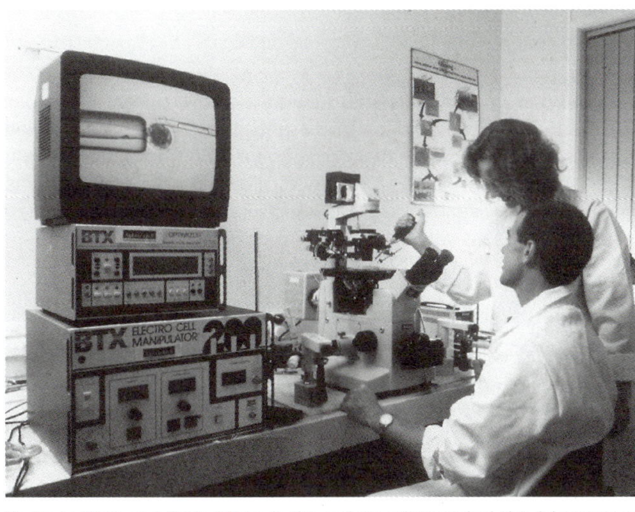

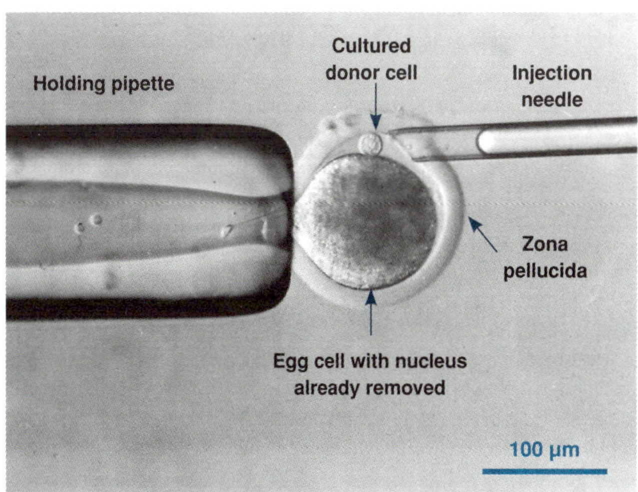

Dr David Wells and Pavla Misica in the embryo micromanipulation laboratory at AgResearch in Hamilton, New Zealand (monitor's image is enlarged on the right).

A single cultured cell is injected underneath the zona pellucida (the outer membrane) and positioned next to the egg cell (step 3 of diagram on previous page).

Adult cloning heralds a new chapter in the breeding of livestock. Traditional breeding methods are slow, unpredictable, and suffer from a time delay in waiting to see what the phenotype is like before breeding the next generation. Adult cloning methods now allow a rapid spread of valuable livestock into commercial use among farmers. It will also allow the livestock industry to respond rapidly to market changes in the demand for certain traits in livestock products. In New Zealand, 10 healthy clones were produced from a single cow (the differences in coat color patterns arise from the random migration of pigment cells in early embryonic development).

Lady is the last surviving cow of the rare Enderby Island (south of N.Z.) cattle breed. Adult cloning was used to produce her genetic duplicate, Elsie (born 31 July 1998). Elsie represents the first demonstration of the use of adult cloning in animal conservation.

1. Explain how cloning using **nuclear transfer** techniques differs from **embryo splitting**:

2. Explain how each of the following events is controlled in the **nuclear transfer** process:

    (a) The switching off of all genes in the donor cell:

    (b) The fusion (combining) of donor cell with enucleated egg cell:

    (c) The activation of the cloned cell into producing an embryo:

3. Describe a potential application of nuclear transfer technology for the cloning of animals:

Stem Cell Technology

Stem cells are undifferentiated cells able to give rise to a number of other specialized cell types. Their two important properties, **self renewal** and **potency**, make them valuable as a source of cell lines for research and therapy. Two types of stem cells are important in medicine and research. **Embryonic stem cells**, which are found in the early embryo, and **adult stem cells**, which occur in some tissues of adults and children. Stem cell research is still at an early stage and much has to be learned about the environments that cells require in order to differentiate into specific cell types. However, the potential applications include tissue engineering and cell therapy to replace diseased or damaged cells with new ones grown in culture.

Embryonic Stem Cells

Embryonic stem cells (ESCs) are pluripotent stem cells from the inner cell mass of blastocysts (below). Blastocysts are embryos of about 50-150 cells that are about five days old. Most ESCs come from IVF embryos, which have been donated for research. When grown *in vitro*, ESCs retain their pluripotency for many cell divisions, provided they are not stimulated to differentiate.

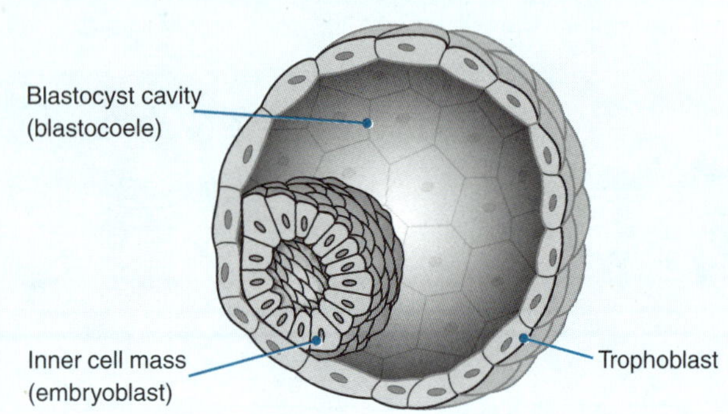

Stem Cell Properties

Self renewal: The ability to divide many times while maintaining an unspecialized state.

Potency: The ability to differentiate into specialized cells.

The Potency of Stem Cells

Totipotent: Stem cells that can differentiate into all the cells in an organism. In humans, only the zygote and its first few divisions are totipotent.

Pluripotent: Stem cells that can become any cells of the body, except extra-embryonic cells, such as the placenta. Embryonic stem cells are pluripotent.

Multipotent: Stem cells that give rise a limited number of cell types, usually related to their tissue of origin (e.g. hematopoietic stem cells give rise to all blood cell types).

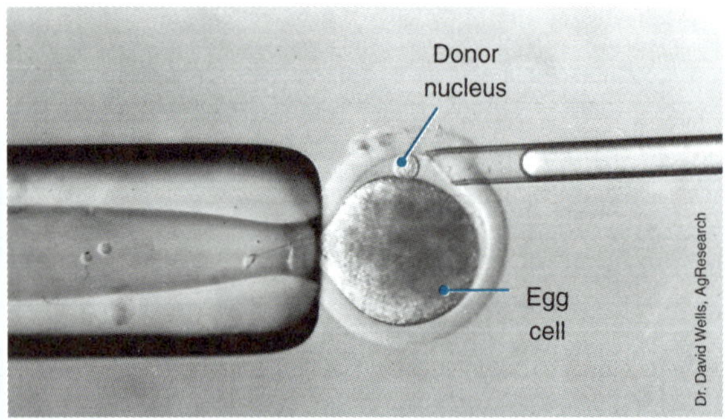

Histocompatibility refers to the compatibility of cells and tissues between different individuals. If donor material is poorly matched to the recipient, the recipient's immune system rejects the donor cells. Stem cell cloning (also called **therapeutic cloning**) provides a way around this problem. Stem cell cloning produces cells that have been derived from the recipient, and are therefore histocompatible. Transplantation success rates are much improved and immunosuppressant drugs are no longer required.

Embryonic Stem Cell Cloning

Somatic cell nuclear transfer can be used to create an embryo and therefore a source of ESCs. When ESCs are given the right growth conditions, they will differentiate into specialized cell types. Scientists can control this process by manipulating the culture conditions to produce cells of a particular type for a particular purpose (e.g. heart cells to replaced damaged heart tissue).

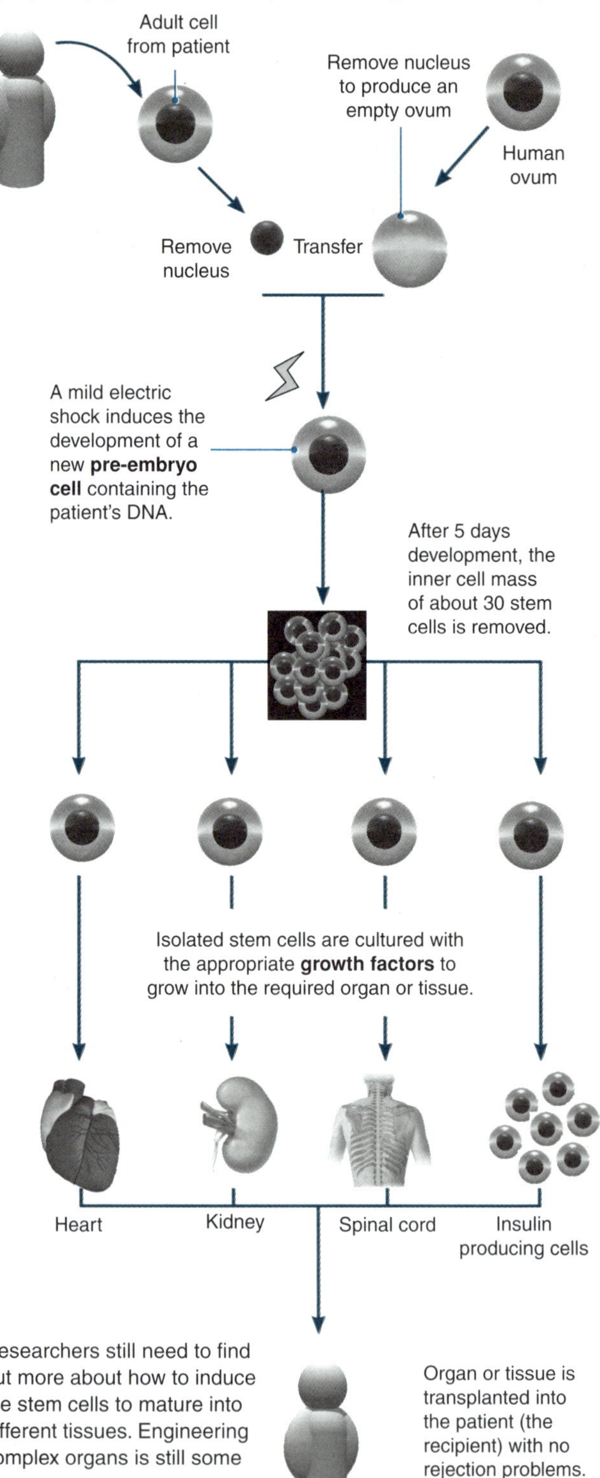

Researchers still need to find out more about how to induce the stem cells to mature into different tissues. Engineering complex organs is still some time away.

Weblinks: Stem Cell Resources

Engineering a Living Skin

New technologies such as cell replacement therapy and tissue engineering require a disease-free and plentiful supply of cells of specific types. Tissue engineering, for example, involves inducing living cells to grow on a scaffold of natural or synthetic material to produce a three-dimensional tissue such as bone or skin.

In 1998, an artificial skin called **Apligraf** became the first product of this type to be approved for use as a biomedical device. It is now widely used in place of skin grafts to treat diabetic ulcers and burns, with the patient's own cells and tissues helping to complete the biological repair. Producing Apligraf is a three stage process (right), which results in a bilayered, living structure capable of stimulating wound repair through its own growth factors and proteins. The cells used to start the culture are usually obtained from discarded neonatal foreskins collected after circumcision. The key to future tissue engineering will be the developments in stem cell research. The best source of stem cells is from very early embryos, but some adult tissues (e.g. bone marrow) also contain stem cells.

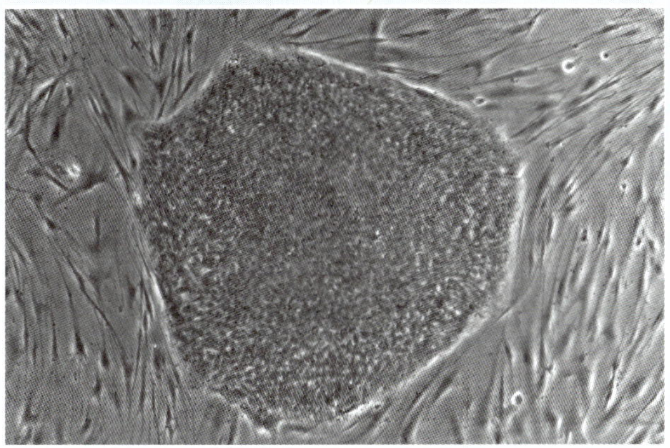

Human embryonic stem cells (ESCs) growing on mouse embryonic fibroblasts. The mouse fibroblasts act as feeder cells for the culture, releasing nutrients and providing a surface for the ESCs to grow on.

Human dermal cells

Day 0

Undifferentiated human dermal cells (fibroblasts) are combined with a gel containing **collagen**, the primary protein of skin. The dermal cells move through the gel, rearranging the collagen and producing a fibrous, living matrix similar to the natural dermis.

Step 1
Form the lower dermal layer

Human epidermal cells

Day 6

Human epidermal cells (called **keratinocytes**) are placed on top of the dermal layer. These cells multiply to cover the dermal layer.

Step 2
Form the upper epidermal layer

Day 10

Exposing the culture to air prompts the epidermal cells to form the outer protective (keratinized) layer of skin. The final size of the Apligraf product is about 75 mm and, from this, tens of thousands of pieces can be made.

Step 3

1. Describe the benefits of using a tissue engineered skin product, such as Apligraf, to treat wounds that require grafts:

2. (a) Describe one of the major difficulties with transplantation of cells:

   (b) How could this problem be overcome?

   (c) Describe one of the ethical concerns associated with this solution:

3. Discuss some of the difficulties that must be overcome when growing *in vitro* tissue cultures:

Cloning and Cell Culture

KEY TERMS: Crossword

Complete the crossword below, which will test your understanding of key terms in this chapter and their meanings.

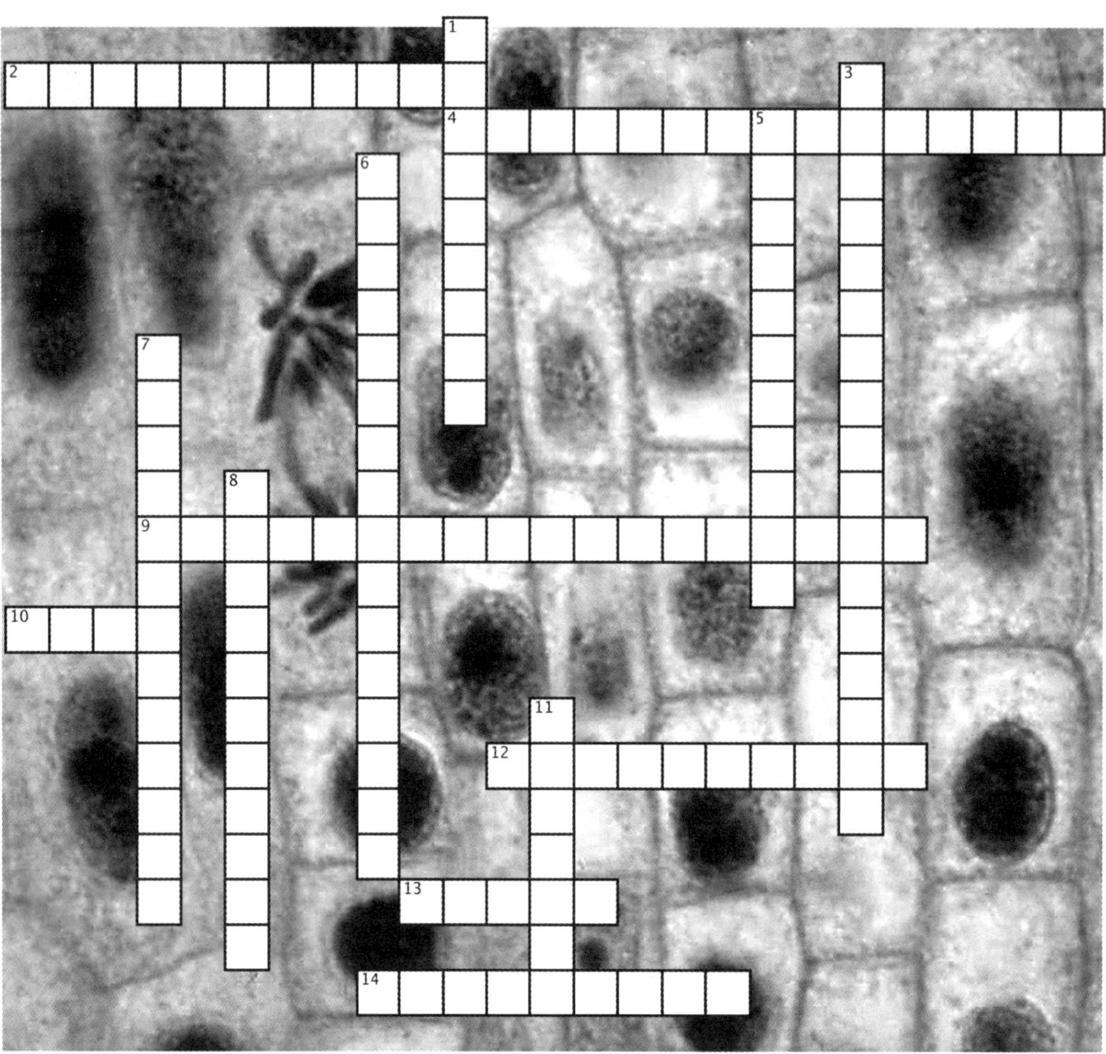

Clues Across

2. Stem cells that give rise a limited number of cell types, usually related to their tissue of origin, are called this.

4. A simple form of cloning that replicates the natural twinning process. (2 words 6, 9)

9. The production of cloned embryonic stem cells for purposes of repairing damaged organs. (2 words 11, 7)

10. The transfer of the nucleus from a somatic cell into an egg from which the nucleus has been removed. (Acronym)

12. This type of cell is produced in the first few divisions of a fertilized egg.

13. An organism that is genetically identical to the parent.

14. Pluripotent stem cells formed in the early embryo are called _ _ _ _ _ _ _ _ _ stem cells.

Clues Down

1. These are unspecialized cells that may differentiate into one of many kinds of cell. (2 words: 4, 5)

3. A multidisciplinary field involving biology, medicine, and engineering which produces laboratory-grown molecules, cells, tissues, or organs to replace or defective or injured body parts. (2 words: 6, 11)

5. Embryonic stem cells are called this.

6. A method of cloning plants using explant tissue which is grown in sterile conditions in a culture vessel.

7. Undifferentiated multipotent cell type found in the tissues or organs of multicellular organisms.(3 words: 5, 4, 4)

8. The ability to go through numerous cycles of cell division while maintaining the undifferentiated state. (2 words: 4, 7)

11. The ability to differentiate into specialized cells.

Chapter 3

Genetic Manipulation

Key terms

annealing
DNA amplification
DNA chip (microarray)
DNA ligase
DNA ligation
DNA (gene) probes
DNA (genetic) screening
gene cloning
gel electrophoresis
gene marker
genetically modified organism (GMO)
gene technology
plasmid
polymerase chain reaction (PCR)
recombinant DNA technology
restriction enzyme
reverse transcriptase
taq polymerase
transgenesis
vector

Key concepts

▶ Biotechnology often makes use of GMOs.

▶ Genetic modification relies on a few basic techniques, widely applied.

▶ Recombinant vectors can be used to introduce novel genetic material into organisms.

▶ GMOs are widely used in industry, agriculture, and medicine to produce valuable commodities.

▶ Genetic modification potentially offers huge benefits, but presents ethical concerns for many.

Learning Objectives

☐ 1. Use the **KEY TERMS** to compile a glossary for this topic.

Basic Principles   pages 60-70, 72-73, also see 114-115

☐ 2. Distinguish **gene technology** from the more general term, biotechnology. Understand that **genetic transfer** involves the insertion of DNA from one organism into another, resulting in a genetically modified organism (**GMO**).

☐ 3. Recognize that the same, relatively few, basic techniques (#4-8) are used in a range of different processes and applications.

☐ 4. Explain the use of **restriction enzymes** in **recombinant DNA technology**.

☐ 5. Explain the technique and purpose of **DNA ligation** and **annealing**, including the role of **DNA ligase**.

☐ 6. Explain the role of **gel electrophoresis** (of DNA) in gene technology.

☐ 7. Describe and explain the role of **polymerase chain reaction** (**PCR**) in **DNA amplification**. Include reference to the role of **Taq polymerase** in this process.

☐ 8. Describe how genes are cloned using microbial host cells (*in vivo* **gene cloning**). Explain how gene expression is achieved in the organism that receives the molecular clone, e.g. in a crop plant where a gene of interest is introduced using the bacterium *Agrobacterium tumefaciens*.

☐ 9. Identify problems with cloning eukaryotic genes and explain how the retorviral enzyme **reverse transcriptase** is used to create a completed artificial gene.

☐ 10. Describe how **DNA** (**gene**) **probes** are used to screen for specific genes (or gene markers). Understand that **DNA chips** (**microarray**) use the same principles as a gene probes, but can screen thousands of sequences at once.

Processes and Applications   pages 71, 74-81

☐ 11. Describe and explain **transgenesis**, including the role of **vectors**, such as **plasmids**, in integrating foreign DNA into another genome. Understand that organisms are usually transformed with recombinant vectors produced using restriction enzymes and DNA ligation.

☐ 12. Describe the range of applications of transgenic organisms. Identify ethical concerns with the use of transgenic organisms. Are these concerns different for transgenic microorganisms, plants, and animals?

☐ 13. Describe the use of gene technology in agriculture. Examples could include:
  • Crop resistance to herbicides and/or insect pests.
  • Expansion of crop growing range (changes in environmental tolerance).
  • The development of new crops or improvement of crop yield or nutritional profile in existing crops (e.g. golden rice).

Weblinks:

*www.thebiozone.com/
weblink/MnB-3725/*

Amazing Organisms, Amazing Enzymes

Before the 1980s scientists knew of only a few organisms that could survive in extreme conditions. Indeed, many scientists believed that life in highly saline or high temperature and pressure environments was impossible. That view changed with the discovery of bacteria inhabiting the deep sea hydrothermal vents. They tolerate temperatures over 110°C and pressures of over 200 atmospheres. Bacteria were also found in volcanic hot pools on land, some surviving at temperatures in excess of 80°C. Most enzymes are denatured at temperatures above 40°C, but these **thermophilic** bacteria have enzymes that are fully functional at high temperatures. This discovery led to the development of one of most important techniques in biotechnology, the **polymerase chain reaction** (PCR).

PCR is a technique, first described in the 1970s, that allows scientists to copy and multiply a piece of DNA millions of times. The DNA is heated to 98°C so that it separates into single strands and polymerase enzyme is added to synthesize new DNA strands from supplied free nucleotides. This earlier technique was labour intensive and expensive because the polymerase denatured at the high temperatures and had to be replaced every cycle. In 1985, a thermophilic polymerase (*Taq* **polymerase**) was isolated from the bacterium *Thermophilus aquaticus,* which inhabited the hot springs of Yellowstone National Park. Isolating this enzyme enabled automation of the PCR process, because the polymerase was stable throughout multiple cycles of synthesis. This led to an rapid growth in biotechnology, and gene technology in particular, because DNA samples could be easily copied for sequencing.

Searching for novel compounds in organisms from extreme environments is important in the development of new biotechnologies. Organisms must have compounds that can work in their specific environment, and the identification and extraction of these may allow them to be adapted for human use. For example, the Antarctic sea sponge *Kirkpatrickia variolosa* produces an alkaloid excreted as a toxic defence to prevent other organisms growing nearby. Tests indicate that this same chemical may have biological activity against cancer cells. Compounds from other sponge species are currently being assessed to treat a range of diseases including cancer, AIDS, tuberculosis and other bacterial infections, and cystic fibrosis.

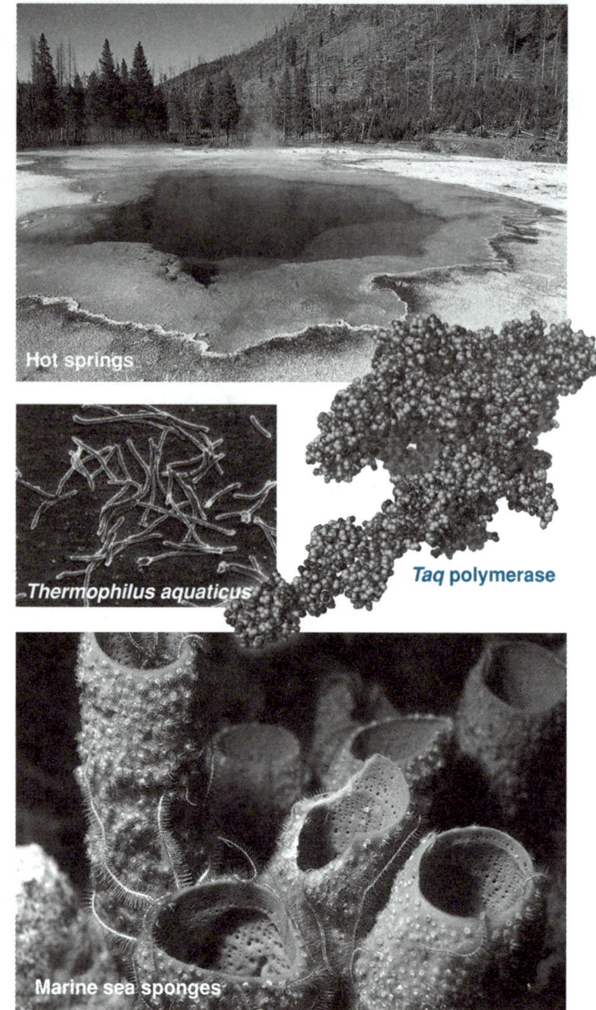

1. Explain why PCR was not a viable technique until the mid 1980s: _______________________________________

2. Explain why *Taq* polymerase was so important in the development of PCR: _______________________________

3. Explain how investigating the lifestyles of other organisms can lead to advances in unrelated areas of science:

What is Genetic Modification?

The genetic modification of organisms is a vast industry, and the applications of the technology are exciting and far reaching. It brings new hope for medical cures, promises to increase yields in agriculture, and has the potential to help solve the world's pollution and resource crises. Organisms with artificially altered DNA are referred to as **genetically modified organisms** or **GMOs**. They may be modified in one of three ways (outlined below). Some of the current and proposed applications of gene technology raise complex ethical and safety issues, where the benefits of their use must be carefully weighed against the risks to human health, as well as the health and well-being of other organisms and the environment as a whole.

Producing Genetically Modified Organisms (GMOs)

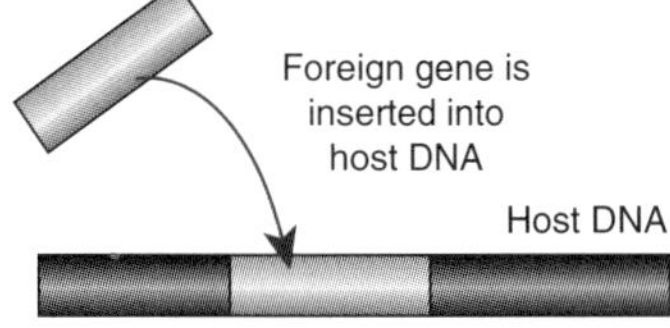

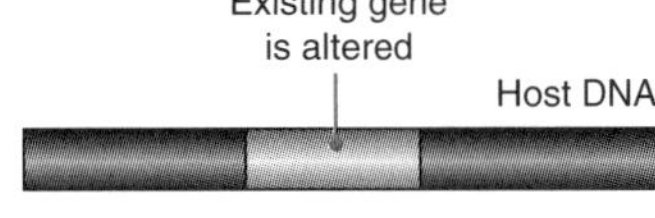

Add a foreign gene

A novel (foreign) gene is inserted from another species. This will enable the GMO to express the trait coded by the new gene. Organisms genetically altered in this way are referred to as **transgenic**.

Alter an existing gene

An existing gene may be altered to make it express at a higher level (e.g. growth hormone) or in a different way (in tissue that would not normally express it). This method is also used for gene therapy.

Delete or 'turn off' a gene

An existing gene may be deleted or deactivated (switched off) to prevent the expression of a trait (e.g. the deactivation of the ripening gene in tomatoes produced the Flavr-Savr tomato).

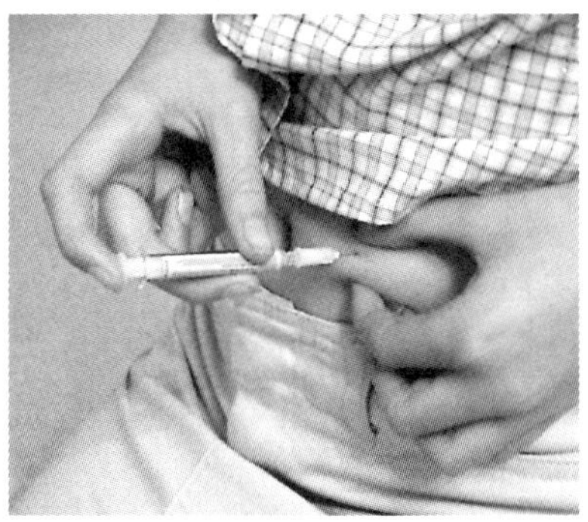

Human insulin, used to treat diabetic patients, is now produced using transgenic bacteria.

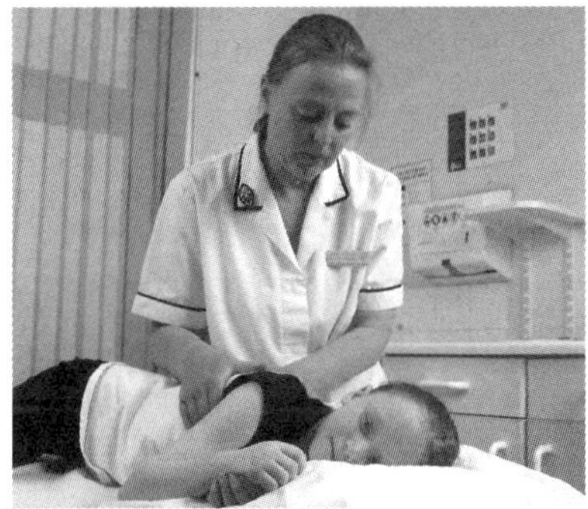

Gene therapy could be used treat genetic disorders, such as cystic fibrosis.

Manipulating gene action is one way in which to control processes such as ripening in fruit.

1. Using examples, discuss the ways in which an organism may be genetically modified (to produce a GMO):

   ____

   ____

   ____

   ____

   ____

   ____

2. Explain how human needs or desires have provided a stimulus for the development of the following biotechnologies:

   (a) Gene therapy: ____

   ____

   ____

   (b) The production and use of transgenic organisms: _______________________________

   ____

   ____

   (c) Plant micropropagation (tissue culture): _____________________________________

   ____

   ____

© BIOZONE International 2013
ISBN: 978-1-927173-72-5
Photocopying Prohibited

Related activities: Applications of GMOs
Weblinks: Biotechnology Tmeline

KNOW

Applications of GMOs

Techniques for genetic manipulation are now widely applied in food and enzyme technology, in industry and medicine, and in agriculture and horticulture. Microorganisms are among the most widely used GMOs, with applications ranging from pharmaceutical production and vaccine development to environmental clean-up. Crops are also popular candidates for genetic modification because they are easily propagated. Crops are commonly engineered for properties such as disease and pest resistance, herbicide resistance, high nutritional value, and environmental tolerance.

Application of GMOs

Extending shelf life

Genetic modification can alter the synthesis of ethylene, which controls the ripening process in fruits. This can delay fruit ripening by up to 6 weeks and extend shelf life. The technique has been used in tomatoes and strawberries.

Pest resistance

Plants can be engineered to produce their own insecticide. For example, potatoes engineered to express a bacterial toxin are resistant to attack from the Colorado potato beetle (above) which has developed resistance to all chemical controls.

Herbicide resistance

Genetically engineered herbicide resistance allows chemical weed killers, e.g. glyphosate, to be used without crop damage. Glyphosate resistant or "Round-Up ready" crops include soy, alfalfa, corn, cotton, canola, and sugar-beet.

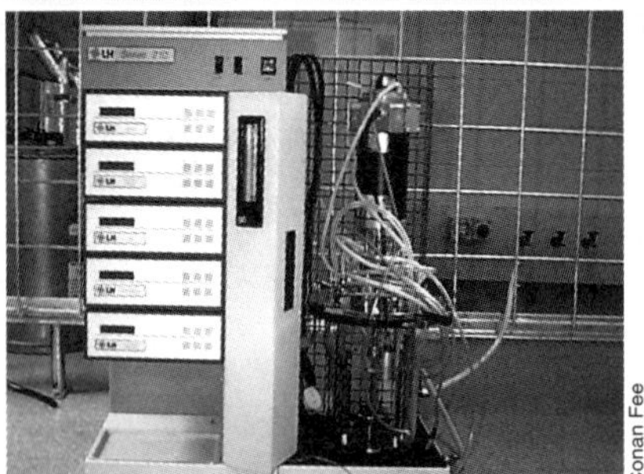

Biofactories

Transgenic bacteria are used to produce desirable products, such as hormones or proteins. Large quantities of a product can be produced using bioreactors (above). Examples: insulin production by recombinant bacteria or yeast, production of bovine growth hormone.

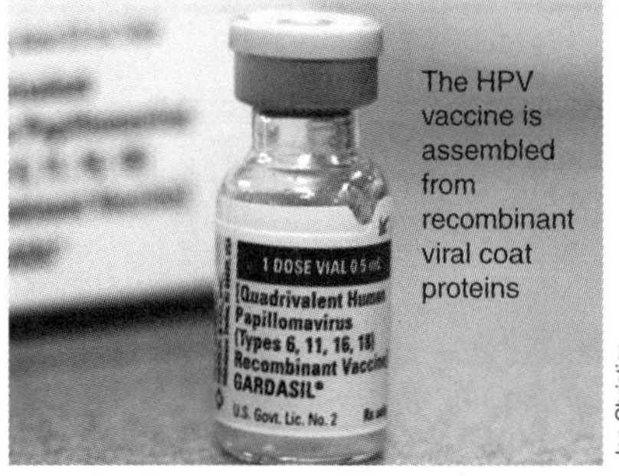

Vaccine development

Recombinant DNA vaccines include the widely used Hepatitis B vaccine and the more recent HPV vaccine. The purified antigenic components of the pathogen (e.g. bacterial cell wall or viral protein coat) are used in the vaccine and there is no risk of contracting the disease itself.

Transgenic Livestock

Research on transgenic livestock is concentrated on improving growth and body composition (e.g. muscle to fat ratio), on disease resistance, and on the quality and properties of animal products such as milk and wool. Some transgenics will secrete valuable human proteins in their milk.

1. In a short account, discuss how genetic modification of organisms has widened the scope of biotechnology:

KNOW

Related activities: *GM Plants-Golden Rice, Using Recombinant Bacteria, Production of Insulin, The Applications of Transgenesis*

Restriction Enzymes

One of the essential tools of genetic engineering is a group of special **restriction enzymes** (also known as restriction endonucleases). These have the ability to cut DNA molecules at very precise sequences of 4 to 8 base pairs called **recognition sites**. These enzymes are the "molecular scalpels" that allow genetic engineers to cut up DNA in a controlled way. Although first isolated in 1970, these enzymes were discovered earlier in many bacteria. The purified forms of these bacterial restriction enzymes are used today as tools to cut DNA (see table on the next page for examples). Enzymes are named according to the bacterial species from which they were first isolated. By using a 'tool kit' of over 400 restriction enzymes recognizing about 100 recognition sites, genetic engineers can isolate, sequence, and manipulate individual genes derived from any type of organism. The sites at which the fragments of DNA are cut may result in overhanging "sticky ends" or non-overhanging "blunt ends". Pieces may later be joined together using an enzyme called **DNA ligase** in a process called **ligation**.

Sticky End Restriction Enzymes

1 A **restriction enzyme** cuts the double-stranded DNA molecule at its specific **recognition** site (see the table on the following page for a representative list of restriction enzymes and their recognition sites).

2 The cuts produce a DNA fragment with two **sticky ends** (ends with exposed nucleotide bases at each end). The piece it is removed from is also left with sticky ends.

Restriction enzymes may cut DNA leaving an overhang or sticky end, without its complementary sequence opposite. DNA cut in such a way is able to be joined to other exposed end fragments of DNA with matching sticky ends. Such joins are specific to their recognition sites.

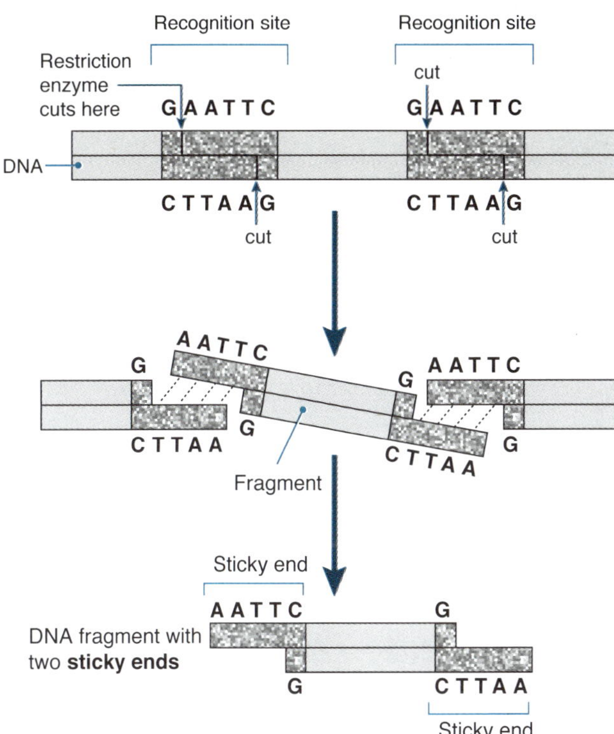

Blunt End Restriction Enzymes

1 A **restriction enzyme** cuts the double-stranded DNA molecule at its specific recognition site (see the table opposite for a representative list of restriction enzymes and their recognition sites).

2 The cuts produce a DNA fragment with two **blunt ends** (ends with no exposed nucleotide bases at each end). The piece it is removed from is also left with blunt ends.

It is possible to use restriction enzymes that cut leaving no overhang. DNA cut in such a way is able to be joined to any other blunt end fragment, but tends to be nonspecific because there are no sticky ends as recognition sites.

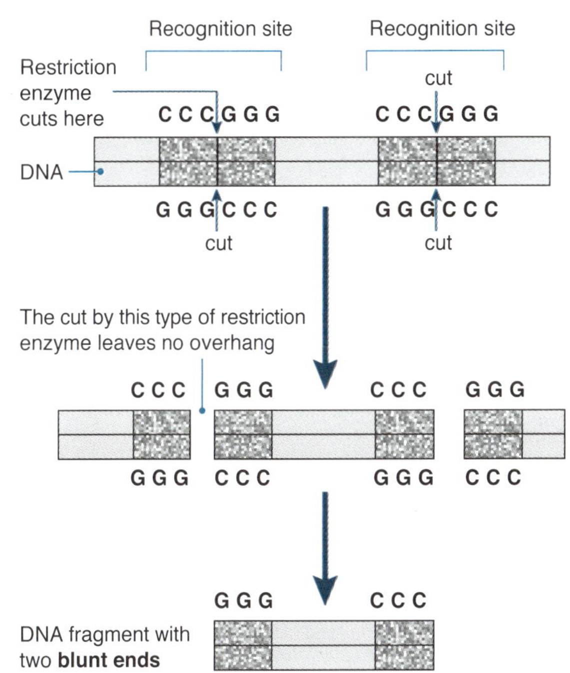

Genetic Manipulation

Related activities: Ligation
Weblinks: Restriction Enzymes Video

KNOW

Recognition sites for selected restriction enzymes

Origin of Restriction Enzymes

Restriction enzymes have been isolated from many bacteria. It was observed that certain *bacteriophages* (viruses that infect bacteria) could not infect bacteria other than their usual hosts. The reason was found to be that other potential hosts could destroy almost all of the phage DNA using *restriction enzymes* present naturally in their cells; a defence mechanism against the entry of foreign DNA. Restriction enzymes are named according to the species they were first isolated from, followed by a number to distinguish different enzymes isolated from the same organism.

Enzyme	Source	Recognition sites
EcoRI	*Escherichia coli* RY13	G A A T T C
BamHI	*Bacillus amyloliquefaciens* H	G G A T C C
HaeIII	*Haemophilus aegyptius*	G G C C
HindIII	*Haemophilus influenzae* Rd	A A G C T T
HpaI	*Haemophilus parainfluenzae*	G T T A A C
HpaII	*Haemophilus parainfluenzae*	C C G G
MboI	*Moraxella bovis*	G A T C
NotI	*Norcardia otitidis-caviarum*	G C G G C C G C
TaqI	*Thermus aquaticus*	T C G A

1. Explain the following terms, identifying their role in recombinant DNA technology:

    (a) Restriction enzyme: ____

    ____

    (b) Recognition site: ____

    ____

    (c) Sticky end: ____

    ____

    (d) Blunt end: ____

    ____

2. The action of a specific sticky end restriction enzyme is illustrated on the opposite page (top). Use the table above to:

    (a) Identify the **restriction enzyme** used: ____

    (b) Name the organism from which it was first isolated: ____

    (c) State the **base sequence** for this restriction enzyme's recognition site: ___________________________

3. A genetic engineer wants to use the restriction enzyme **BamHI** to cut the DNA sequence below:

    (a) Consult the table above and state the recognition site for this enzyme: ____________________________

    (b) Circle every **recognition site** on the DNA sequence below that could be cut by the enzyme **BamHI**:

```
         10             20             30             40             50             60
|AATGGGTACG CACAGTGGAT CCACGTAGTA TGCGATGCGT AGTGTTTATG GAGAGAAGAA|
         70             80             90            100            110            120
|AACGCGTCGC CTTTTATCGA TGCTGTACGG ATGCGGAAGT GGCGATGAGG ATCCATGCAA|
        130            140            150            160            170            180
|TCGCGGCCGA TCGXGTAATA TATCGTGGCT GCGTTTATTA TCGTGACTAG TAGCAGTATG|
        190            200            210            220            230            240
|CGATGTGACT GATGCTATGC TGACTATGCT ATGTTTTTAT GCTGGATCCA GCGTAAGCAT|
        250            260            270            280            290            300
|TTCGCTGCGT GGATCCCATA TCCTTATATG CATATATTCT TATACGGATC GCGCACGTTT|
```

    (c) State how many fragments of DNA were created by this action: _____________________________________

4. When restriction enzymes were first isolated in 1970, there were not many applications to which they could be put to use. Now, they are an important tool in genetic engineering. Describe the human needs and demands that have driven the development and use of restriction enzymes in genetic engineering:

    ____

    ____

    ____

Ligation

DNA fragments produced using restriction enzymes may be reassembled by a process called **ligation**. Pieces are joined together using an enzyme called **DNA ligase**. DNA of different origins produced in this way is called **recombinant DNA** (because it is DNA that has been recombined from different sources). The combined techniques of using restriction enzymes and ligation are the basic tools of genetic engineering (also known as recombinant DNA technology).

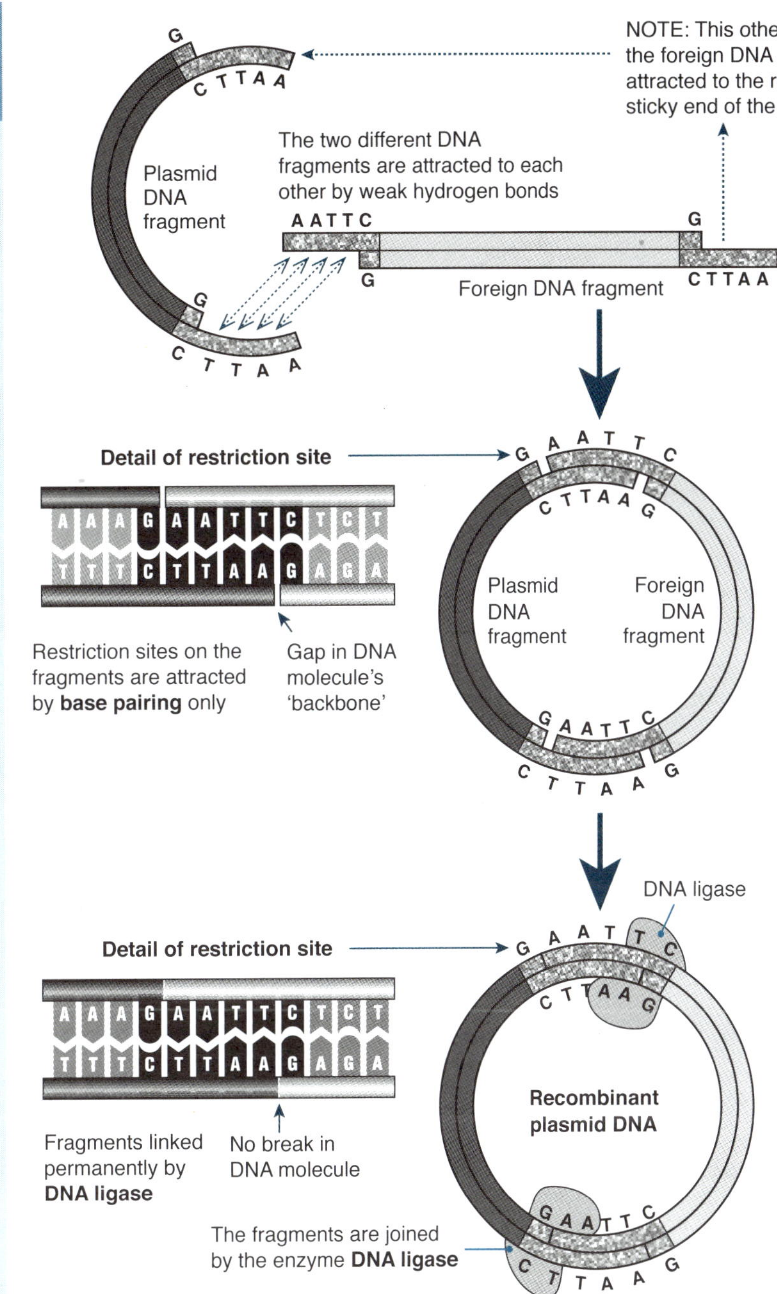

1. Explain in your own words the two main steps in the process of joining two DNA fragments together:

   (a) Annealing: ____

   ____

   (b) DNA ligase: ____

   ____

2. Briefly state the **usual role** of DNA ligase in a cell (Hint: Refer to a reference on DNA replication): ____

3. Explain why **ligation** can be considered the reverse of the **restriction enzyme** process: ____

   ____

© BIOZONE International 2013
ISBN: 978-1-927173-72-5
Photocopying Prohibited

Related activities: Restriction Enzymes

KNOW

Cloning a Gene *In Vivo*

It is possible to use recombinant DNA techniques to insert a gene of interest into another organism, and use that organism's replication machinery to clone the gene. This is called *in vivo gene cloning*. A **vector** is needed to transfer the foreign genetic material into another cell. Features of a good vector include being able to replicate inside their host organism, having one or more sites at which a restriction enzyme can cut, and having a **genetic marker** that allows them to be easily identified. Bacterial plasmids are commonly used as vectors because they are easy to manipulate, their restriction sites are well known, and they are readily taken up by cells in culture. Once the recombinant plasmid vector (containing the desired gene) has been taken up by bacterial cells the gene can be replicated many times as the bacteria grow and divide.

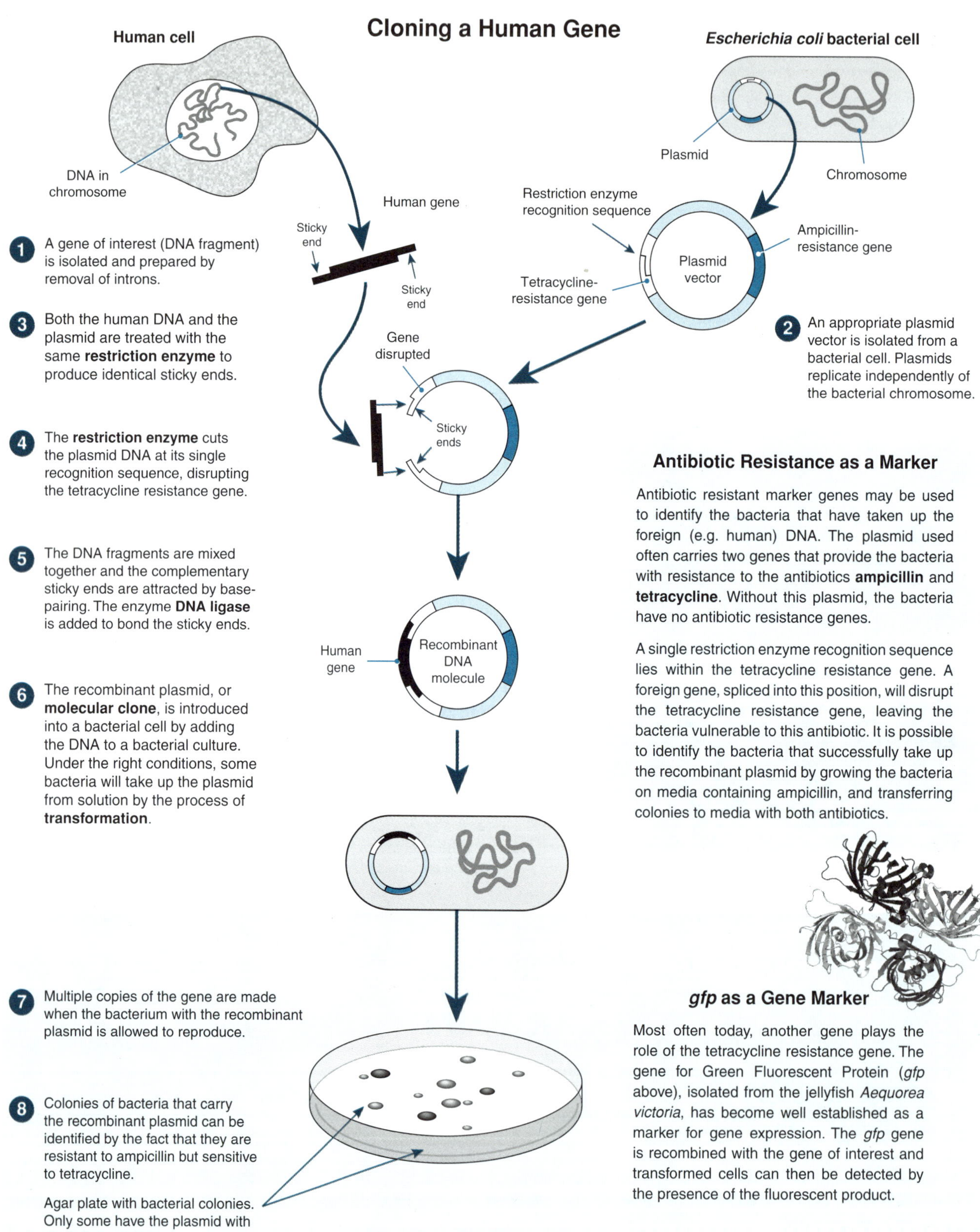

1. A gene of interest (DNA fragment) is isolated and prepared by removal of introns.

2. An appropriate plasmid vector is isolated from a bacterial cell. Plasmids replicate independently of the bacterial chromosome.

3. Both the human DNA and the plasmid are treated with the same **restriction enzyme** to produce identical sticky ends.

4. The **restriction enzyme** cuts the plasmid DNA at its single recognition sequence, disrupting the tetracycline resistance gene.

5. The DNA fragments are mixed together and the complementary sticky ends are attracted by base-pairing. The enzyme **DNA ligase** is added to bond the sticky ends.

6. The recombinant plasmid, or **molecular clone**, is introduced into a bacterial cell by adding the DNA to a bacterial culture. Under the right conditions, some bacteria will take up the plasmid from solution by the process of **transformation**.

7. Multiple copies of the gene are made when the bacterium with the recombinant plasmid is allowed to reproduce.

8. Colonies of bacteria that carry the recombinant plasmid can be identified by the fact that they are resistant to ampicillin but sensitive to tetracycline.

Agar plate with bacterial colonies. Only some have the plasmid with the human gene.

Antibiotic Resistance as a Marker

Antibiotic resistant marker genes may be used to identify the bacteria that have taken up the foreign (e.g. human) DNA. The plasmid used often carries two genes that provide the bacteria with resistance to the antibiotics **ampicillin** and **tetracycline**. Without this plasmid, the bacteria have no antibiotic resistance genes.

A single restriction enzyme recognition sequence lies within the tetracycline resistance gene. A foreign gene, spliced into this position, will disrupt the tetracycline resistance gene, leaving the bacteria vulnerable to this antibiotic. It is possible to identify the bacteria that successfully take up the recombinant plasmid by growing the bacteria on media containing ampicillin, and transferring colonies to media with both antibiotics.

gfp as a Gene Marker

Most often today, another gene plays the role of the tetracycline resistance gene. The gene for Green Fluorescent Protein (*gfp* above), isolated from the jellyfish *Aequorea victoria*, has become well established as a marker for gene expression. The *gfp* gene is recombined with the gene of interest and transformed cells can then be detected by the presence of the fluorescent product.

KNOW

Related activities: *Using Recombinant Bacteria*
Weblinks: *Gene Cloning*

Making a Clone Library

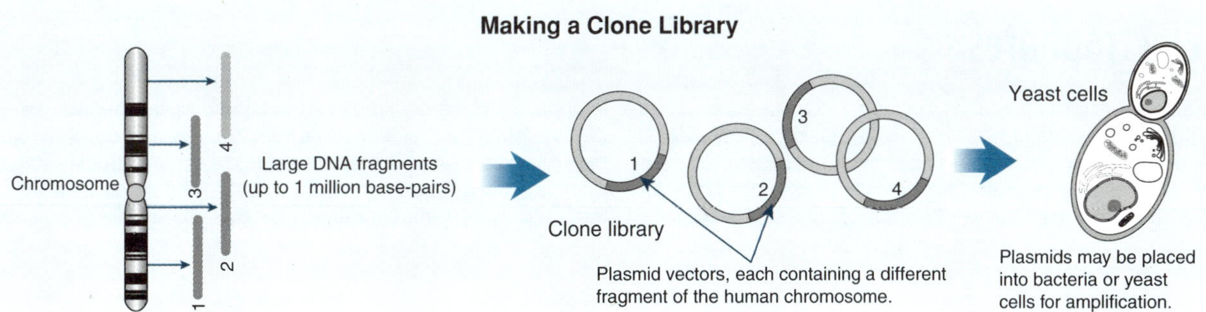

A **clone library** is a collection of DNA from a single organism created by *in vivo* cloning. The libraries are used to find genes of interest. Restriction enzymes cut DNA into fragments of varying lengths. Small fragments are inserted into vectors, such as plasmids, and large fragments can be packaged as artificial chromosomes. The genetic material is mixed with a host organism, usually bacteria for plasmids, and yeast cells for artificial chromosomes, where it is taken up into the cells. As the cells grow and divide, the number of DNA fragments is amplified. The fragments can then be cultured and sequenced.

1. Explain why it might be desirable to use *in vivo* methods to clone genes rather than PCR (*ex vivo* gene cloning):

2. Explain when it may not be desirable to use bacteria to clone genes:

3. Explain how a human gene is removed from a chromosome and placed into a plasmid.

4. A bacterial plasmid replicates at the same rate as the bacteria. If a bacteria containing a recombinant plasmid replicates and divides once every thirty minutes, calculate the number of plasmid copies there will be after twenty four hours:

5. When cloning a gene using **plasmid vectors**, the bacterial colonies containing the recombinant plasmids are mixed up with colonies that have none. All the colonies look identical, but some have taken up the plasmids with the human gene, and some have not. Explain how the colonies with the recombinant plasmids are identified:

6. Explain why the *gfp* marker is a more desirable gene marker than genes for antibiotic resistance:

7. Viruses are also used for *in vivo* gene cloning even though they have no replication machinery themselves. Explain how viruses can be used to clone genes:

© BIOZONE International 2013
ISBN: 978-1-927173-72-5
Photocopying Prohibited

Gel Electrophoresis

Gel electrophoresis is a method that separates large molecules (including nucleic acids or proteins) on the basis of size, electric charge, and other physical properties. Such molecules possess a slight electric charge (see DNA below). To prepare DNA for gel electrophoresis the DNA is often cut up into smaller pieces. This is done by mixing DNA with restriction enzymes in controlled conditions for about an hour. Called **restriction digestion**, it produces a range of DNA fragments of different lengths. During electrophoresis, molecules are forced to move through the pores of a **gel** (a jelly-like material), when the electrical current is applied. Active electrodes at each end of the gel provide the driving force. The electrical current from one electrode repels the molecules while the other electrode simultaneously attracts the molecules. The frictional force of the gel resists the flow of the molecules, separating them by size. Their rate of migration through the gel depends on the strength of the electric field, size and shape of the molecules, and on the ionic strength and temperature of the buffer in which the molecules are moving. After staining, the separated molecules in each lane can be seen as a series of bands spread from one end of the gel to the other.

Analysing DNA using Gel Electrophoresis

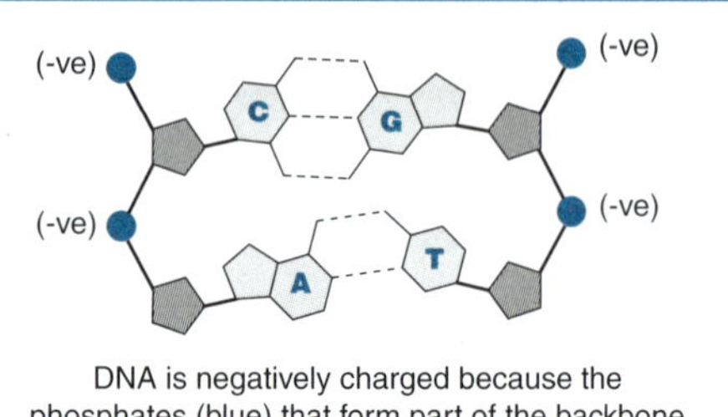

DNA is negatively charged because the phosphates (blue) that form part of the backbone of a DNA molecule have a negative charge.

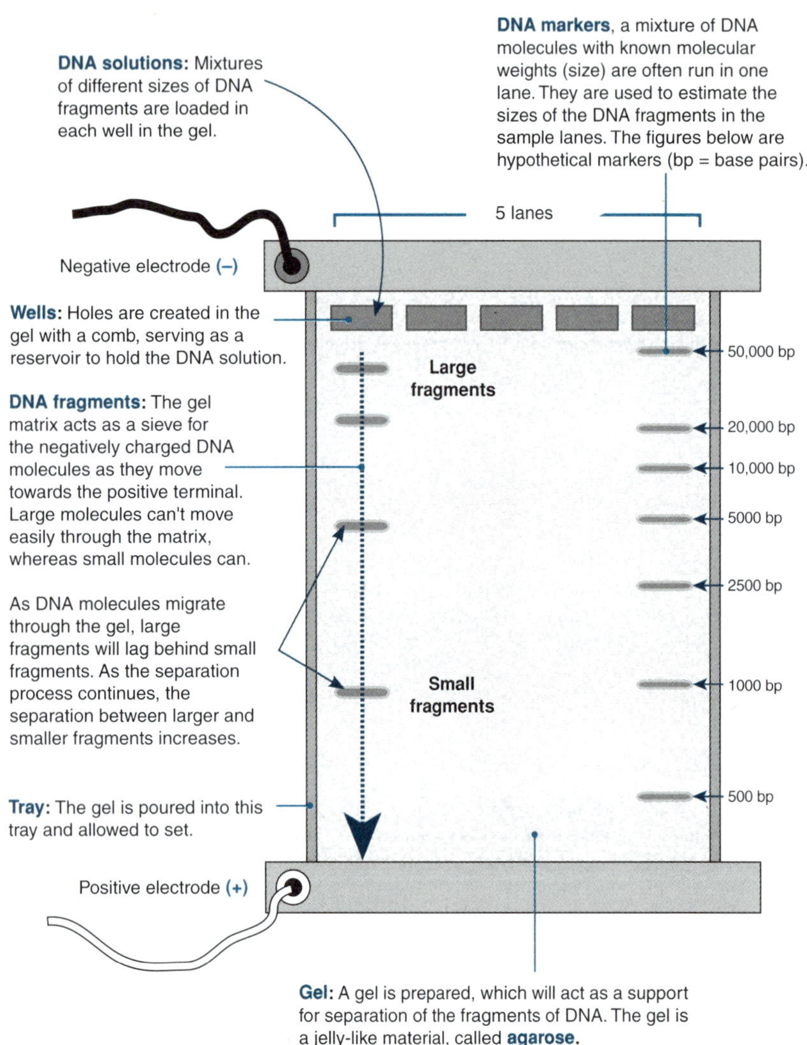

Gel: A gel is prepared, which will act as a support for separation of the fragments of DNA. The gel is a jelly-like material, called **agarose**.

Steps in the process of gel electrophoresis of DNA

1. A tray is prepared to hold the gel matrix.

2. A gel comb is used to create holes in the gel. The gel comb is placed in the tray.

3. Agarose gel powder is mixed with a buffer solution (this carries the DNA in a stable form). The solution is heated until dissolved and poured into the tray and allowed to cool.

4. The gel tray is placed in an electrophoresis chamber and the chamber is filled with buffer, covering the gel. This allows the electric current from electrodes at either end of the gel to flow through the gel.

5. DNA samples are mixed with a "loading dye" to make the DNA sample visible. The dye also contains glycerol or sucrose to make the DNA sample heavy so that it will sink to the bottom of the well.

6. A safety cover is placed over the gel, electrodes are attached to a power supply and turned on.

7. When the dye marker has moved through the gel, the current is turned off and the gel is removed from the tray.

8. DNA molecules are made visible by staining the gel with **methylene blue** or ethidium bromide which binds to DNA and will fluoresce in UV light.

1. Explain the purpose of gel electrophoresis: ____

____

____

2. Describe the two forces that control the speed at which fragments pass through the gel:

(a) ____

(b) ____

3. Explain why the smallest fragments travel through the gel the fastest: ________________________

____

____

© BIOZONE International 2013
ISBN: 978-1-927173-72-5
Photocopying Prohibited

KNOW

Related activities: DNA Profiling Using PCR, Automated DNA Sequencing
Weblinks: Gel Electrophoresis Video

Screening for Genes

A **DNA probe** (also called a hybridization probe) is a fragment of DNA or RNA used to detect the presence of nucleotide sequences that are complementary to the probe sequence. DNA probes can therefore identify the presence and location of individual genes. This has many useful applications including screening for particular genetic defects (where the gene sequence or a marker for it is known) and constructing a gene map of the chromosomes. The probes have either a radioactive label (e.g. ^{32}P) or a fluorescent dye so that it can be visualized on an electrophoresis gel or X-ray film.

Making and Using a DNA Probe

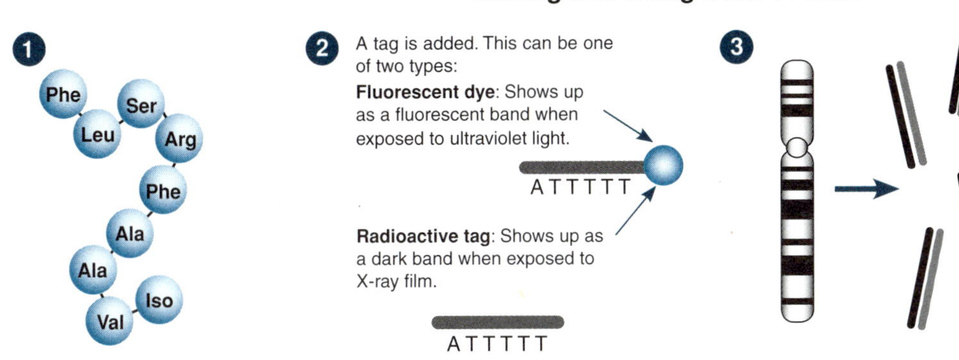

The protein product of a gene is isolated and its amino acid sequence is determined.

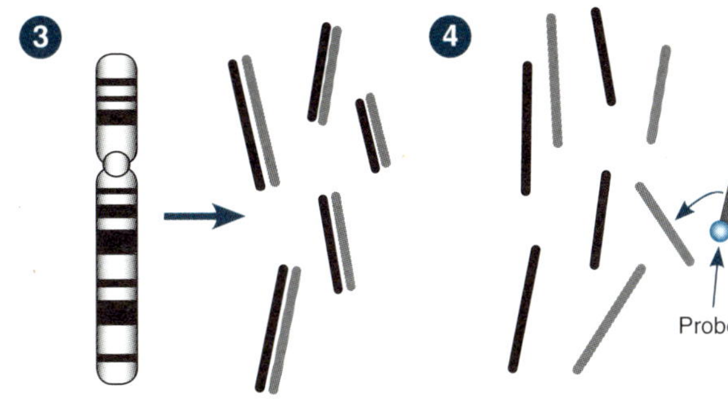

The DNA sequence for the protein product is identified from the amino acid sequence. The DNA sequence is artificially manufactured.

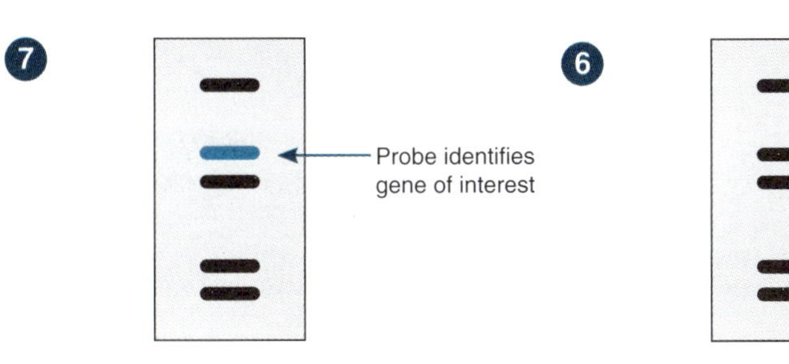

The DNA sequence being probed is cut into fragments using restriction enzymes.

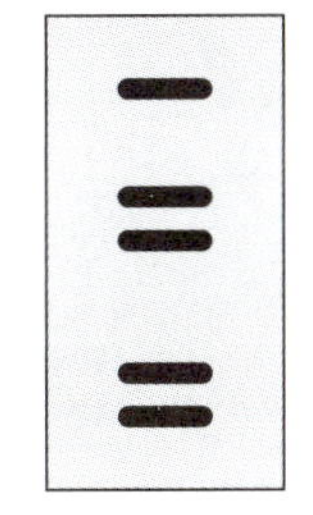

The DNA fragments are denatured, forming single stranded DNA. The probe is added to the DNA fragments.

5 If a complementary sequence is present, the probe will bind to it by base pairing.

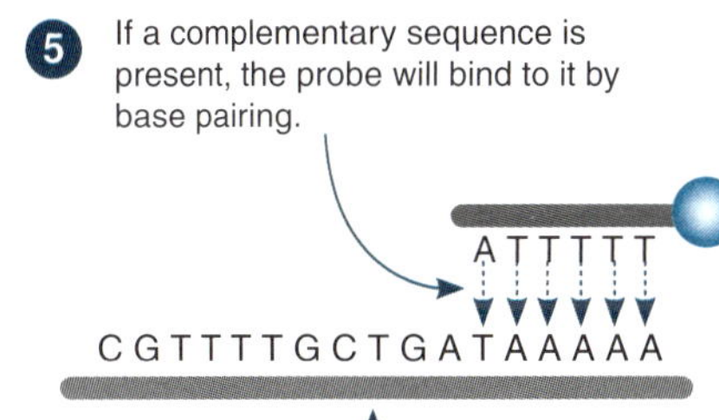

Target DNA strand (contains the complementary sequence to that of the probe).

7

Probe identifies gene of interest

The gel is viewed by fluorescent light or on X-ray film (depending on the type of probe used). If the probe has bound to a gene, the label makes it visible.

6

The DNA fragments are run on an electrophoresis gel. The fragments are separated by size.

1. What is the purpose of a DNA probe? ____

____

2. Explain why a DNA probe can be used to identify a gene or DNA sequence: ____________________

____

____

3. Why does the DNA have to be denatured before adding the probe? _____________________________

____

____

4. How is the presence of a specific DNA sequence or gene visualized? __________________________

____

____

5. Using a textbook, or the internet for reference, describe some specific situations in which DNA probes are used:

____

____

____

____

Genetic Manipulation

Related activities: Determining Gene Function

KNOW

Cloning Eukaryotic Genes: Problems and Solutions

Not all the DNA in a eukaryotic gene is translated during protein synthesis. **Introns** are sequences of a gene's DNA that do not code for proteins. In eukaryotic cells, before mRNA from a transcribed gene is translated into a protein, the introns are removed. The DNA sequences that are left behind are called **exons**, and the mRNA is called mature mRNA. Exons code for specific proteins. The presence of protein coding and non-protein coding DNA sequences presents a problem when preparing a eukaryotic gene for insertion into a bacterial cell. Prokaryotic cells generally do not distinguish between introns and exons. The solution is to engineer a eukaryotic gene that can be copied, translated and used by the prokaryote. This is achieved using the retroviral enzyme **reverse transcriptase**, which copies the mature mRNA (containing exons only) to produce a complementary strand of DNA. This task is important in both *in vitro* and *in vivo* gene cloning because it produces a gene that is ready for amplification.

Preparing a Gene for Cloning

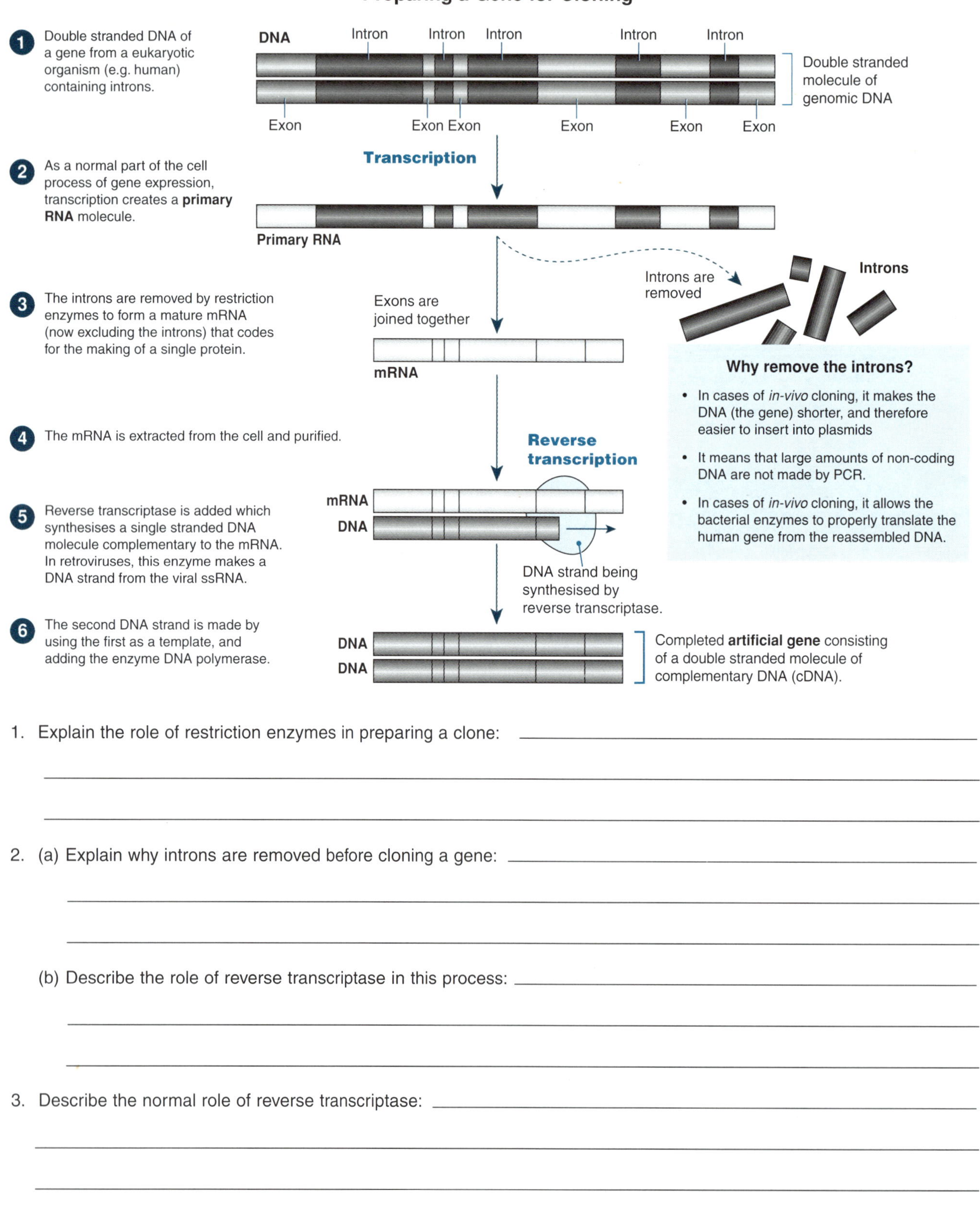

1. Double stranded DNA of a gene from a eukaryotic organism (e.g. human) containing introns.

2. As a normal part of the cell process of gene expression, transcription creates a **primary RNA** molecule.

3. The introns are removed by restriction enzymes to form a mature mRNA (now excluding the introns) that codes for the making of a single protein.

4. The mRNA is extracted from the cell and purified.

5. Reverse transcriptase is added which synthesises a single stranded DNA molecule complementary to the mRNA. In retroviruses, this enzyme makes a DNA strand from the viral ssRNA.

6. The second DNA strand is made by using the first as a template, and adding the enzyme DNA polymerase.

1. Explain the role of restriction enzymes in preparing a clone: ____

____

____

2. (a) Explain why introns are removed before cloning a gene: ____

____

____

(b) Describe the role of reverse transcriptase in this process: ____

____

____

3. Describe the normal role of reverse transcriptase: ____

____

____

____

© BIOZONE International 2013
ISBN: 978-1-927173-72-5
Photocopying Prohibited

KNOW   ***Related activities:*** *Cloning a Gene In Vivo, Polymerase Chain Reaction*

The Applications of Transgenesis

Transgenesis is the insertion of a gene from one species into another that would not normally contain the gene. Organisms which have undergone transgenesis are called **transgenic organisms**. The genes are inserted using vectors or by direct insertion of the DNA. Transgenesis allows direct modification of a genome so traits can be introduced that are not naturally present in a species. Transgenesis has many applications, including improving crop yields, production of herbicide resistant plants, enhancement of desirable features in livestock, production of human proteins, and the treatment of genetic defects through gene therapy. Cloning, or selectively breeding transgenic organisms ensures the introduced gene is inherited in following generations. One method of producing a transgenic organism, pronuclear injection, is described below.

Pronuclear Injection

A gene that has been transferred into another organism is called a **transgene**. Genes can be introduced directly into an animal cell by microinjection. Multiple copies of the desired transgene are injected via a glass micropipette into a recently fertilized egg cell, which is then transferred to a surrogate mother. Transgenic mice and livestock are produced in this way. However, the process is inefficient: only 2-3% of eggs give rise to transgenic animals and only a proportion of these animals express the transgene adequately.

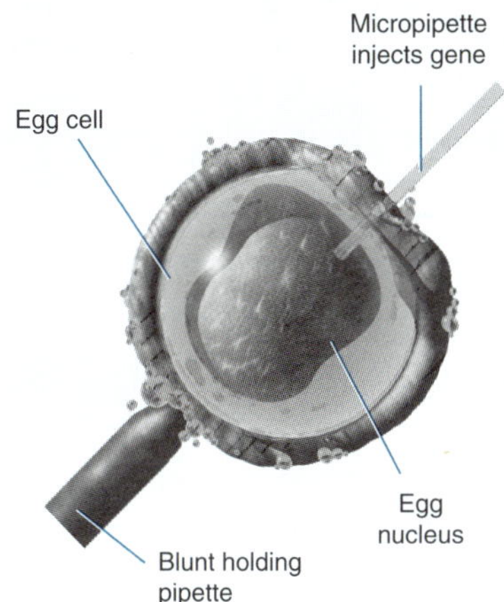

Creating Transgenic Mice Using Pronuclear Injection

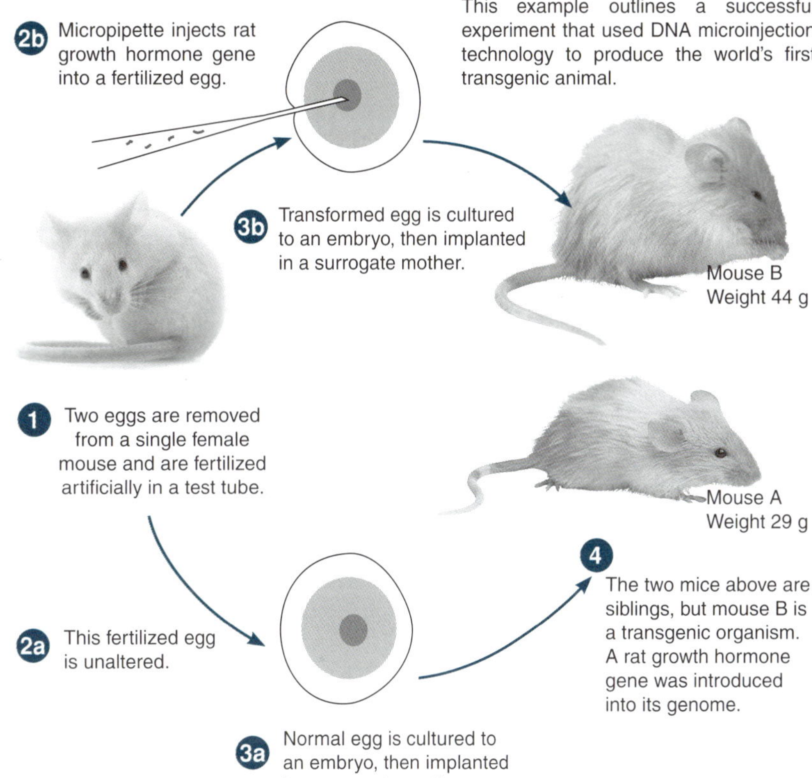

Applications of Transgenesis

Modifying crops

Transgenesis has been used in many types of crop plants. Some have been modified to include genes that produce insecticides, such as Bt cotton (above). Golden rice contains genes from a bacterium and a daffodil plant to improve its nutritional value.

Medical research

The effect of a gene can be studied in a living organism by inserting genes into model animals. Rhesus macaques have been engineered to provide models for studying the effects and potential treatments of diseases such as Huntington's and Parkinson's.

Livestock improvement

Transgenic sheep have been used to enhance wool production in flocks. The keratin protein of wool contains large amounts of the amino acid cysteine. Injecting developing sheep with the genes for the enzymes that generate cysteine produces woollier sheep.

Animals as Biofactories

Transgenic animals can be used as biofactories, to produce certain proteins. Transgenic sheep with the human gene for the -1-antitrypsin protein, produce the protein in their milk. The antitrypsin is extracted from the milk, and used to treat hereditary emphysema.

1. What is transgenesis? ____

____

2. Describe an application of transgenesis: ____________________________

____

____

Related activities: Vectors for Gene Therapy, Some Common Techniques in Genetic Engineering

KNOW

Polymerase Chain Reaction

Many procedures in DNA technology (such as DNA sequencing and DNA profiling) require substantial amounts of DNA to work with. Some samples, such as those from a crime scene or fragments of DNA from a long extinct organism, may be difficult to get in any quantity. The diagram below describes the laboratory process called **polymerase chain reaction (PCR)**.

Using this technique, vast quantities of DNA identical to trace samples can be created. This process is often termed **DNA amplification**. Although only one cycle of replication is shown below, following cycles replicate DNA at an exponential rate. PCR can be used to make billions of copies in only a few hours.

A single cycle of PCR

A DNA sample (called target DNA) is obtained. It is denatured (DNA strands are separated) by heating at 98°C for 5 minutes.

The sample is cooled to 60°C. Primers are annealed (bonded) to each DNA strand. In PCR, the primers are short strands of DNA; they provide the starting sequence for DNA extension.

Free nucleotides and the enzyme DNA polymerase are added. DNA polymerase binds to the primers andsynthesises complementary strands of DNA, using the free nucleotides.

After one cycle, there are now two copies of the original DNA.

Repeat cycle of heating and cooling until enough copies of the target DNA have been produced

Loading tray
Prepared samples in PCR tubes are placed in the loading tray and the lid is closed.

Temperature control
Inside the machine are heating and refrigeration mechanisms to rapidly change the temperature.

Dispensing pipette
Pipettes with disposable tips are used to dispense DNA samples into the PCR tubes.

Thermal Cycler

Amplification of DNA can be carried out with simple-to-use machines called thermal cyclers. Once a DNA sample has been prepared, in just a few hours the amount of DNA can be increased billions of times. Thermal cyclers are in common use in the biology departments of universities, as well as other kinds of research and analytical laboratories. The one pictured on the left is typical of this modern piece of equipment.

DNA quantitation
The amount of DNA in a sample can be determined by placing a known volume in this quantitation machine. For many genetic engineering processes, a minimum amount of DNA is required.

Controls
The control panel allows a number of different PCR programmes to be stored in the machine's memory. Carrying out a PCR run usually just involves starting one of the stored programmes.

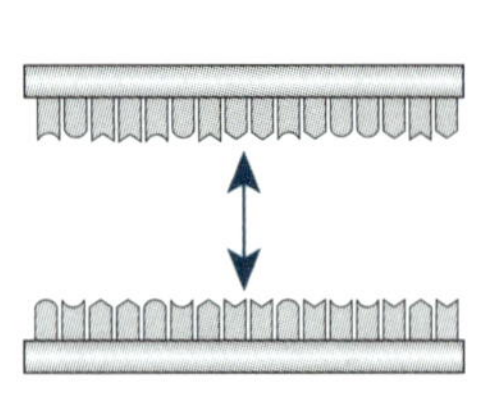

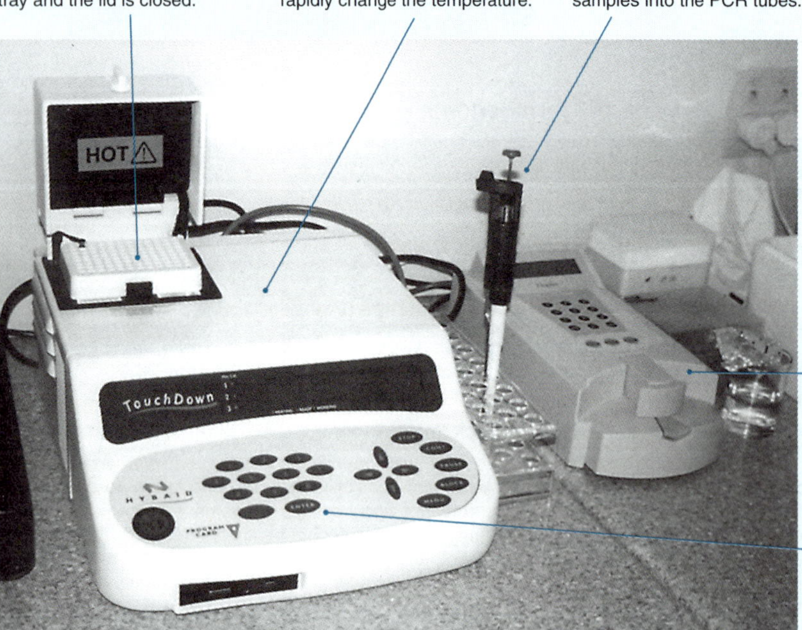

1. Explain the purpose of PCR: ____

____

____

____

© BIOZONE International 2013
ISBN: 978-1-927173-72-5
Photocopying Prohibited

Related activities: Automated DNA Sequencing, DNA Profiling Using PCR

2. Briefly describe how the **polymerase chain reaction** works: _______________________________________

____

____

____

____

____

____

____

3. Describe three situations where only very small DNA samples may be available for sampling and PCR could be used:

(a) ____

____

(b) ____

____

(c) ____

____

4. After only two cycles of replication, four copies of the double-stranded DNA exist. Calculate how much a DNA sample will have increased after:

(a) 10 cycles: _______________   (b) 25 cycles: _______________

5. The risk of contamination in the preparation for PCR is considerable.

(a) Explain what the effect would be of having a single molecule of unwanted DNA in the sample prior to PCR:

____

____

____

(b) Describe two possible sources of DNA contamination in preparing a PCR sample:

Source 1: ____

Source 2: ____

(c) Describe two precautions that could be taken to reduce the risk of DNA contamination:

Precaution 1: ____

____

Precaution 2: ____

____

6. Describe two other genetic engineering/genetic manipulation procedures that require PCR amplification of DNA:

(a) ____

____

____

(b) ____

____

____

Genetic Manipulation

GM Plants - Golden Rice

The Issue

▶ **Beta-carotene** (β-carotene) is a precursor to **vitamin A** which is involved in many functions including vision, immunity, fetal development, and skin health.

▶ Vitamin A deficiency is common in developing countries where up to 500,000 children suffer from night blindness, and death rates due to infections are high due to a lowered immune response.

▶ Providing enough food containing useful quantities of β-carotene is difficult and expensive in many countries.

Concept 1	Concept 2	Concept 3	Concept 4
Rice is a staple food in many developing countries. It is grown in large quantities and is available to most of the population, but it lacks many of the essential nutrients required by the human body for healthy development. It is low in β-carotene.	Rice plants produce β-carotene but not in the edible rice **endosperm**. Engineering a new biosynthetic pathway would allow β-carotene to be produced in the endosperm. Genes expressing enzymes for carotene synthesis can be inserted into the rice genome.	The enzyme **carotene desaturase (CRT1)** in the soil bacterium *Erwinia uredovora*, catalyses multiple steps in carotenoid biosynthesis. **Phytoene synthase (PSY)** overexpresses a colorless carotene in the daffodil plant *Narcissus pseudonarcissus*.	DNA can be inserted into an organism's genome using a suitable **vector**. ***Agrobacterium tumefaciens*** is a tumor-forming bacterial plant pathogen that is commonly used to insert novel DNA into plants.

The Development of Golden Rice

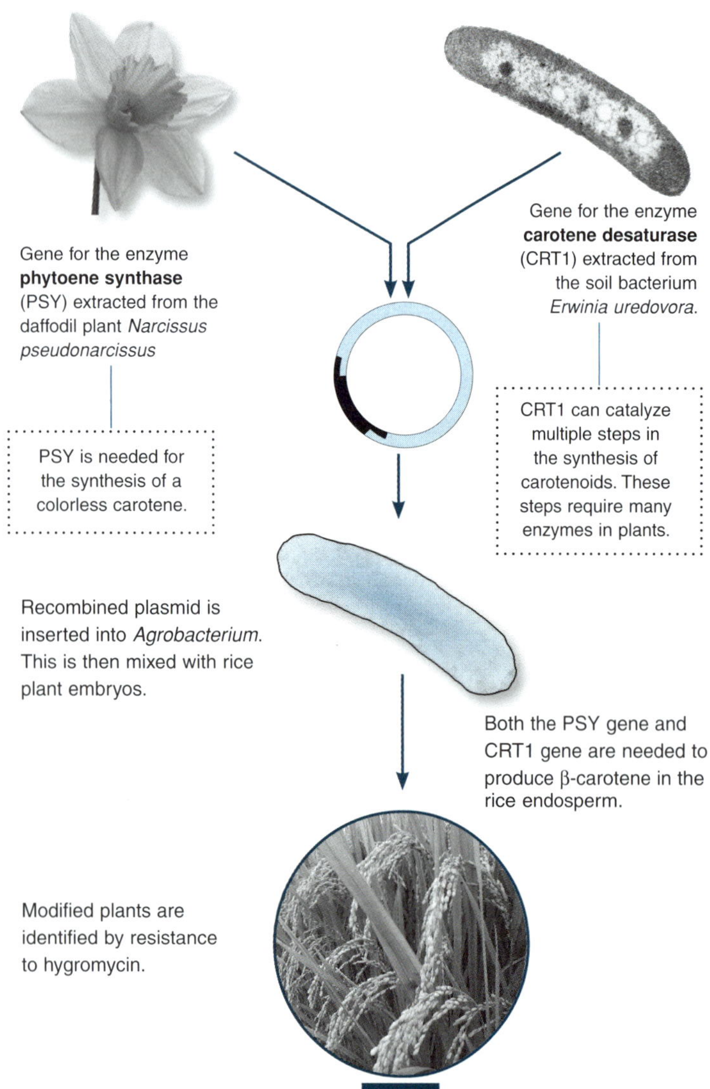

Techniques

The **PSY** gene from daffodils and the **CRT1** gene from *Erwinia uredovora* are sequenced.

DNA sequences are synthesized into packages containing the CRT1 or PSY gene, terminator sequences, and **endosperm specific promoters** (these ensure expression of the gene only in the edible portion of the rice).

The *Ti* **plasmid** from *Agrobacterium* is modified using restriction enzymes and DNA ligase to delete the tumor-forming gene and insert the synthesized DNA packages. A gene for resistance to the antibiotic **hygromycin** is also inserted so that transformed plants can be identified later. The parts of the *Ti* plasmid required for plant transformation are retained.

Modified *Ti* plasmid is inserted into the bacterium.

Agrobacterium is incubated with rice plant embryo. Transformed embryos are identified by their resistance to hygromycin.

Outcomes

The rice produced had endosperm with a distinctive yellow color. Under greenhouse conditions golden rice (**SGR1**) contained 1.6 µg per g of carotenoids. Levels up to five times higher were produced in the field, probably due to improved growing conditions.

Further Applications

Further research on the action of the PSY gene identified more efficient methods for the production of β-carotene. The second generation of golden rice now contains up to 37 µg per g of carotenoids. Golden rice was the first instance where a complete biosynthetic pathway was engineered. The procedures could be applied to other food plants to increase their nutrient levels.

   Related activities: Cloning a Gene In Vivo

The ability of *Agrobacterium* to transfer genes to plants is exploited for crop improvement. The tumor-inducing *Ti* plasmid is modified to delete the tumor-forming gene and insert a gene coding for a desirable trait. The parts of the *Ti* plasmid required for plant transformation are retained.

Soybeans are one of the many food crops that have been genetically modified for broad spectrum herbicide resistance. The first GM soybeans were planted in the US in 1996. By 2007, nearly 60% of the global soybean crop was genetically modified; the highest of any other crop plant.

GM cotton was produced by inserting the gene for the BT toxin into its genome. The bacterium *Bacillus thuringiensis* naturally produces BT toxin, which is harmful to a range of insects, including the larvae that eat cotton. The BT gene causes cotton to produce this insecticide in its tissues.

1. Describe the basic methodology used to create golden rice: _______________________________

____

____

____

____

2. Explain how scientists ensured β-carotene was produced in the endosperm: _______________

____

____

____

3. What property of *Agrobacterium tumefaciens* makes it an ideal vector for introducing new genes into plants?

____

____

____

____

4. (a) How could this new variety of rice reduce disease in developing countries? _______________

____

____

____

(b) Absorption of vitamin A requires sufficient dietary fat. Explain how this could be problematic for the targeted use of golden rice in developing countries:

____

____

5. As well as increasing nutrient content as in golden rice, other traits of crop plants are also desirable. For each of the following traits, suggest features that could be desirable in terms of increasing yield:

(a) Grain size or number: ____

(b) Maturation rate: ____

(c) Pest resistance: ____

Using Recombinant Bacteria

The Issue

- The enzymes used in the food industry have traditionally been extracted from their original plant, animal, or bacterial source. This can be costly.
- **Chymosin** (**rennin**) is an enzyme that digests milk proteins. It is the active ingredient in rennet, a substance used in cheese-making to form the curd.
- Traditionally rennin is extracted from "chyme", i.e. the stomach secretions of suckling calves (hence its name of chymosin).
- By the 1960s, a shortage of chymosin was limiting the volume of cheese produced.
- Enzymes from fungi were used as an alternative but were unsuitable because they caused variations in the cheese flavor.

Concept 1	Concept 2	Concept 3	Concept 4	Concept 5
Enzymes are proteins made up of amino acids. The amino acid sequence of chymosin can be determined and the mRNA coding sequence for its translation identified.	**Reverse transcriptase** can be used to synthesize a DNA strand from the mRNA. This process produces DNA without the introns, which cannot be processed by bacteria.	DNA can be cut at specific sites using **restriction enzymes** and rejoined using **DNA ligase.** New genes can be inserted into self-replicating bacterial **plasmids**.	Under certain conditions, bacteria are able to lose or take up plasmids from their environment. Bacteria are readily grown in vat cultures at little expense.	The protein in made by the bacteria in large quantities.

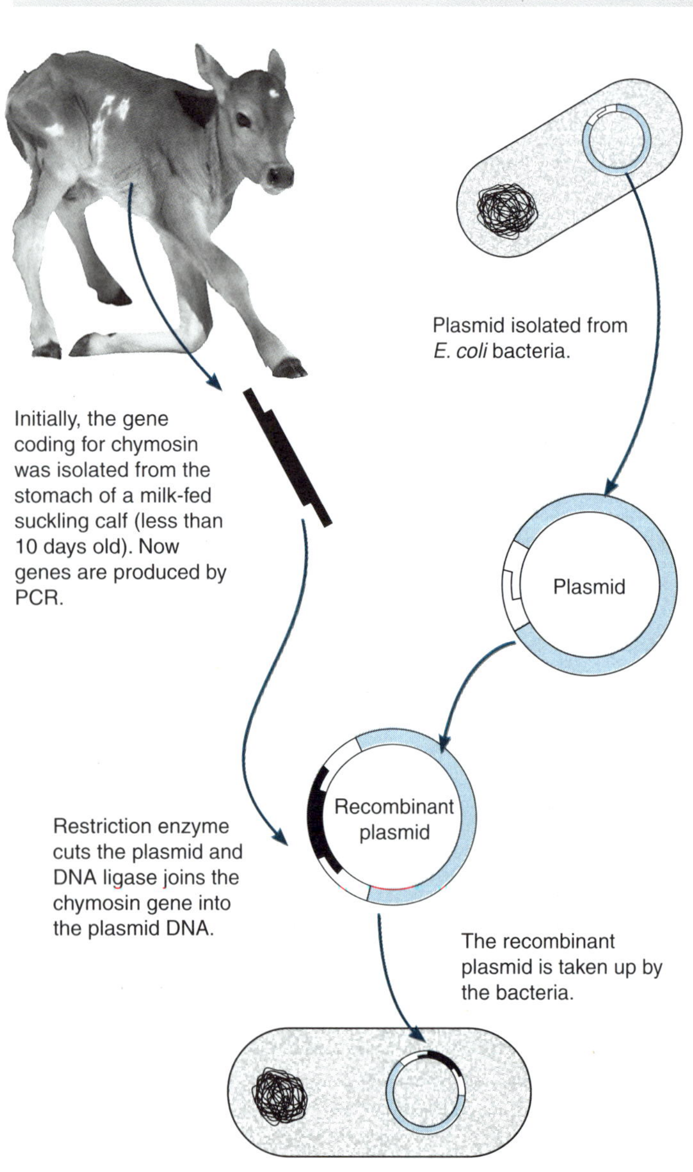

Initially, the gene coding for chymosin was isolated from the stomach of a milk-fed suckling calf (less than 10 days old). Now genes are produced by PCR.

Restriction enzyme cuts the plasmid and DNA ligase joins the chymosin gene into the plasmid DNA.

The recombinant plasmid is taken up by the bacteria.

Transformed bacterial cells are grown in a vat culture

Techniques

The amino acid sequence of chymosin is first determined and the RNA codons for each amino acid identified.

mRNA matching the identified sequence is isolated from the stomach of young calves. **Reverse transcriptase** is used to transcribe mRNA into DNA. The DNA sequence can also be made synthetically once the sequence is determined.

The DNA is amplified using PCR.

Plasmids from *E. coli* bacteria are isolated and cut using **restriction enzymes.** The DNA sequence for chymosin is inserted using **DNA ligase**.

Plasmids are returned to *E. coli* by placing the bacteria under conditions that induce them to take up plasmids.

Outcomes

The transformed bacteria are grown in vat culture. Chymosin is produced by *E. coli* in packets within the cell that are separated during the processing and refining stage.

Recombinant chymosin entered the marketplace in 1990. It established a significant market share because cheesemakers found it to be cost effective, of high quality, and in consistent supply. Most cheese is now produced using recombinant chymosin such as CHY-MAX.

Further Applications

A large amount of processing is required to extract chymosin from *E.coli*. There are now a number of alternative bacteria and fungi that have been engineered to produce the enzyme. Most chymosin is now produced using the fungi **Aspergillus niger** and **Kluyveromyces lactis**. Both are produced in a similar way as that described for *E. coli*.

© BIOZONE International 2013
ISBN: 978-1-927173-72-5
Photocopying Prohibited

KNOW

Related activities: *Production of Insulin, Cloning a Gene In Vivo*

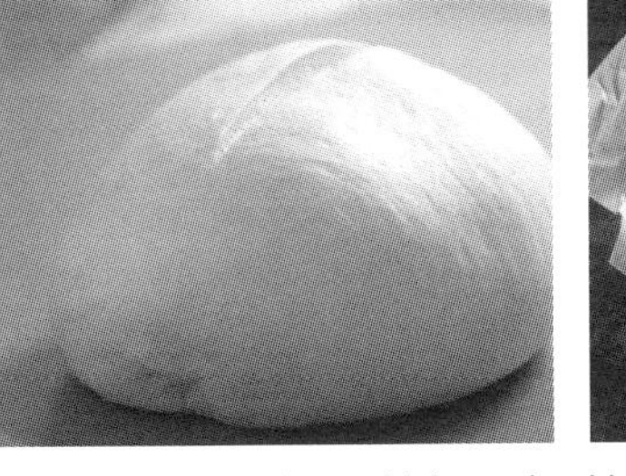

Enzymes from GMOs are widely used in the baking industry. Maltogenic alpha amylase from *Bacillus subtilis* bacteria is used as an anti-staling agent to prolong shelf life. Hemicellulases from *B. subtilis* and xylanase from the fungus *Aspergillus oryzae* are used for improvement of dough, crumb structure, and volume during the baking process.

Lipase from *Aspergillus oryzae* is used in processing of palm oil to produce low cost cocoa butter substitutes (above), which have a similar 'mouth feel' to cocoa butter.

Acetolactate decarboxylase from *B. subtilis* is one of several enzymes used in the brewing industry. It reduces maturation time of the beer by by-passing a rate-limiting step.

1. Describe the main use of chymosin: ____

   ____

2. What was the traditional source of chymosin? _______________________________________

   ____

3. Summarize the key concepts that led to the development of the technique for producing chymosin:

   (a) Concept 1: ____

   (b) Concept 2: ____

   (c) Concept 3: ____

   (d) Concept 4: ____

   (e) Concept 5: ____

4. Discuss how the gene for chymosin was isolated and how the technique could be applied to isolating other genes:

   ____

   ____

   ____

   ____

   ____

   ____

   ____

5. Describe three advantages of using chymosin produced by GE bacteria over chymosin from traditional sources:

   (a) ____

   ____

   (b) ____

   ____

   (c) ____

6. Explain why the fungus *Aspergillus niger* is now more commonly used to produce chymosin instead of *E. coli*:

   ____

   ____

   ____

Genetic Manipulation

Food for the Masses

It is estimated that by 2050 the world population will reach between 9 and 10 billion people. Currently 1 billion people (one sixth of the world's population) are undernourished. If trends continue, 1.5 billion people will be living under the threat of starvation by 2050, and by 2100 (if global warming is taken into account) nearly half the world's population could be threatened with food shortages. The solution to the problem of food production is complicated. Most of the suitable crop-growing land has already been developed, and accounts for 37% of the Earth's land area, leaving little room for more agriculture. Development of new fast growing and high yield crops appears to be a major part of the solution, but many crops can only be grown under a narrow range of conditions or are susceptible to disease. Moreover, the farming and irrigation of some areas is difficult, costly, and damaging to the environment because vast amounts of water are diverted from their natural courses. **Genetic modification** of plants may help to solve some of these problems by producing plants that will require less intensive culture or that will grow in areas previously considered not suitable for agriculture.

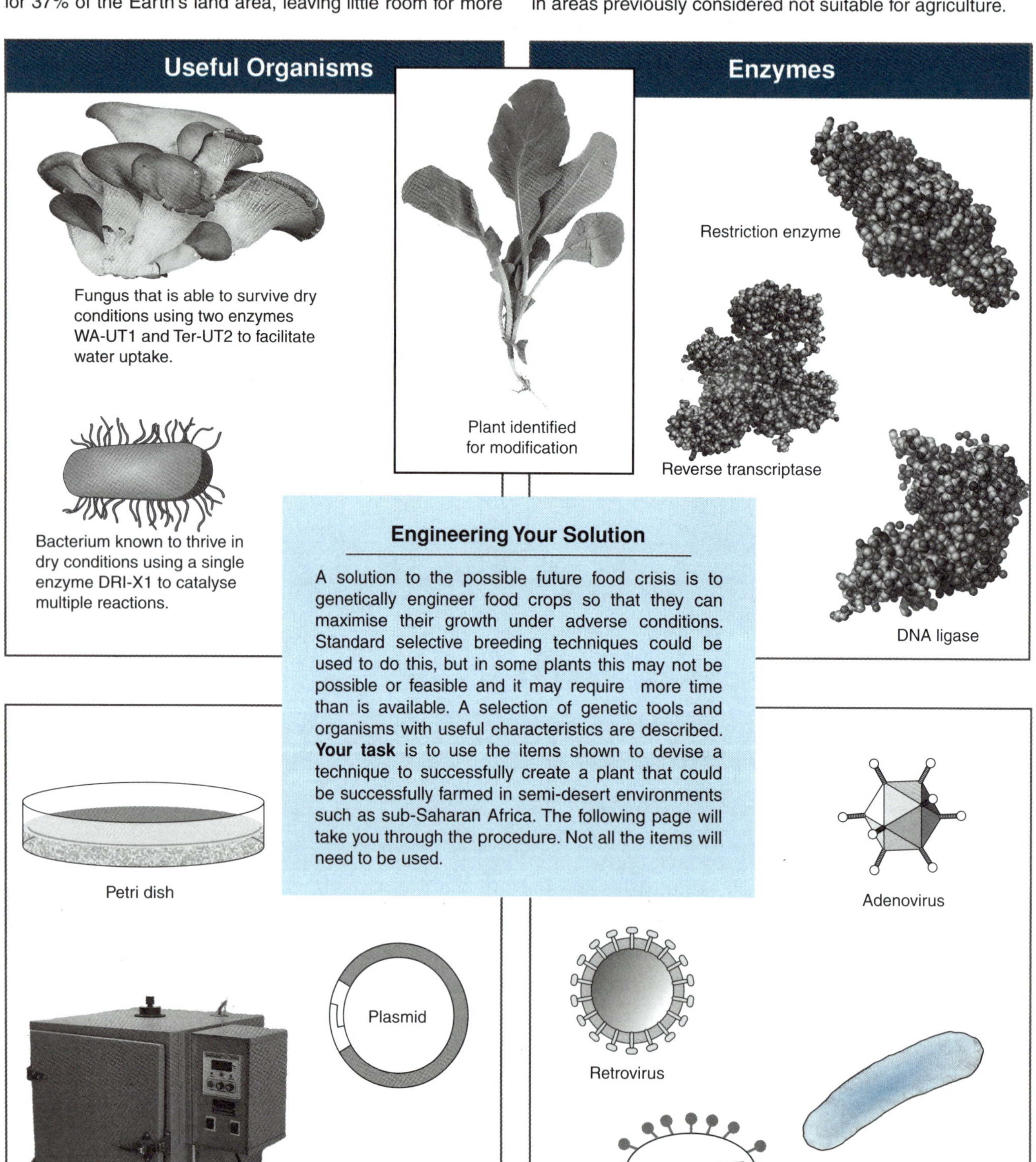

© BIOZONE International 2013
ISBN: 978-1-927173-72-5
Photocopying Prohibited

TEST

Related activities: Restriction Enzymes, Ligation, GM Plants-Golden Rice

1. Identify the organism you would chose as a 'donor' of drought survival genes and explain your choice:

____

2. Describe a process to identify and isolate the required gene(s) and identify the tools to be used: _______________

____

____

____

____

____

3. Identify a vector for the transfer of the isolated gene(s) into the crop plant and explain your decision: _______________

____

4. Explain how the isolated gene(s) would be integrated into the vector's genome: _______________

____

____

____

____

____

5. (a) Explain how the vector will transform the identified plant: _______________

____

____

(b) Identify the stage of development at which the plant would most easily be transformed. Explain your choice:

____

____

____

6. Explain how the transformed plants could be identified: _______________

____

____

____

____

____

7. Explain how a large number of plants can be grown from the few samples that have taken up the new DNA:

____

____

____

____

____

Genetic Manipulation

The Ethics of GM Technology

The risks associated with using **genetically modified organisms** (GMOs) have been the subject of much debate in recent times. Most experts agree that, provided GMOs are tested properly, the health risks to individuals should be minimal from plant products, although minor problems will occur. Health risks from animal GMOs are potentially more serious, especially when the animals are for human consumption. The potential benefits to be gained from the use of GMOs creates enormous pressure to apply the existing technology. However, there are many concerns, including the environmental and socio-economic effects, and problems of unregulated use. There is also concern about the environmental and economic costs of possible GMO accidents. GMO research is being driven by heavy investment on the part of biotechnology companies seeking new applications for GMOs. Currently a matter of great concern to consumers is the adequacy of government regulations for the labelling of food products with GMO content. This may have important trade implications for countries exporting and importing GMO produce.

Some important points about GMOs

1. The modified DNA is in every cell of the GMO.

2. The mRNA is only expressed in specific tissues.

3. The foreign protein is only expressed in particular tissues but it may circulate in the blood or lymph or be secreted (e.g. milk).

4. In animals, the transgene is only likely to be transmitted from parent to offspring. However, viral vectors may enable accidental transfer of the transgene between unrelated animals.

5. In plants, transmission of the transgene in GMOs is possible by pollen, cuttings, and seeds (even between species).

6. If we eat the animal or plant proper, we will also be eating DNA. The DNA will remain 'intact' if raw, but "degraded" if cooked.

7. Non-transgenic food products may be processed using genetically modified bacteria or yeast, and cells containing their DNA may be in the food product.

8. A transgenic product (e.g. a protein, polypeptide or a carbohydrate) may be in the GMO, but not in the portions sold to the consumer.

Potential effects of GMOs on the world

1. Increase in food production.

2. Decrease in use of pesticides, herbicides and animal remedies.

3. Improvement in the health of the human population and the medicines used to achieve it.

4. Possible development of transgenic products which may be harmful to some (e.g. new proteins causing allergies).

5. May have little real economic benefit to farmers (and the consumer) when increased production (as little as 10%) is weighed against cost, capital, and competition.

6. Possible (uncontrollable) spread of transgenes into other species: plants, indigenous species, animals, and humans.

7. Concerns that the release of GMOs into the environment may be irreversible.

8. Economic sanctions resulting from a consumer backlash against GMO foods and products.

9. Animal welfare and ethical issues: GM animals may suffer poor health and reduced life span.

10. GMOs may cause the emergence of pest, insect, or microbial resistance to traditional control methods.

11. May create a monopoly and dependence of developing countries on companies who are seeking to control the world's commercial seed supply.

GMO protestors are arrested
© Greenpeace

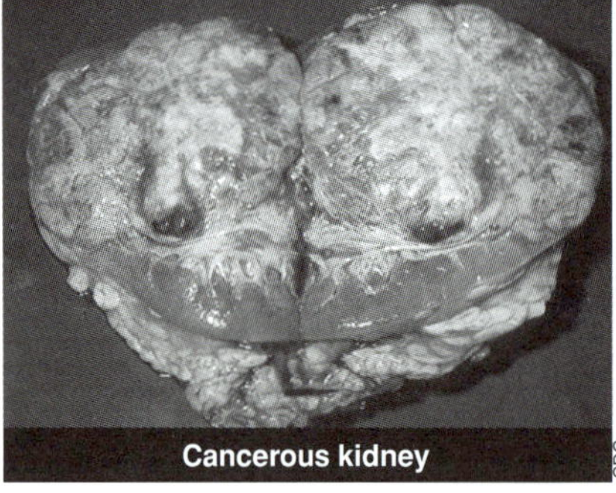
Cancerous kidney
CDC

Protest against GMOs in the environment
© Greenpeace

Issue: The accidental release of GMOs into the environment.

Problem: Recombinant DNA may be taken up by non-target organisms. These then may have the potential to become pests or cause disease.

Solution: Rigorous controls on the production and release of GMOs. GMOs could have specific genes deleted so that their growth requirements are met only in controlled environments.

Issue: A new gene or genes may disrupt normal gene function.

Problem: Gene disruption may trigger cancer. Successful expression of the desired gene is frequently very low.

Solution: A combination of genetic engineering, cloning, and genetic screening so that only those cells that have been successfully transformed are used to produce organisms.

Issue: Targeted use of transgenic organisms in the environment.

Problem: Once their desired function, e.g. environmental clean-up, is completed, they may be undesirable invaders in the ecosystem.

Solution: GMOs can be engineered to contain "suicide genes" or metabolic deficiencies so that they do not survive for long in the new environment after completion of their task.

1. Why are genetically modified (GM) plants thought to pose a greater environmental threat than GM animals?

____

____

____

____

© BIOZONE International 2013
ISBN: 978-1-927173-72-5
Photocopying Prohibited

KNOW

Related activities: *GM Plants- Golden Rice, Using Recombinant Bacteria, The Applications of Transgenesis, Production of Insulin*

2. Describe an advantage and a problem with the use of genetically engineered herbicide resistant crop plants:

   (a) Advantage: ____

   ____

   (b) Problem: ____

   ____

3. Describe an advantage and a problem with using tropical crops genetically engineered to grow in cold regions:

   (a) Advantage: ____

   ____

   (b) Problem: ____

   ____

4. Describe an advantage and a problem with using crops that are genetically engineered to grow in marginal habitats (for example, in very saline or poorly aerated soils):

   (a) Advantage: ____

   ____

   (b) Problem: ____

   ____

5. Describe two uses of transgenic animals within the livestock industry:

   (a) ____

   (b) ____

6. Some years ago, Britain banned the import of a GM, pest resistant corn variety containing marker genes for ampicillin antibiotic resistance. Suggest why the use of antibiotic-resistance genes as markers is no longer common practice:

   ____

   ____

7. Many agricultural applications of DNA technology make use of transgenic bacteria which infect plants and express a foreign gene. Explain one advantage of each of the following applications of genetic engineering to crop biology:

   (a) Development of nitrogen-fixing *Rhizobium* bacteria that can colonize non-legumes such as corn and wheat:

   ____

   (b) Addition of transgenic *Pseudomonas fluorescens* bacteria into seeds (bacterium produces a pathogen-killing toxin):

   ____

8. Some of the public's fears and concerns about genetically modified food stem from moral or religious convictions, while others have a biological basis and are related to the potential biological threat posed by GMOs.
   (a) Conduct a class discussion or debate to identify these fears and concerns, and list them below:

   ____

   ____

   ____

   ____

   (b) Identify which of those you have listed above pose a real biological threat: _______________________________

   ____

   ____

   ____

Genetic Manipulation

KEY TERMS: Mix and Match

INSTRUCTIONS: *Test your vocabulary by matching each term to its correct definition, as identified by its preceding letter code.*

annealing

DNA amplification

DNA chip (microarray)

DNA ligase

DNA ligation

DNA (gene) probe

DNA (genetic) screening

gene cloning

gel electrophoresis

gene marker

genetically modified organism (GMO)

gene technology

plasmid

polymerase chain reaction (PCR)

recombinant DNA technology

restriction enzyme

reverse transcriptase

taq polymerase

transgenesis

vector

A   An enzyme that is able to cut a length of DNA at a specific sequence or site.

B   A process that is used to separate different lengths of DNA by placing them in a gel matrix placed in a buffered solution through which an electric current is passed.

C   DNA analysis to detect the presence of a gene(s) associated with an inherited disorder.

D   An array of thousands of DNA probes that can be used to measure the level of gene expression or to search for novel genes.

E   The repairing or attaching of fragmented DNA by ligase enzymes.

F   Technology used to produce DNA that has had a new sequence added so that the original sequence has been changed.

G   Making identical copies of a piece of DNA, either *in-vitro* (by PCR) or *in-vivo*, using an organism.

H   An organism that has had part of its DNA sequence altered either by the removal or insertion of a piece of DNA

I   Short sequence of labeled DNA (e.g. radioactively labeled) which is introduced to a DNA sample in order detect complementary DNA sequences for analysis.

J   The process of introducing DNA from one species into the DNA of another.

K   The attachment of a DNA primer to a length of DNA as a starter point for the process of replication by a polymerase enzyme.

L   Enzyme that is capable of joining fragments of DNA together.

M   A small circular piece of DNA commonly found in bacteria.

N   A reaction that is used to amplify fragments of DNA using cycles of heating and cooling (abbreviation).

O   A thermostable DNA polymerase named after the bacterium it was originally isolated from. Because of its thermal stability, it is used in PCR

P   The process of producing more copies of a length of DNA, normally using PCR.

Q   An organism or artificial vehicle that is capable of transferring a DNA sequence to another organism.

R   Enzyme capable of copying RNA into DNA.

S   A gene, with an identifiable effect, used to determine if a piece of DNA has been successfully inserted into the host organism

T   The manipulation of DNA and gene sequences in order to modify the characteristics of organisms.

VOCAB

Chapter 4

Biotechnology in Medicine

Key terms

gene knockdown

gene knockout

gene marker

gene probes

gene therapy

genetic (DNA) screening

monoclonal antibodies

pre-implantation genetic diagnosis

recombinant DNA vaccine

transgenesis

vaccine

vector

Key concepts

▶ DNA can be screened for particular sequences.

▶ Gene function can be determined by studying the effect of gene inactivation.

▶ Monoclonal antibodies have wide applications in the diagnosis and treatment of disease.

▶ Recombinant DNA techniques can be used to produce proteins, vaccines, and pharmaceuticals.

▶ Gene therapy can be used to treat genetic defects.

Learning Objectives

☐ 1. Use the **KEY TERMS** to compile a glossary for this topic.

Detecting and Studying Disorders   pages 85-88

☐ 2. Describe the use of **gene probes** and **gene markers** in genetic screening. Describe the applications of genetic screening, including:
   • pre-symptomatic testing for adult-onset disorders, e.g. Huntington's disease
   • **pre-implantation genetic diagnosis** (PGD)
   • prenatal diagnostic testing

☐ 3. Discuss the ethical issues associated with genetic screening.

☐ 4. Explain how the function of genes can be determined using **gene knockout** and **gene knockdown** techniques. Discuss the application of these studies and identify the sorts of information they provide.

Diagnosis and Treatment of Disease   pages 71, 83-84, 89-98

☐ 5. Describe the production and applications of **monoclonal antibodies**. Using a specific example, e.g. Herceptin, explain how monoclonal antibodies can be used to target a disease.

☐ 6. Describe how human proteins, e.g. human insulin, can be produced using gene cloning and industrial-scale fermentation technology.

☐ 7. Describe the use of transgenic livestock as biofactories to produce human proteins, such as alpha-1-antitrypsin and interferon. Discuss the medical applications of these (and other) proteins.

☐ 8. Describe the advantages (over traditional methods) of using recombinant DNA technology to produce valuable commodities, such as human proteins. Evaluate any disadvantages with reference to traditional methods of production.

☐ 9. Describe the principles involved in the production of a **vaccine**. Distinguish between subunit and whole-agent vaccines and between inactivated (dead) and live (attenuated) vaccines. Contrast the risks and benefits associated with live and dead vaccines.

☐ 10. Explain the production and application of **recombinant DNA vaccines**, identifying existing and future benefits of these over vaccines produced by traditional methods.

☐ 11. Outline the principles of **gene therapy**. Identify the criteria that must be met before gene therapy can be considered as a potentially viable treatment. Identify vectors used in gene therapy and the advantages and disadvantages of each.

☐ 12. Using an appropriate example, explain the techniques involved in gene therapy, including the **vectors** used, and delivery systems for these vectors. With reference to your specific example, discuss the difficulties currently encountered in improving the success of gene therapy.

Weblinks:

www.thebiozone.com/
weblink/MnB-3725/

Production of Insulin

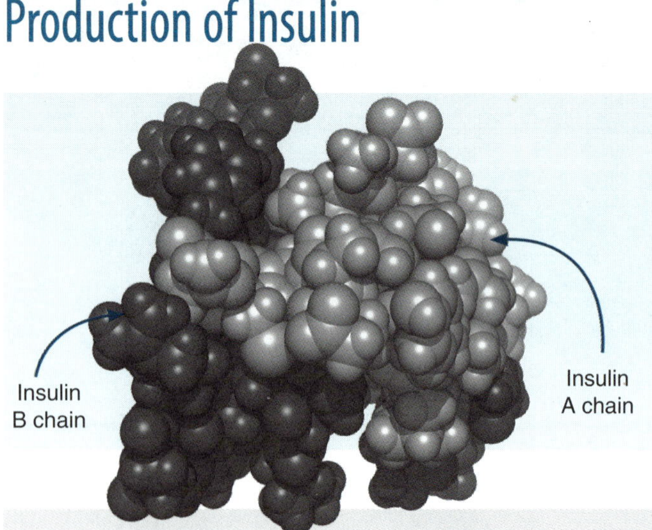

The Issue

▶ **Type I diabetes mellitus** is a metabolic disease caused by a lack of **insulin**. Around 25 people in every 100,000 suffer from type I diabetes.

▶ It is treatable only with injections of insulin.

▶ In the past, insulin was taken from the pancreases of cows and pigs and purified for human use. The method was expensive and some patients had severe allergic reactions to the foreign insulin or its contaminants.

Concept 1

DNA can be cut at specific sites using **restriction enzymes** and joined together using **DNA ligase**. New genes can be inserted into self-replicating bacterial **plasmids** at the point where the cuts are made.

Concept 2

Plasmids are small, circular pieces of DNA found in some bacteria. They usually carry genes useful to the bacterium. *E. coli* plasmids can carry promoters required for the transcription of genes.

Concept 3

Under certain conditions, Bacteria are able to lose or pick up plasmids from their environment. Bacteria can be readily grown in vat cultures at little expense.

Concept 4

The DNA sequences coding for the production of the two polypeptide chains (A and B) that form human insulin can be isolated from the human genome.

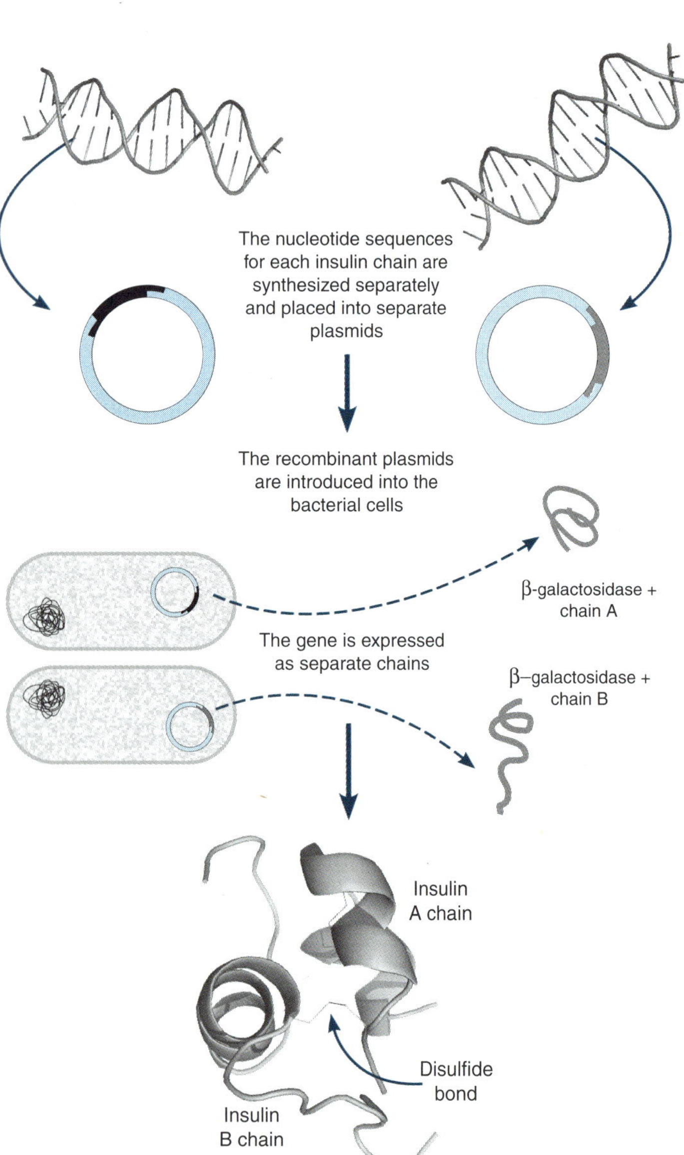

Techniques

The **gene** is **chemically synthesized** as two nucleotide sequences, one for the **insulin A chain** and one for the **insulin B chain**. The two sequences are small enough to be inserted into a plasmid.

Plasmids are extracted from *Escherichia coli*. The gene for the bacterial enzyme β-**galactosidase** is located on the plasmid. To make the bacteria produce insulin, the insulin gene must be linked to the β-galactosidase gene, which carries a promoter for transcription.

Restriction enzymes are used to cut plasmids at the appropriate site and the A and B insulin sequences are inserted. The sequences are joined with the plasmid DNA using **DNA ligase**.

The **recombinant plasmids** are inserted back into the bacteria by placing them together in a culture that favors plasmid uptake by bacteria.

The bacteria are then grown and multiplied in vats under carefully controlled growth conditions.

Outcomes

The product consists partly of β-galactosidase, joined with either the A or B chain of insulin. The chains are extracted, purified, and mixed together. The A and B insulin chains connect via **disulfide cross linkages** to form the functional insulin protein. The insulin can then be made ready for injection in various formulations.

Further Applications

The techniques involved in producing human insulin from genetically modified bacteria can be applied to a range of human proteins and hormones. Proteins currently being produced include human growth hormone, interferon, and factor VIII.

© BIOZONE International 2013
ISBN: 978-1-927173-72-5
Photocopying Prohibited

Related activities: Restriction Enzymes, Ligation

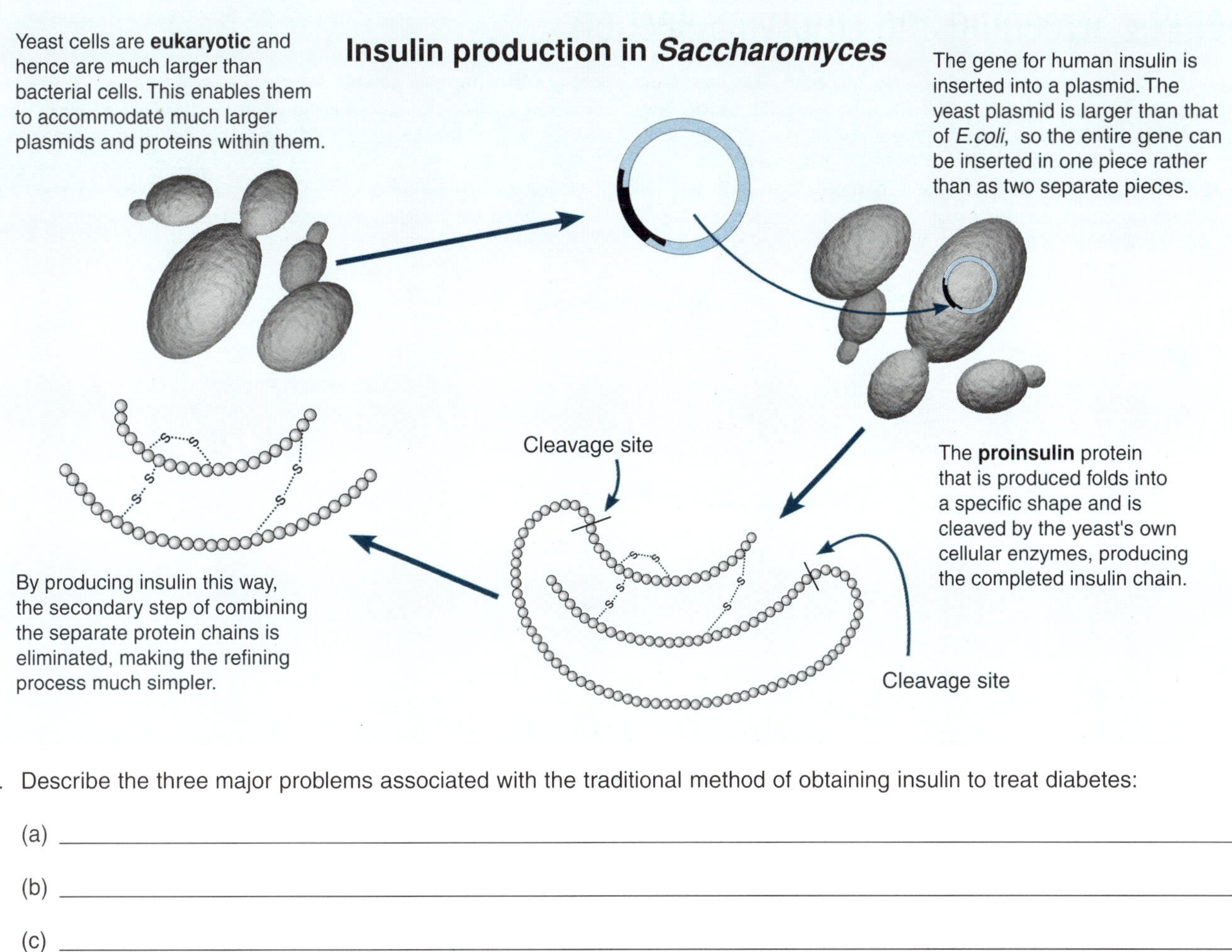

1. Describe the three major problems associated with the traditional method of obtaining insulin to treat diabetes:

    (a) ____

    (b) ____

    (c) ____

2. Explain the reasoning behind using *E. coli* to produce insulin and the benefits that GM technology has brought to diabetics:

    ____

    ____

    ____

    ____

3. Explain why, when using *E. coli*, the insulin gene is synthesized as two separate A and B chain nucleotide sequences:

    ____

    ____

4. Why are the synthetic nucleotide sequences ('genes') 'tied' to the β-galactosidase gene? ______________________

    ____

    ____

5. Yeast (*Saccharomyces cerevisiae*) is also used in the production of human insulin. Discuss the differences in the production of insulin using yeast and *E. coli* with respect to:

    (a) Insertion of the gene into the plasmid: ____

    ____

    ____

    (b) Secretion and purification of the protein product: ______________________________________

    ____

    ____

    ____

Genetic Screening and Embryo Selection

Many diseases, such as Huntington's disease, are known to be caused by specific gene defects. The **genetic screening** of gametes, embryos, or individuals for some diseases is now possible. **Pre-implantation genetic diagnosis** (or pre-implantation genetic screening) tests gametes and embryos for a specific genetic disorder before implantation into the uterus occurs. Genetic screening is usually carried out when at least one of the parents suffers from, or is a carrier for, a certain disease. Screening makes it highly likely that the resulting baby will be free of the disease. PGD can also be used to determine the sex of the embryo, and has lead to the ethically debatable practice of sex selection. PGD can also be used in livestock improvement to screen for genetic markers for preferred genes (e.g. for high milk production, or high meat yields).

Embryo Selection

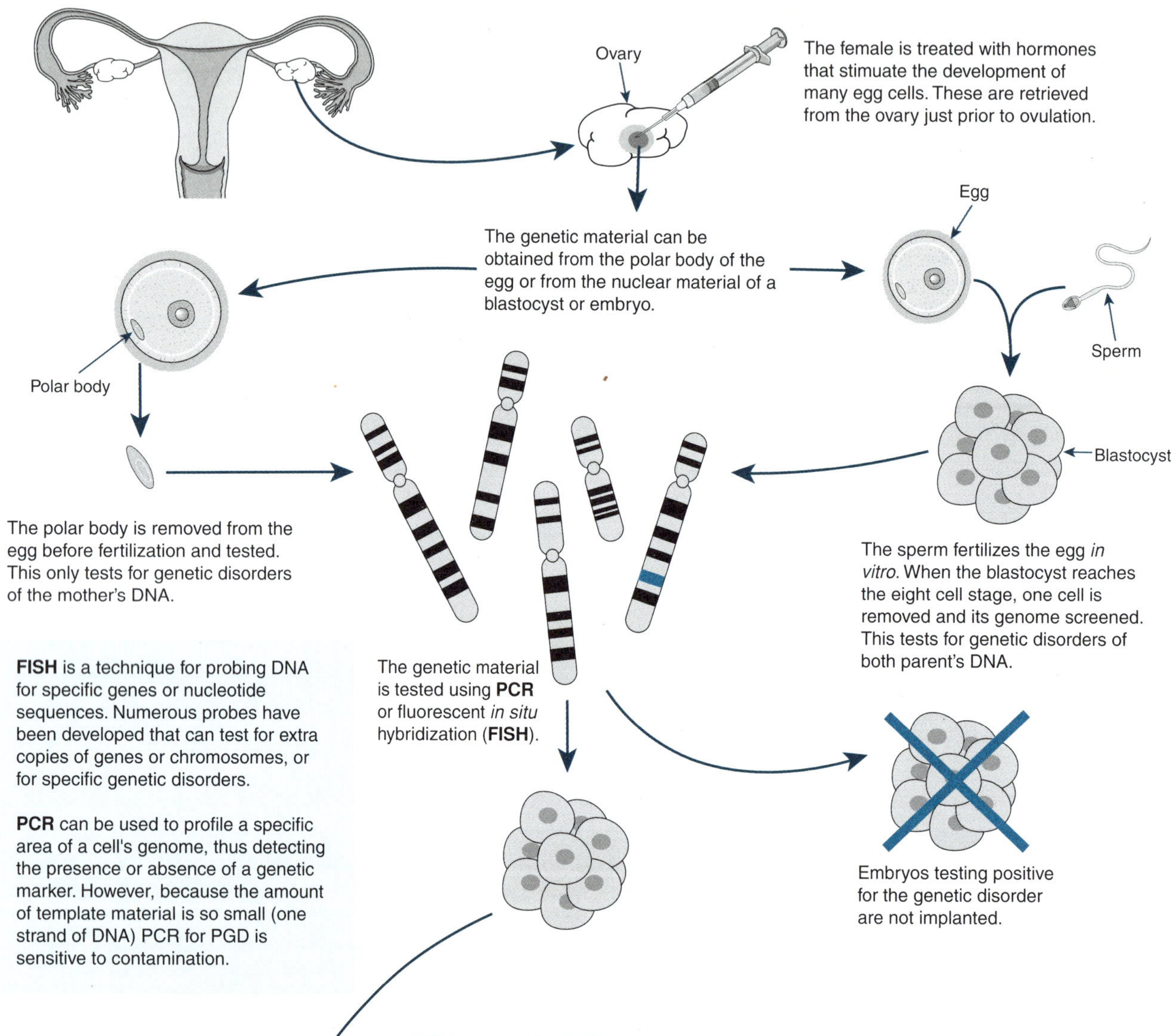

Ovary

The female is treated with hormones that stimuate the development of many egg cells. These are retrieved from the ovary just prior to ovulation.

The genetic material can be obtained from the polar body of the egg or from the nuclear material of a blastocyst or embryo.

Egg

Sperm

Polar body

Blastocyst

The polar body is removed from the egg before fertilization and tested. This only tests for genetic disorders of the mother's DNA.

The sperm fertilizes the egg *in vitro*. When the blastocyst reaches the eight cell stage, one cell is removed and its genome screened. This tests for genetic disorders of both parent's DNA.

FISH is a technique for probing DNA for specific genes or nucleotide sequences. Numerous probes have been developed that can test for extra copies of genes or chromosomes, or for specific genetic disorders.

PCR can be used to profile a specific area of a cell's genome, thus detecting the presence or absence of a genetic marker. However, because the amount of template material is so small (one strand of DNA) PCR for PGD is sensitive to contamination.

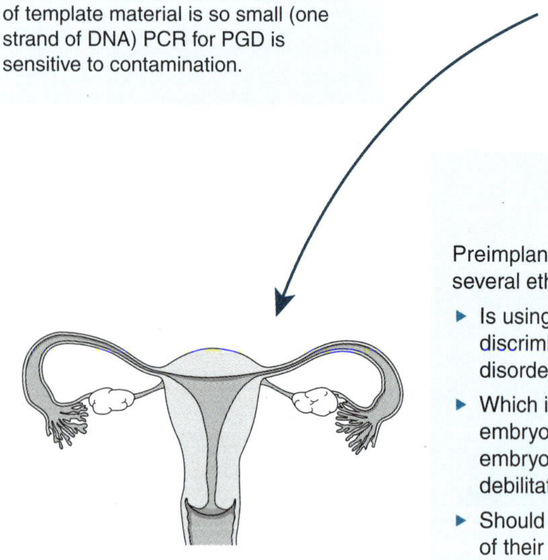

The genetic material is tested using **PCR** or fluorescent *in situ* hybridization (**FISH**).

Embryos testing positive for the genetic disorder are not implanted.

The Ethics of PGD

Preimplantation genetic diagnosis raises several ethical issues:

▶ Is using PGD to obtain healthy embryos discriminating against people with genetic disorders?

▶ Which is more ethical: the destruction of an embryo with a genetic disorder, or letting the embryo grow knowing that it will develop a debilitating or untreatable disease?

▶ Should parents be allowed to decide the sex of their child?

▶ PDG allows affected gametes and embryos to be discarded prior to implantation. Is this a better option than terminating a pregnancy once a genetic disorder has been discovered?

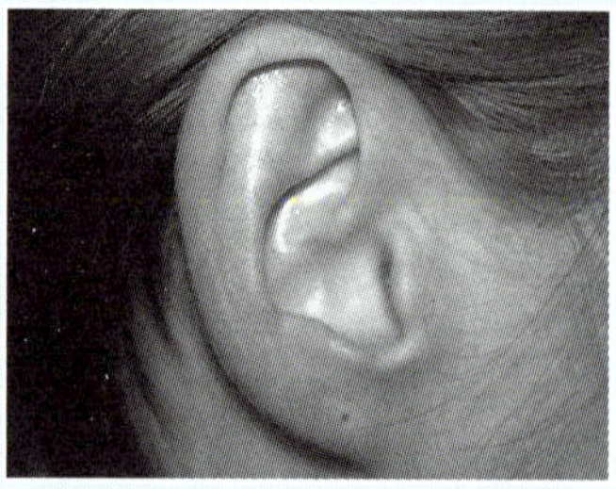

In the United States, up to 3% of PGD is used to select embryos *with* a genetic disorder. This most often occurs when parents have a particular disorder and want their child to have it too. For example, genetic deafness.

Embryos that test negative for the genetic disorder are implanted into the uterus.

Related activities: Screening for Genes

1. What is the main purpose of preimplantation genetic diagnosis (PGD)? ___________________________

____

2. Write a short paragraph that would explain the procedure for PGD to prospective parents: ___________________

____

____

____

____

____

____

3. Explain why using the polar body to test for genetic disorders does not give a full diagnosis of the resulting embryo:

____

____

____

4. Explain why using PCR in PGD could give a false response: ____

____

____

____

5. How can PGD be used for livestock improvement? ____

____

____

____

____

6. Discuss some of the ethical issues involved in PGD. Discuss what limitations (if any) should be placed on its use:

____

____

____

____

____

____

____

____

____

____

____

Determining Gene Function

Determining the function of a gene has several applications. It provides an understanding of how organisms develop, it can be used to develop treatments for genetic diseases, or for improving livestock and crops. One of the best ways to determine the function of a gene is to produce an individual with a non-functional version of the gene. The gene's function can be determined by comparing the development of the normal and altered individuals.

In classical genetics, this is done using mutant organisms with defects in particular genes. However, natural mutations may not occur in the gene being studied, so a modern solution is required. One technique for doing this is called **gene knockout** in which the target gene is altered to become non-functional. A second technique is called **gene knockdown** where the mRNA of the gene is altered to become non-functional.

Creating Gene Knockout Mice

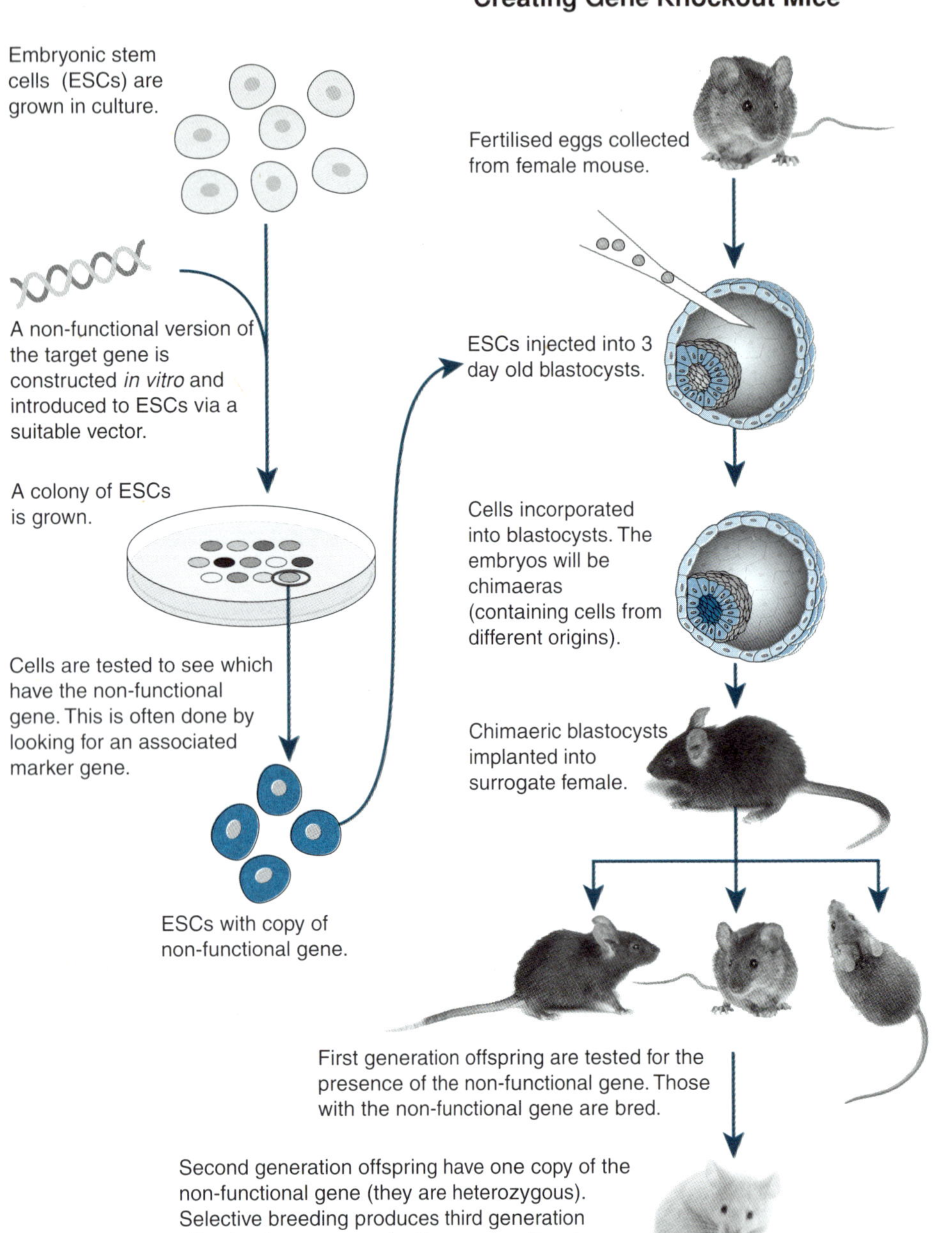

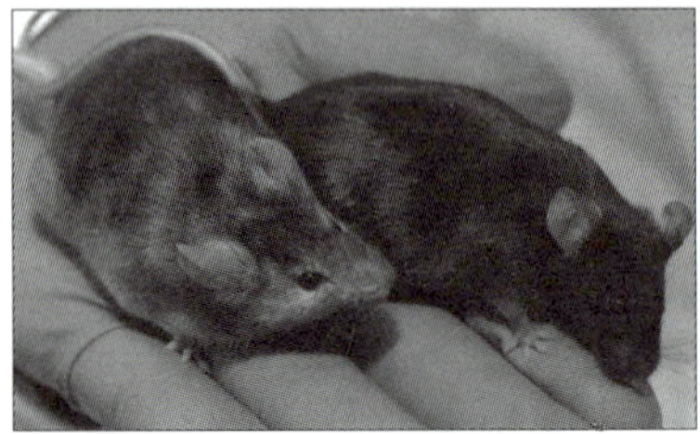

Gene knockout mice are commonly used to determine the effect of genes that humans and mice both have in common. Mice are used because they are the most closely related laboratory animal species to humans to which the gene knockout technique can easily be applied.

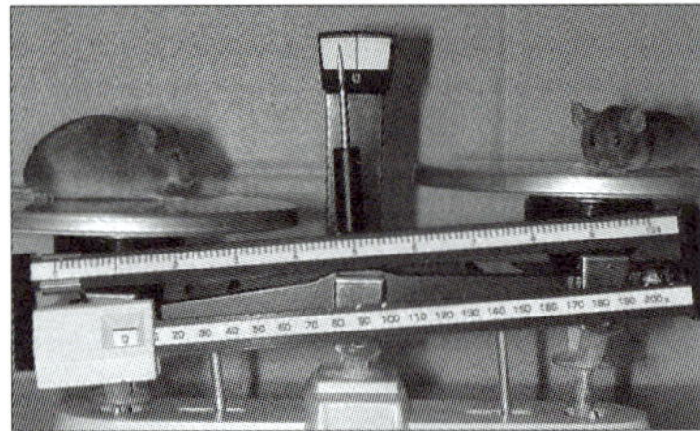

Several thousand strains of knockout mice have now been bred. The knockout mouse above left was created as a model for obesity.

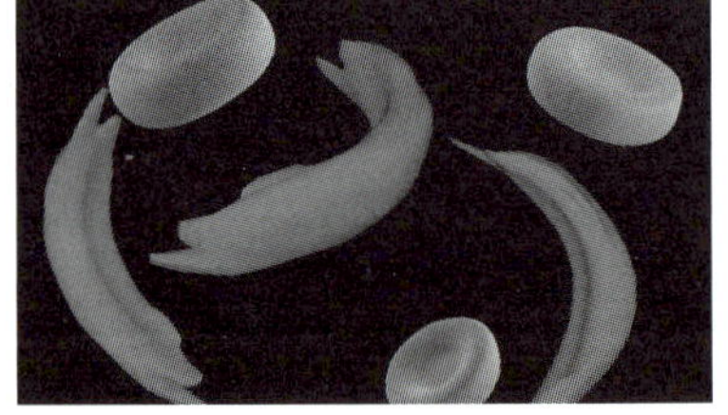

Recently, gene knockout has been used to knockout the BCL11A gene that would usually cause sickle cell disease to develop in mice. The research is helping to develop a drug treatment for human sufferers of sickle cell disease.

1. (a) Describe how gene function was studied before the development of gene knockout: _______________________

____

____

   (b) Why was this method not as efficient as gene knockout? _______________________

____

____

____

© BIOZONE International 2013
ISBN: 978-1-927173-72-5
Photocopying Prohibited

KNOW

Related activities: The Applications of Transgenesis
Weblinks: Gene Knockout in Mouse

Gene Knockdown

Gene knockdown is a technique where the mRNA product of a gene is targeted and disrupted so it can't carry out its normal function. **Double stranded RNA (dsRNA)** is introduced into the cells being studied. The dsRNA is processed to produce **small interfering RNA (siRNA)**. These bind to the mRNA product of the target gene, and inactivate it (right).

Organisms can be engineered so that their DNA is modified to carry the code for the dsRNA. A vector is used to introduce the new DNA code into the zygote of the organism. All the cells of the individual will carry the DNA code for the dsRNA. This is important because it means the gene knockdown can produce its effects in the very first generation (unlike gene knockout). However, gene knockdown is not always 100% effective (hence its name).

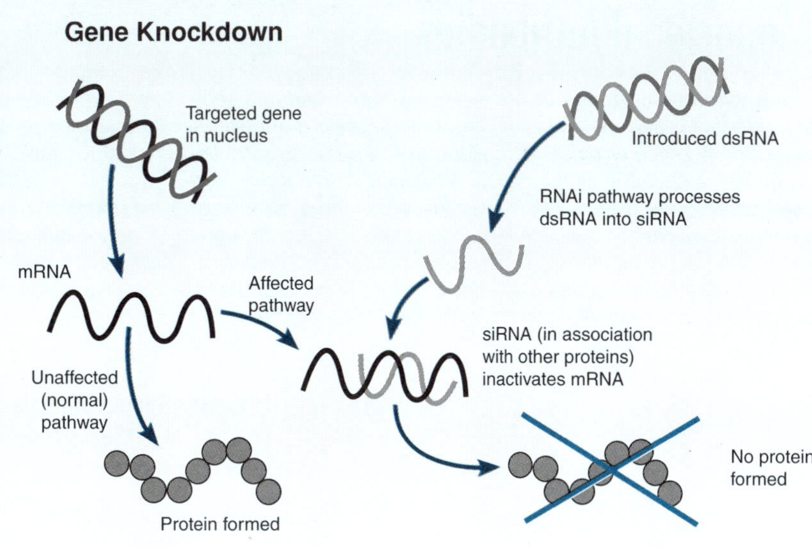

2. In the process of creating a **gene knockout** mouse:

   (a) Where does the non-functional gene come from? ____

   ____

   (b) How is the non-functional gene introduced into the blastocysts? _________________________________

   ____

   ____

   (c) Explain why only some of the cells in the first generation of mice will have the non-functional gene:

   ____

   ____

   ____

   (d) Explain how a mouse that is homozygous for the non-functional gene is produced: ________________

   ____

   ____

   ____

3. (a) Explain how gene knockout produces its effects compared to gene knockdown: __________________

   ____

   ____

   ____

   (b) Describe two other differences between gene knockout and gene knockdown: _________________

   ____

   ____

   ____

4. Describe some uses of gene knockout and gene knockdown: ______________________________________

   ____

   ____

   ____

   ____

Monoclonal Antibodies

A **monoclonal antibody** is an artificially produced antibody that binds to and neutralizes only one specific **antigen**. A monoclonal antibody binds an antigen in the same way that a normally produced antibody does. Monoclonal antibodies are used as diagnostic tools (e.g. detecting pregnancy) or to treat some types of cancer or autoimmune diseases. Therapeutic uses are still limited because the antibodies produced are from non-human cells and can cause side effects. In the future, production of monoclonal antibodies from human cells will probably result in fewer side effects. Monoclonal antibodies are produced in the laboratory by stimulating the production of B-cells in mice injected with the antigen. These B-cells produce an antibody against a specific antigen. Once isolated, they are made to fuse with immortal tumor cells, and they can be cultured indefinitely in a suitable growing medium (below). Monoclonal antibodies are useful for three reasons: they are all the same (i.e. clones), they can be produced in large quantities, and they are highly specific.

Making Monoclonal Antibodies

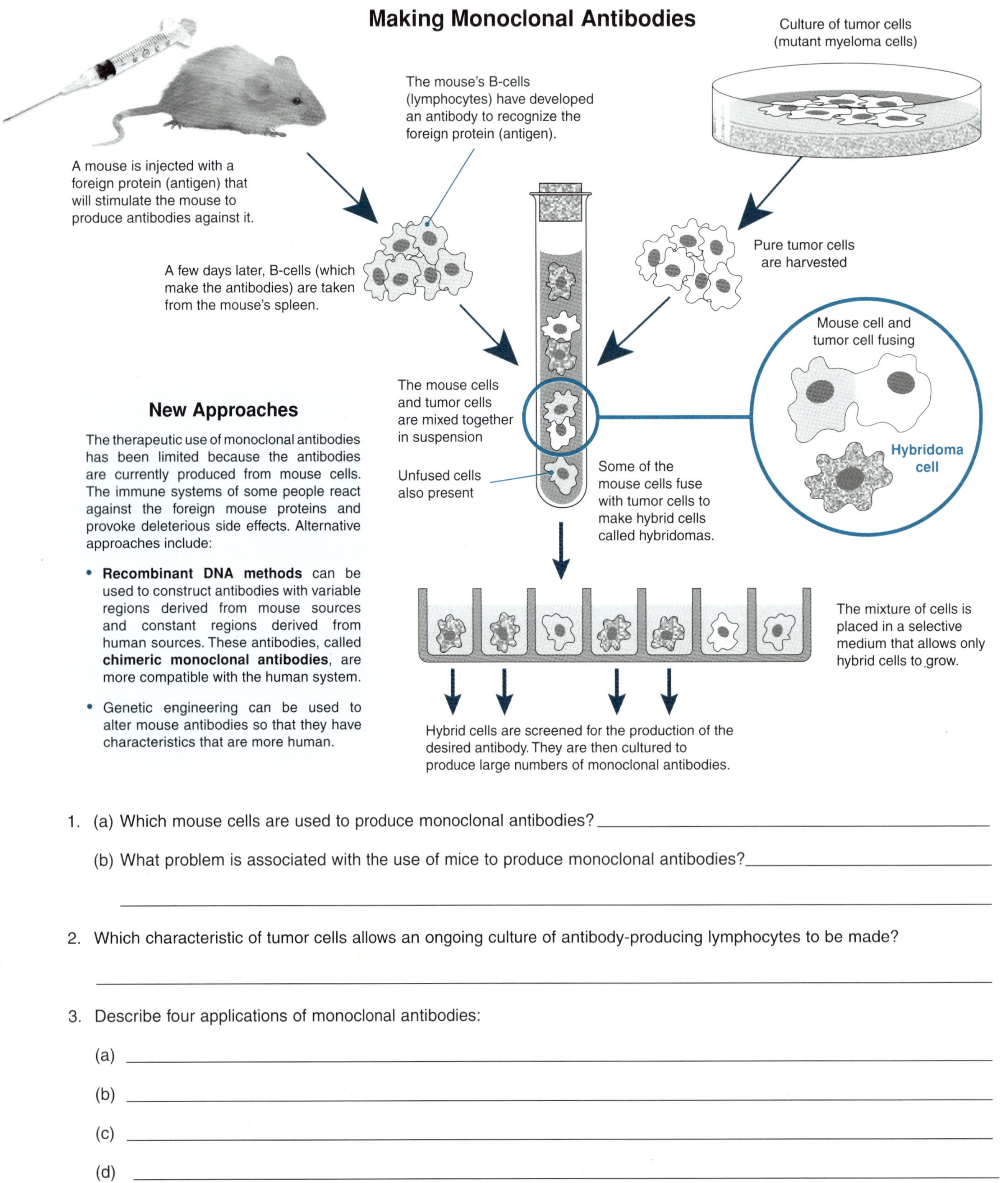

New Approaches

The therapeutic use of monoclonal antibodies has been limited because the antibodies are currently produced from mouse cells. The immune systems of some people react against the foreign mouse proteins and provoke deleterious side effects. Alternative approaches include:

- **Recombinant DNA methods** can be used to construct antibodies with variable regions derived from mouse sources and constant regions derived from human sources. These antibodies, called **chimeric monoclonal antibodies**, are more compatible with the human system.

- Genetic engineering can be used to alter mouse antibodies so that they have characteristics that are more human.

1. (a) Which mouse cells are used to produce monoclonal antibodies? _______________________________________

   (b) What problem is associated with the use of mice to produce monoclonal antibodies?_____________________

   ____

2. Which characteristic of tumor cells allows an ongoing culture of antibody-producing lymphocytes to be made?

   ____

3. Describe four applications of monoclonal antibodies:

   (a) ____

   (b) ____

   (c) ____

   (d) ____

© BIOZONE International 2013
ISBN: 978-1-927173-72-5
Photocopying Prohibited

KNOW

Related activities: Herceptin: A Modern Monoclonal
Weblinks: Monoclonal Antibody Production

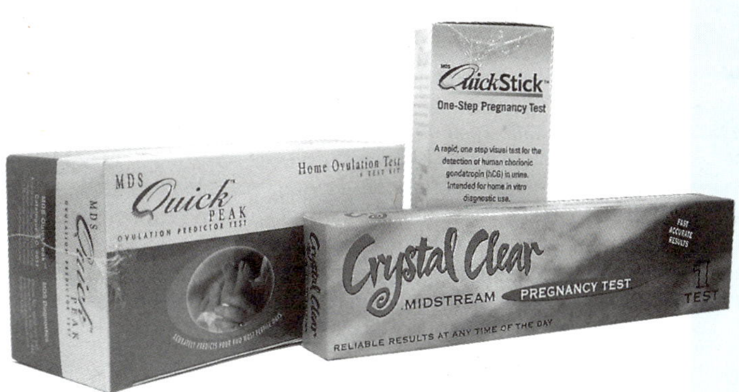

Detecting Pregnancy using Monoclonal Antibodies

When a woman becomes pregnant, a hormone called **human chorionic gonadotropin** (HCG) is released. HCG accumulates in the bloodstream and is excreted in the urine. Antibodies can be produced against HCG and used in simple test kits (below) to determine if a woman is pregnant. Monoclonal antibodies are also used in other home testing kits, such as those for detecting ovulation time (far left).

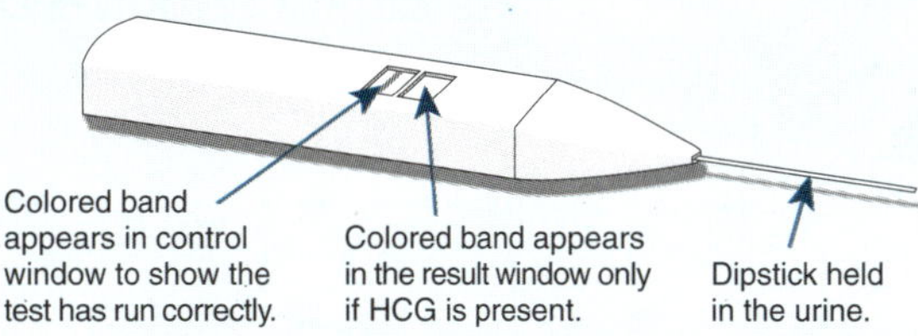

Other Applications of Monoclonal Antibodies

Diagnostic uses

- Detecting the presence of pathogens such as *Chlamydia* and streptococcal bacteria, distinguishing between *Herpesvirus* I and II, and diagnosing AIDS.
- Measuring protein, toxin, or drug levels in serum.
- Blood and tissue typing.
- Detection of antibiotic residues in milk.

Therapeutic uses

- Neutralizing endotoxins produced by bacteria in blood infections.
- Used to prevent organ rejection, e.g. in kidney transplants, by interfering with the T-cells involved with the rejection of transplanted tissue.
- Used in the treatment of some auto-immune disorders such as rheumatoid arthritis and allergic asthma. The monoclonal antibodies bind to and inactivate factors involved in the cascade leading to the inflammatory response.
- Immunodetection and immunotherapy of cancer. Herceptin is a monoclonal antibody for the targeted treatment of breast cancer. Herceptin recognizes receptor proteins on the outside of cancer cells and binds to them. The immune system can then identify the antibodies as foreign and destroy the cell.
- Inhibition of platelet clumping, which is used to prevent reclogging of coronary arteries in patients who have undergone angioplasty. The monoclonal antibodies bind to the receptors on the platelet surface that are normally linked by fibrinogen during the clotting process.

How home pregnancy detection kits work

The test area of the dipstick (below) contains two types of antibodies: free monoclonal antibodies and capture monoclonal antibodies, bound to the substrate in the test window.

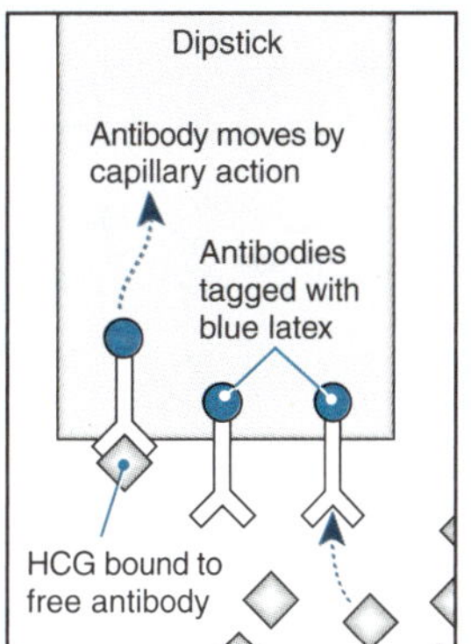

The free antibodies are specific for HCG and are color-labeled. HCG in the urine of a pregnant woman binds to the free antibodies on the surface of the dipstick. The antibodies then travel up the dipstick by capillary action.

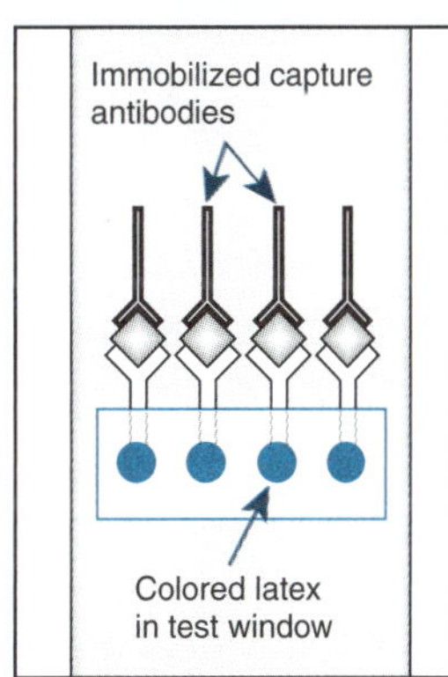

The capture antibodies are specific for the HCG-antibody complex. The HCG-antibody complexes traveling up the dipstick are bound by the immobilized capture antibodies, forming a sandwich. The color labeled antibodies then create a visible color change in the test window.

4. For each of the following applications, suggest why an antibody-based test or therapy is so valuable:

(a) Detection of toxins or bacteria in perishable foods: ______________________________________

____

____

(b) Detection of pregnancy without a doctor's prescription: ______________________________________

____

(c) Targeted treatment of tumors in cancer patients: ______________________________________

____

Herceptin: A Modern Monoclonal

Herceptin is the patented name of a **monoclonal antibody** for the targeted treatment of breast cancer. This drug (chemical name Trastuzumab) recognizes and is specific to the receptor proteins on the outside of cancer cells that are produced by the **proto-oncogene HER2**. The HER2 (**H**uman **E**pidermal growth factor **R**eceptor **2**) gene codes for cell surface proteins that signal to the cell when it should divide. Cancerous cells contain 20-30% more of the HER2 gene than normal cells and this causes **over-expression** of HER2, and large amounts of HER2 protein.

The over-expression causes the cell to divide more often than normal, producing a tumor. Cancerous cells are designated **HER2+** indicating receptor protein over-expression. The immune system fails to destroy these cells because they are not recognized as being abnormal. Herceptin's role is to recognize and bind to the HER2 protein on the surface of the cancerous cell. The immune system can then identify the antibodies as foreign and destroy the cell. The antibody also has the effect of blocking the cell's signalling pathway and thus stops the cell from dividing.

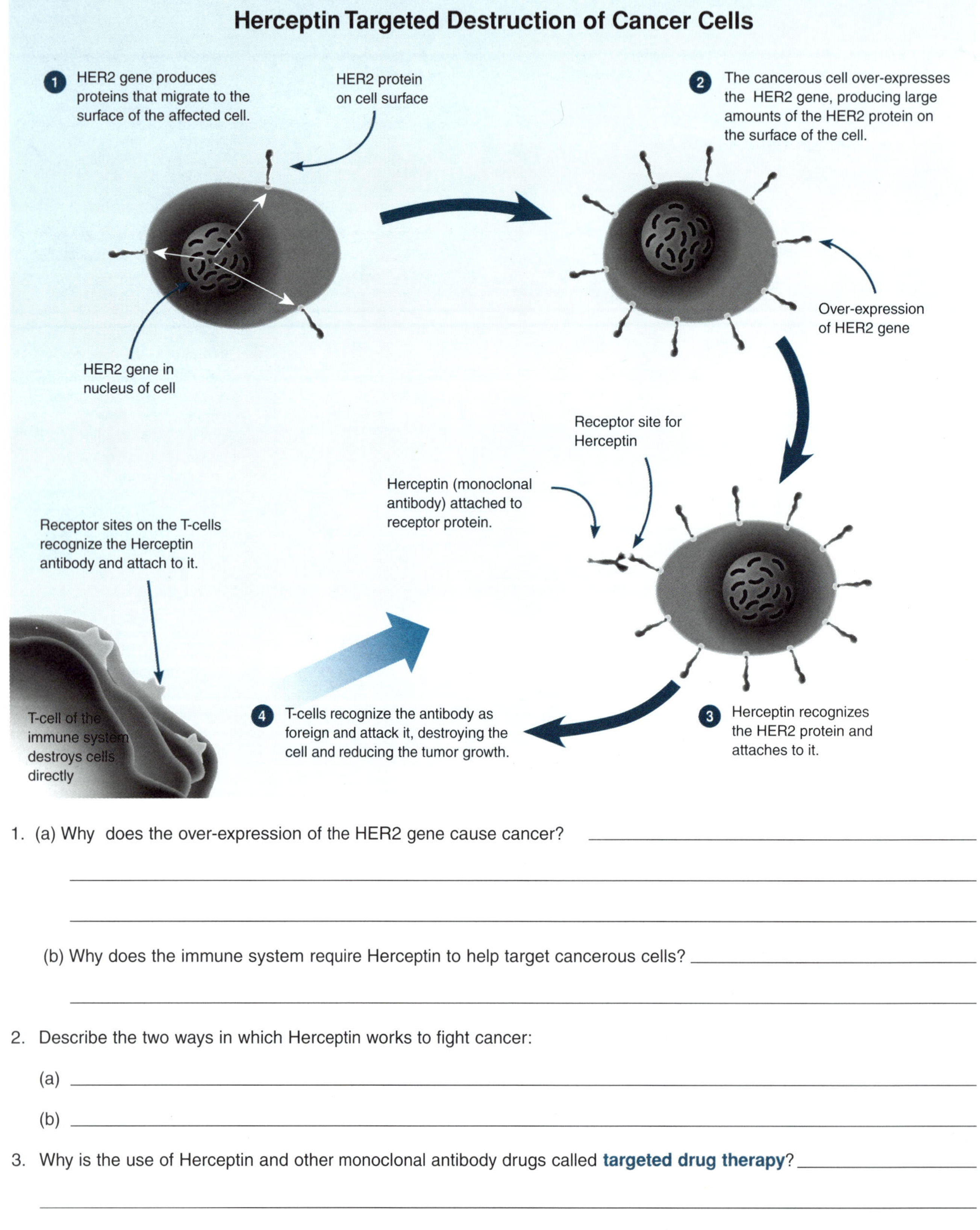

Herceptin Targeted Destruction of Cancer Cells

1. (a) Why does the over-expression of the HER2 gene cause cancer? _______________________________

____

____

   (b) Why does the immune system require Herceptin to help target cancerous cells? _______________________

____

2. Describe the two ways in which Herceptin works to fight cancer:

   (a) ____

   (b) ____

3. Why is the use of Herceptin and other monoclonal antibody drugs called **targeted drug therapy**? _______________

____

____

KNOW

Related activities: Monoclonal Antibodies

Weblinks: How Herceptin Works

Vaccines and Vaccination

Vaccines operate on the principle that they alert the immune system to the presence of a pathogen by introducing harmless but recognisably foreign antigens against which the body can form antibodies. There are two basic types of vaccine: subunit vaccines and whole-agent vaccines. **Whole-agent vaccines** contain complete nonvirulent microbes, either **inactivated** (killed), or alive but **attenuated** (weakened). Attenuated viruses make very effective vaccines and often provide life-long immunity without the need for booster immunizations. Killed viruses are less effective and many vaccines of this sort have now been replaced by newer subunit vaccines. **Subunit vaccines** contain only the parts of the pathogen that induce the immune response. They are safer than attenuated vaccines because they cannot reproduce in the recipient, and they produce fewer adverse effects because they contain little or no extra material. There are several ways to make subunit vaccines but, in all cases, the subunit vaccine loses its ability to cause disease while retaining its antigenic properties. Some of the most promising vaccines under development consist of naked DNA which is injected into the body and produces an antigenic protein. The safety of DNA vaccines is uncertain but they show promise against rapidly mutating viruses such as influenza and HIV.

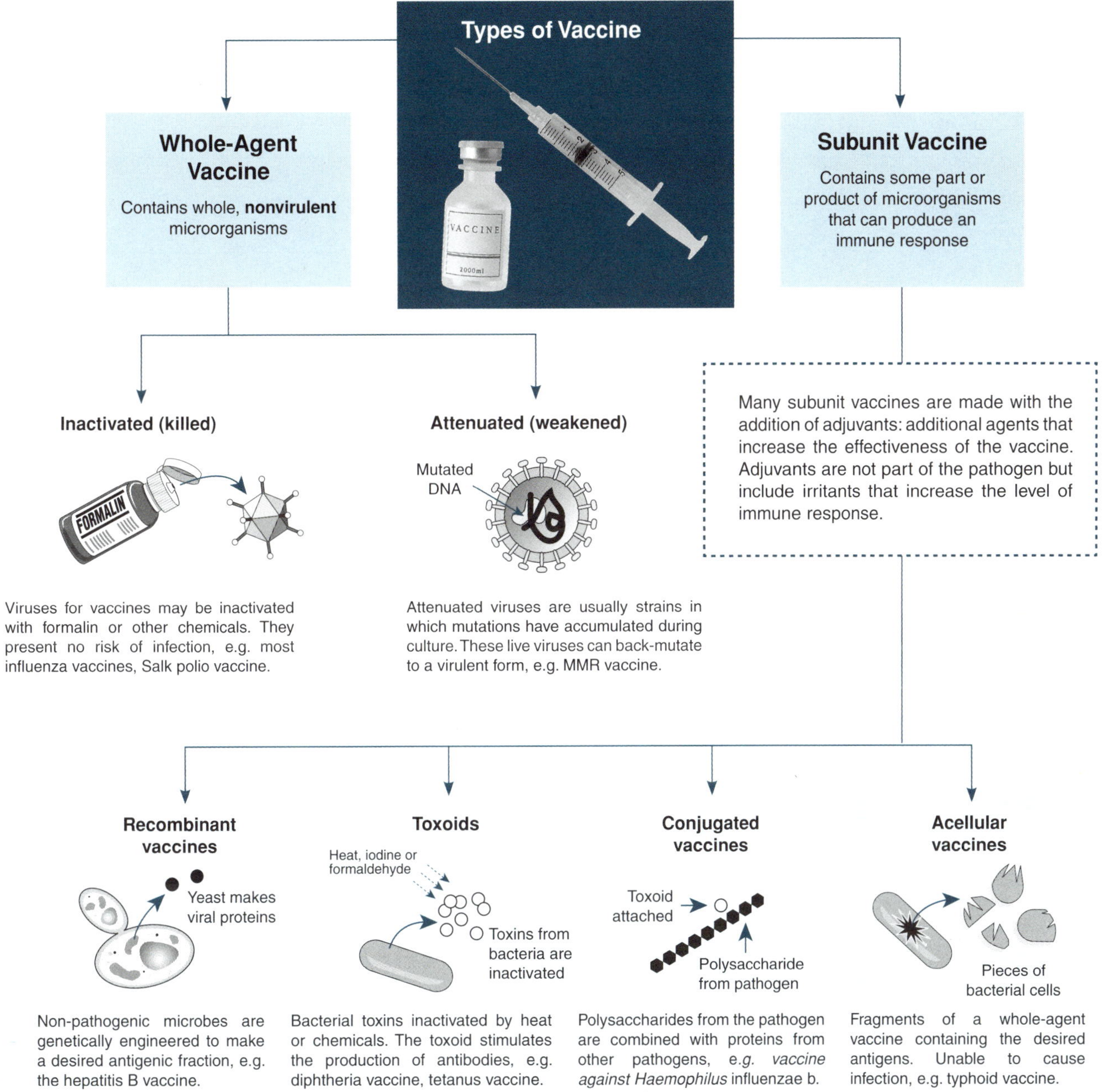

1. **Attenuated viruses** provide long term immunity to their recipients and generally do not require booster shots. Why do you think attenuated viruses provide such effective long-term immunity when inactivated viruses do not?

____

____

____

____

Related activities: Edible Vaccines

KNOW

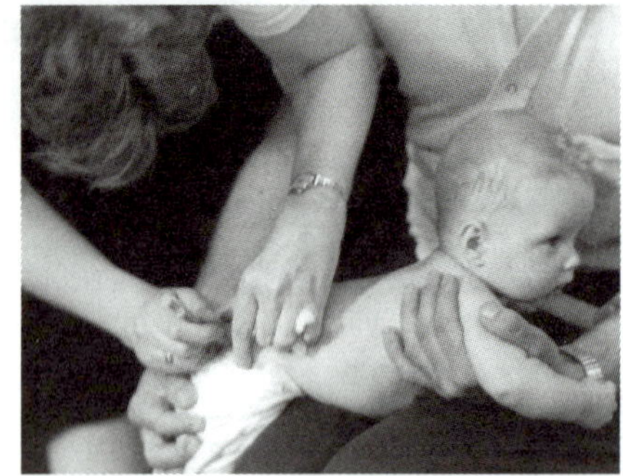
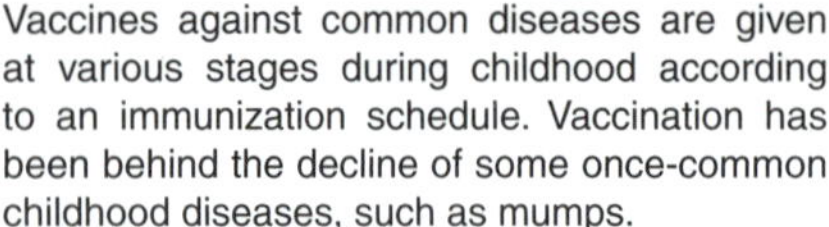

Vaccines against common diseases are given at various stages during childhood according to an immunization schedule. Vaccination has been behind the decline of some once-common childhood diseases, such as mumps.

Many childhood diseases for which vaccination programmes exist are kept at a low level because of **herd immunity**. If most of the population is immune, those that are not immunized may be protected because the disease is uncommon.

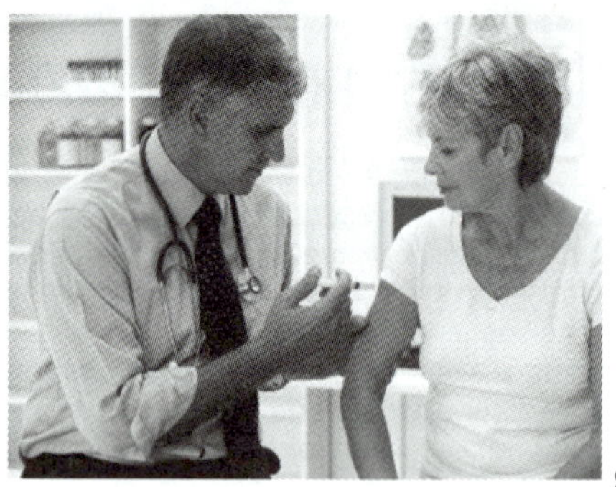

Most vaccinations are given in childhood, but adults may be vaccinated against a disease (e.g. TB, influenza) if they are in a high risk group (e.g. the elderly) or if they are travelling to a region in the world where a disease is prevalent.

2. Describe briefly **how** each of the following types of vaccine are made and name an **example** of each:

    (a) Whole-agent vaccine: ____

    (b) Subunit vaccine: ____

    (c) Inactivated vaccine: ____

    (d) Attenuated vaccine: ____

    (e) Recombinant vaccine: ____

    (f) Toxoid vaccine: ____

    (g) Conjugated vaccine: ____

    (h) Acellular vaccine: ____

3. (a) Describe an advantage of creating vaccines using **recombinant DNA technology**: _______________________

    (b) Draw a simple **diagram** to illustrate the use of the recombinant method to manufacture a vaccine:

Edible Vaccines

Although still a few years away, the development of edible vaccines produced by transgenic plants using **recombinant DNA technology** will overcome many of the problems faced when using traditional vaccines. Plants engineered to contain the vaccine can be grown locally, in the area where vaccination is required, overcoming the logistic and economic problems of transporting prepared vaccines over long distances. Most importantly, edible vaccines do not require syringes, saving money and eliminating the risk of infection from contaminated needles. One method (below) used to generate edible vaccines relies on the bacterium *Agrobacterium tumefaciens* to deliver the genes for viral or bacterial antigens into plant cells (e.g. potatoes).

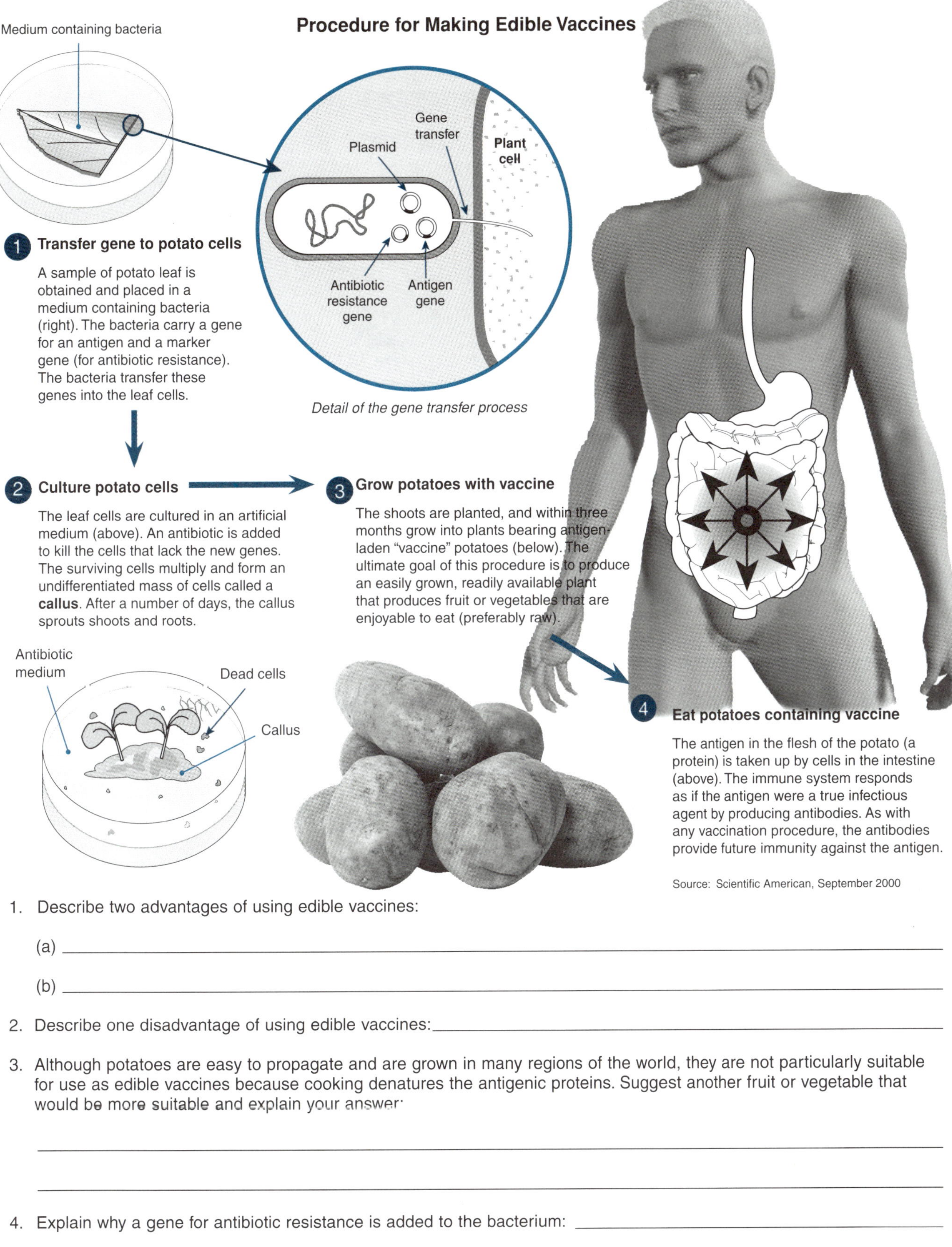

Procedure for Making Edible Vaccines

1 Transfer gene to potato cells

A sample of potato leaf is obtained and placed in a medium containing bacteria (right). The bacteria carry a gene for an antigen and a marker gene (for antibiotic resistance). The bacteria transfer these genes into the leaf cells.

2 Culture potato cells

The leaf cells are cultured in an artificial medium (above). An antibiotic is added to kill the cells that lack the new genes. The surviving cells multiply and form an undifferentiated mass of cells called a **callus**. After a number of days, the callus sprouts shoots and roots.

3 Grow potatoes with vaccine

The shoots are planted, and within three months grow into plants bearing antigen-laden "vaccine" potatoes (below). The ultimate goal of this procedure is to produce an easily grown, readily available plant that produces fruit or vegetables that are enjoyable to eat (preferably raw).

4 Eat potatoes containing vaccine

The antigen in the flesh of the potato (a protein) is taken up by cells in the intestine (above). The immune system responds as if the antigen were a true infectious agent by producing antibodies. As with any vaccination procedure, the antibodies provide future immunity against the antigen.

Source: Scientific American, September 2000

1. Describe two advantages of using edible vaccines:

   (a) ____

   (b) ____

2. Describe one disadvantage of using edible vaccines: ____

3. Although potatoes are easy to propagate and are grown in many regions of the world, they are not particularly suitable for use as edible vaccines because cooking denatures the antigenic proteins. Suggest another fruit or vegetable that would be more suitable and explain your answer:

   ____

   ____

4. Explain why a gene for antibiotic resistance is added to the bacterium: _______________________________

   ____

Related activities: Vaccines and Vaccination

KNOW

Gene Therapy

Gene therapy uses gene technology to treat disease by correcting or replacing faulty genes. Although varying in detail, all gene therapies are based around the same technique. Normal (non-faulty) DNA containing the correct gene is inserted into a vector, a carrier which transfers the DNA into the patient's cells. This process is called **transfection**. The vector is introduced into a sample of the patient's cells, and these are cultured to amplify the correct gene. The cultured cells are then transferred back to the patient. The use of altered stem cells instead of mature somatic cells has so far achieved longer lasting results in many patients. The treatment of somatic cells or stem cells is therapeutic (provides a benefit) but the changes are not inherited. **Germline therapy** (modification of the gametes) would enable genetic changes to be passed on. Gene therapy has had limited success because transfection of targeted cells is inefficient, and the side effects can be severe or even fatal. However, gene therapy to treat SCID, a genetic disease affecting the immune system, has had some success.

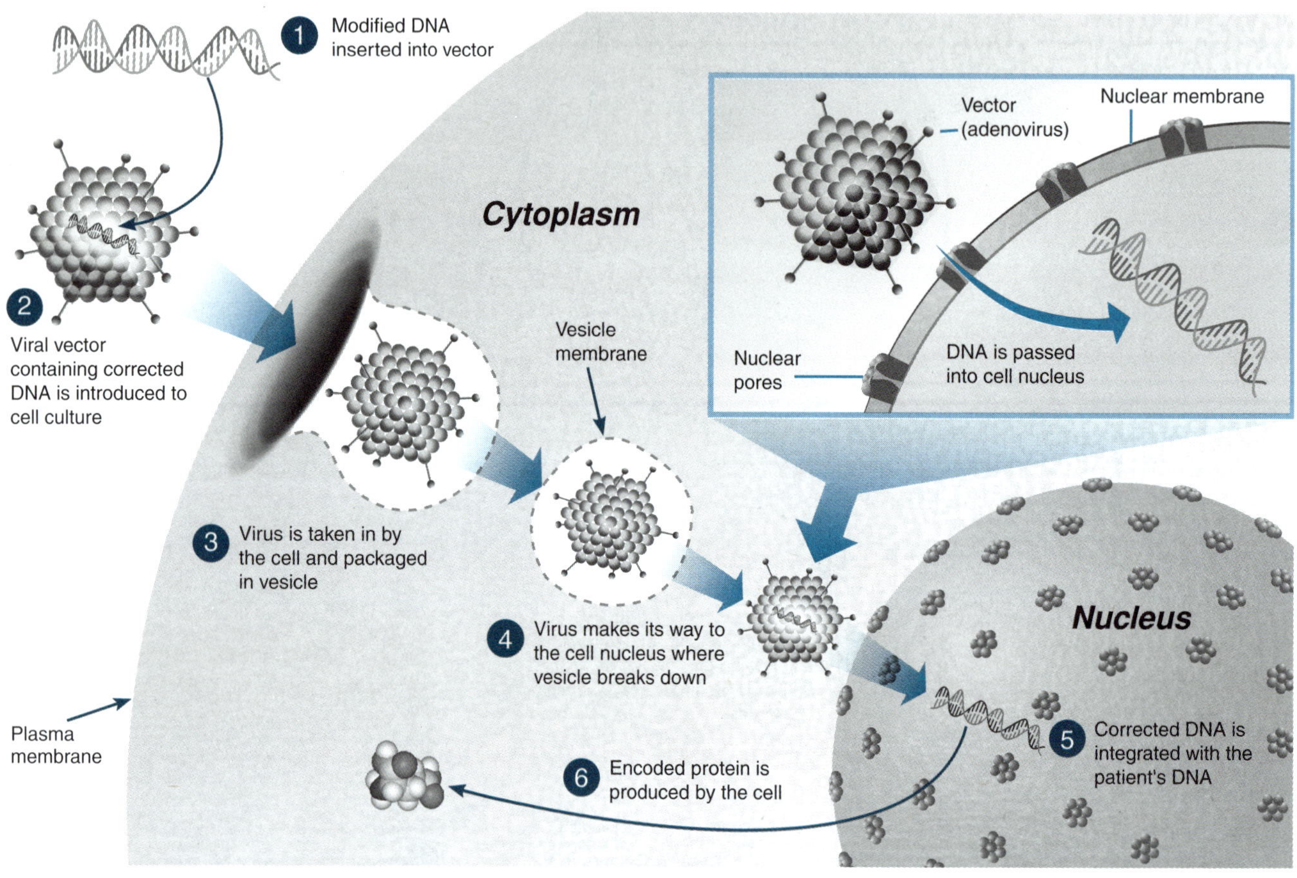

1. (a) Describe the general principle of gene therapy: ___________________________________

    ____

    ____

   (b) Describe the medical areas where gene therapy might be used:_________________________

    ____

    ____

2. Explain the significance of transfecting **germline cells** rather than **somatic cells**: ___________

    ____

    ____

3. Explain the purpose of **gene amplification** in gene therapy: __________________________

    ____

    ____

    ____

© BIOZONE International 2013
ISBN: 978-1-927173-72-5
Photocopying Prohibited

KNOW

Related activities: Vectors for Gene Therapy
Weblinks: Gene Therapy Video

Vectors for Gene Therapy

Gene therapy usually requires a **vector** (carrier) to introduce the DNA to a cell. **Retroviral vectors** are most often used to deliver the selected gene to the target cells. Other commonly used vectors include adenoviral vectors, liposomes, and injection of naked plasmid DNA. Some of the advantages and disadvantages for each vector are given below.

Vectors that can be used for gene therapy			
Retrovirus	**Adenovirus**	**Liposome**	**Naked DNA**
Insert size: 8000 bases	8000 bases	>20,000 bases	>20,000 bases
Integration: Yes	No	No	No
In vivo delivery: Poor	High	Variable	Poor
Advantages • Integrate genes into the chromosomes of the human host cell. • Offers chance for long-term stability.	• Modified for gene therapy, they infect human cells and express the normal gene. • Most do not cause disease. • Have a large capacity to carry foreign genes.	• Liposomes seek out target cells using sugars in their membranes that are recognised by cell receptors. • They have no viral genes that may cause disease.	• They have no viral genes that may cause disease. • Expected to be useful for vaccination.
Disadvantages • Many infect only cells that are dividing. • Genes integrate randomly into chromosomes, so might disrupt useful genes in the host cell.	• Viruses may have poor survival due to attack by the host's immune system. • Genes may function only sporadically because they are not integrated into the host cell's chromosome.	• Less efficient than viruses at transferring genes into cells, but recent work on using sugars to aid targeting have improved success rate.	• Unstable in most tissues of the body. • Inefficient at gene transfer.

In the table above, the following terms are defined as follows: **Naked DNA**: the genes are applied by ballistic injection (firing using a gene gun) or by regular hypodermic injection of plasmid DNA. **Insert size**: size of gene that can be inserted into the vector. **Integration**: whether or not the gene is integrated into the host DNA (chromosomes). **In vivo delivery**: ability to transfer a gene directly into a patient.

1. (a) Describe the features of viruses that make them well suited as **vectors** for gene therapy: _______________

   ____

   ____

   (b) Identify two problems with using viral vectors for gene therapy: _______________

   ____

   ____

2. (a) Suggest why it may be beneficial for a (therapeutic) gene to integrate into the patient's chromosome:

   ____

   ____

   (b) Explain why this has the potential to cause problems for the patient: _______________

   ____

3. (a) Suggest why naked DNA is likely to be unstable within a patient's tissues: _______________

   ____

   (b) Suggest why enclosing the DNA within liposomes might provide greater stability: _______________

   ____

Related activities: Gene Therapy, Gene Delivery Systems

KNOW

Gene Delivery Systems

The mapping of the human genome has improved the feasibility of gene therapy as a option for treating a variety of diseases. However, it still remains technically difficult to deliver genes successfully to a patient. Gene therapy success rates have generally been poor. Any improvements have been short-lived, or counteracted by adverse side effects. The inserted genes may reach only about 1% of target cells. Those that reach their target may work inefficiently and produce too little protein, too slowly to be of benefit. Many patients also have immune reactions to the vectors used in gene transfer. One of the first gene therapy trials was for cystic fibrosis (CF). CF was an obvious candidate for gene therapy because, in most cases, the disease is caused by a single, known gene mutation. However, despite its early promise, gene therapy for this disease has been disappointing (below right). Severe Combined Immune Deficiency (SCID) is another candidate for gene therapy, again because the disease is caused by single, known mutation (below left). Gene therapies for this disease have so far proved promising.

Treating SCID using Gene Therapy

The most common form of **SCID** (Severe Combined Immune Deficiency) is X-linked SCID, which results from mutations to a gene on the X chromosome encoding a protein that forms part of a receptor complex for numerous types of leukocytes. A less common form of the disease, (ADA-SCID) is caused by a defective gene that codes for the enzyme adenosine deaminase (ADA).

Both of these types of SCID lead to immune system failure. A common treatment for SCID is bone marrow transplant, but this is not always successful and runs the risks of infection from unscreened viruses. **Gene therapy** appears to hold the best chances of producing a cure for SCID because the mutation affects only one gene whose location is known. DNA containing the corrected gene is placed into a gutted retrovirus and introduced to a sample of the patient's bone marrow. The treated cells are then returned to the patient.

In some patients with ADA-SCID, treatment was so successful that supplementation with purified ADA was no longer required. The treatment carries risks though. In early trials, two of ten treated patients developed leukemia when the corrected gene was inserted next to a gene regulating cell growth.

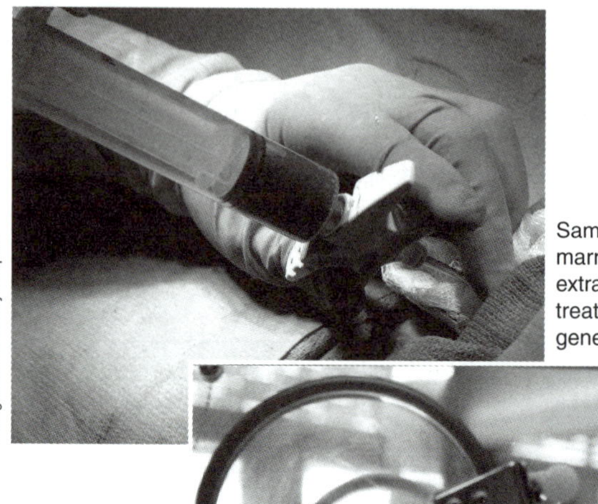

Samples of bone marrow being extracted prior to treatment with gene therapy.

Detection of SCID is difficult for the first months of an infant's life due to the mother's antibodies being present in the blood. Suspected SCID patients must be kept in sterile conditions at all times to avoid infection.

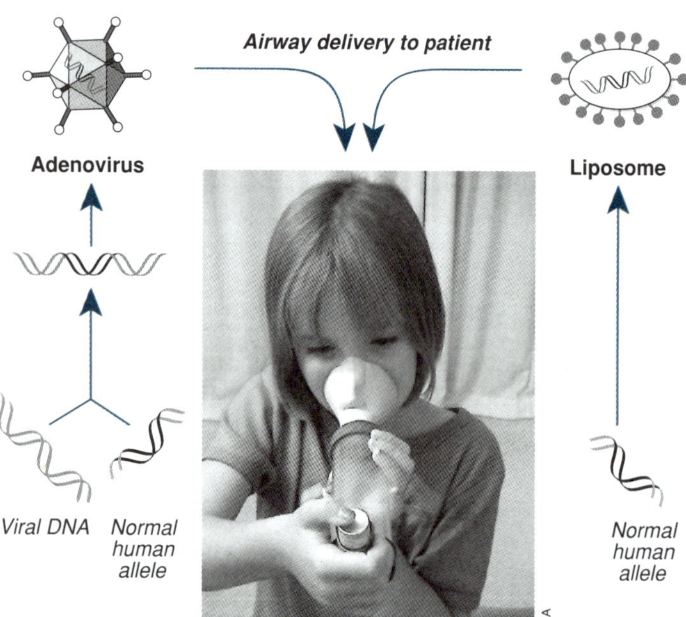

An **adenovirus** that normally causes colds is genetically modified to make it safe and to carry the normal (unmutated) CFTR ('cystic fibrosis') gene.

Liposomes are tiny fat globules. Normal CF genes are enclosed in liposomes, which fuse with plasma membranes and deliver the genes into the cells.

Gene Therapy - Potential Treatment for Cystic Fibrosis?

Cystic fibrosis (CF) is caused by a mutation to the gene coding for a chloride ion channel important in creating sweat, digestive juices, and mucus. The dysfunction results in abnormally thick, sticky mucus that accumulates in the lungs and intestines. The identification and isolation of the CF gene in 1989 meant that scientists could look for ways in which to correct the genetic defect rather than just treating the symptoms using traditional therapies.

The main target of CF gene therapy is the lung, because the progressive lung damage associated with the disease is eventually lethal.

In trials, normal genes were isolated and inserted into patients using vectors such as adenoviruses and liposomes, delivered via the airways (left). The results of trials were disappointing: on average, there was only a 25% correction, the effects were short lived, and the benefits were quickly reversed. Alarmingly, the adenovirus used in one of the trials led to the death of one patient.

Source: Cystic Fibrosis Trust, UK.

Related activities: Gene Therapy, Vectors for Gene Therapy

1. A great deal of current research is being devoted to discovering a gene therapy solution to treat **cystic fibrosis** (CF):

(a) Describe the symptoms of CF: ____

____

____

(b) Explain why this genetic disease has been so eagerly targeted by gene therapy researchers: _______________

____

____

____

____

(c) Outline some of the problems so far encountered with gene therapy for CF: _______________________________

____

____

____

____

____

2. Identify two vectors for introducing healthy CFTR genes into CF patients.

(a) Vector 1: ____

(b) Vector 2: ____

3. (a) Describe the difference between X-linked SCID and ADA-SCID: _______________________________

____

(b) Identify the vector used in the treatment of SCID: _______________________________________

____

4. Briefly outline the differences in the gene therapy treatment of CF and SCID: _______________________________

____

____

____

____

5. Changes made to chromosomes as a result of gene therapy involving somatic cells are not inherited. Germ-line gene therapy has the potential to cure disease, but the risks and benefits are still not clear. For each of the points outlined below, evaluate the risk of germ-line gene therapy relative to somatic cell gene therapy and explain your answer:

(a) Chance of interfering with an essential gene function: _______________________________________

____

____

____

(b) Misuse of the therapy to selectively alter phenotype: _______________________________________

____

____

____

KEY TERMS: Crossword

Complete the crossword below, which will test your understanding of key terms in this chapter and their meanings.

Clues Across

1. The testing of embryos so that embryos with genetic disorders are not implanted into the prospective mother. (Acronym)

10. A vaccine produced using genetically engineered DNA. (2 words: 11, 7)

11. A substance used to stimulate the production of antibodies and provide immunity against a specific disease.

Clues Down

2. The insertion of normal or genetically altered genes into cells, usually to replace defective genes. (2 words: 4, 7)

3. A technique for determining gene function where the where the mRNA of the gene is altered to become non-functional. (2 words: 4, 9)

4. Integration of a foreign gene conferring a new property in the recipient organism.

5. An artificially produced antibody that binds to only one specific protein. (2 words: 10, 8)

6. Short sequence of labeled DNA (e.g. radioactively labeled) which is introduced to a DNA sample in order detect complementary DNA sequences for analysis. (2 words: 4, 5)

7. DNA analysis to detect the presence of a gene(s) associated with an inherited disorder. (2 words: 7, 9)

8. A length of DNA that is associated with a particular gene. It is not necessarily the gene of interest itself, but it is linked to and inherited with the gene of interest. (2 words: 4, 6)

9. A technique for determining gene function where the target gene is altered to become non-functional. (2 words: 4, 8)

VOCAB

Chapter 5

Genome Research

Key concepts

- ► Genome research (or **genomics**) involves sequencing, assembling, and analyzing the structure and function of genomes.

- ► Genomics involves the use of recombinant DNA technology, DNA sequencing methods, and **bioinformatics**.

- ► The information provided by genomics is used for forensic analysis, to screen for disease, select for traits, and determine gene function.

Key terms

bioinformatics

DNA (gene) probes

DNA (genetic) profiling

DNA chip (microarray)

forensic

gel electrophoresis

gene marker

genomics

Human Genome Project

marker assisted selection

microsatellites (STRs)

polymerase chain reaction (PCR)

proteomics

quantitative trait

quantitative trait loci

recombinant DNA technology

selective breeding

SNPs

Learning Objectives

☐ 1. Use the **KEY TERMS** to compile a glossary for this topic.

DNA Sequencing and Genome Analysis pages 100-108

☐ 2. Recognize that **DNA sequencing** refers to the determination of the nucleotide base sequence in DNA. It may be applied to individual genes, clusters of genes, full chromosomes or entire genomes. Appreciate that several methods of DNA sequencing exist and that the need for high throughput determination of sequences has driven the development of the technology.

☐ 3. Describe the use of **PCR**, radioactive labeling, and **gel electrophoresis** in DNA sequencing. Describe the role of automated DNA sequencing in the feasibility of large scale genome analyses. Identify applications of this technology.

☐ 4. Describe the aim of the collaborative project known as the **Human Genome Project** (HGP). Describe possible applications of the information provided by the HGP and other genome projects. Identify areas of further development in genome analysis, e.g. determining when and where genes are expressed, and determining the role of the gene products (a field known as **proteomics**).

DNA Profiling pages 109-112

☐ 5. Know that **DNA profiling** relies on the presence of highly variable repetitive sequences in an individual's DNA.

☐ 6. Describe DNA profiling using PCR, including the role of the following:
   (a) **Microsatellites** (**STRs**) in providing identifiable variation.
   (b) PCR in amplifying the microsatellites.
   (c) Gel electrophoresis in visualizing the PCR products for comparison.

☐ 7. Discuss the applications of DNA profiling, e.g. in **forensic** analysis and in determining pedigrees for animal breeding purposes.

DNA Microarrays pages 113-114

☐ 8. Describe the construction of a **DNA chip (microarray)**, identifying the principles by which the chip operates. Appreciate that a microarray is a progression of basic DNA probe technology.

☐ 9. Describe how microarrays are used to study the expression of genes. Describe the applications of this research in medicine and in agriculture.

DNA Markers and Marker Assisted Selection pages 115-116

☐ 10. Explain how DNA probes and genetic markers are used in **marker assisted selection** for **quantitative traits** in livestock breeds.

Weblinks:

www.thebiozone.com/
weblink/MnB-3725/

Automated DNA Sequencing

The process of determining the DNA sequence of an organism can be automated using gel electrophoresis machines that can sequence up to 600 bases at a time. Automation made sequencing faster and less costly and thus made large-scale genome sequencing projects possible. Automated sequencing analyses the light signals from nucleotides labeled with fluorescent dyes. Computer analysis of the data is then used to assemble the sequence. The basic automation method is outlined below. The new so-called next-generation high throughput sequencers extend this process across millions of reactions in parallel and are capable of producing thousands to millions of sequences at the same time.

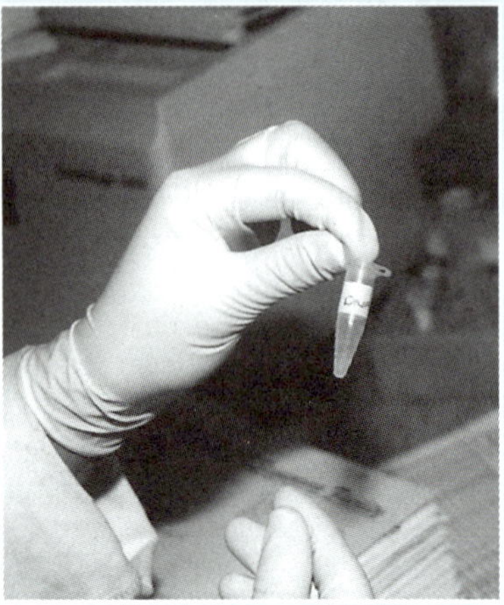

1. DNA sample arrives
Purified DNA samples may contain linear DNA or plasmids. The sample should contain about 1×10^{11} DNA molecules. The sample is checked to ensure that there is enough DNA present in the sample to work with.

2. Primer and reaction mix added
A **DNA primer** is added to the sample which provides a starting sequence for synthesis. Also added is the **sequencing reaction mix** containing the *polymerase enzyme* and free nucleotides, some which are labeled with dye.

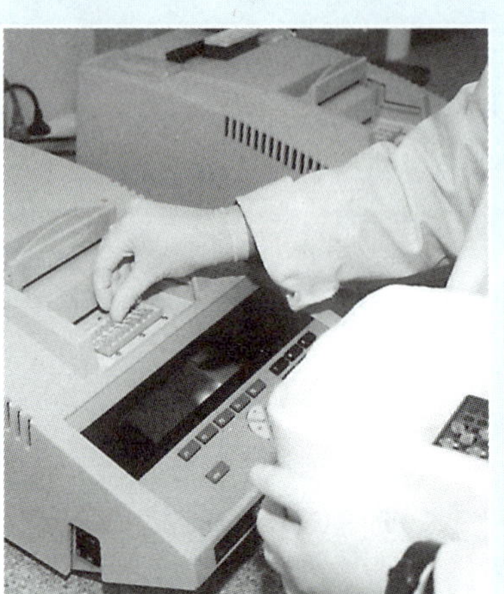

3. Create dye-labeled fragments
A PCR machine creates fragments of DNA complementary to the original template DNA. Each fragment is tagged with a fluorescent dye-labeled nucleotide. Running for 25 cycles, it creates 25×10^{11} single-stranded DNA molecules.

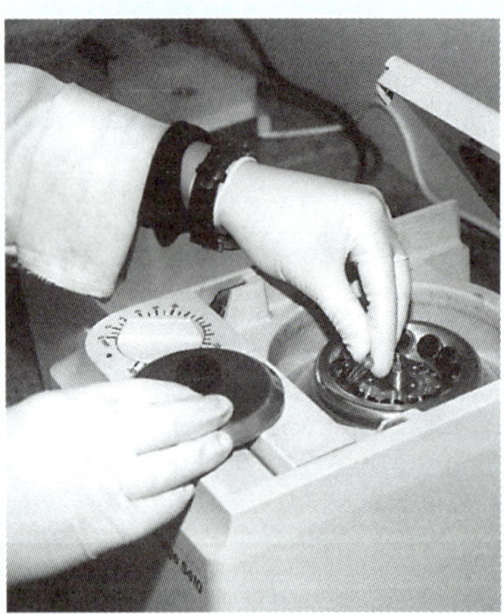

4. Centrifuge to create DNA pellet
The sample is chemically precipitated and centrifuged to settle the DNA fragments as a solid pellet at the bottom of the tube. Unused nucleotides, still in the liquid, are discarded.

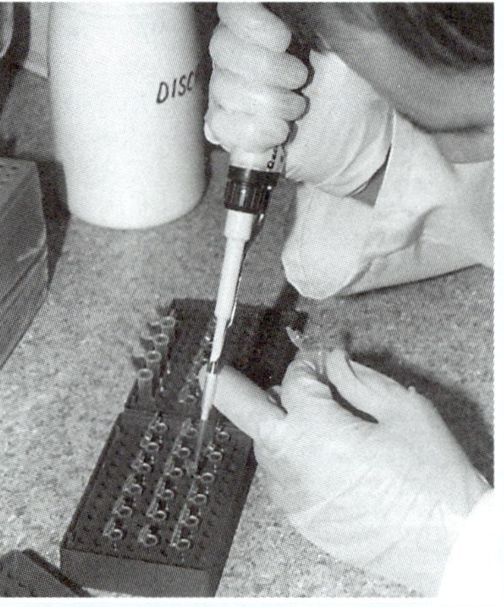

5. DNA pellet washed, buffer added
The pellet is washed with ethanol, dried, and a gel loading buffer is added. All that remains now is single stranded DNA with one dye-labeled nucleotide at the end of each molecule.

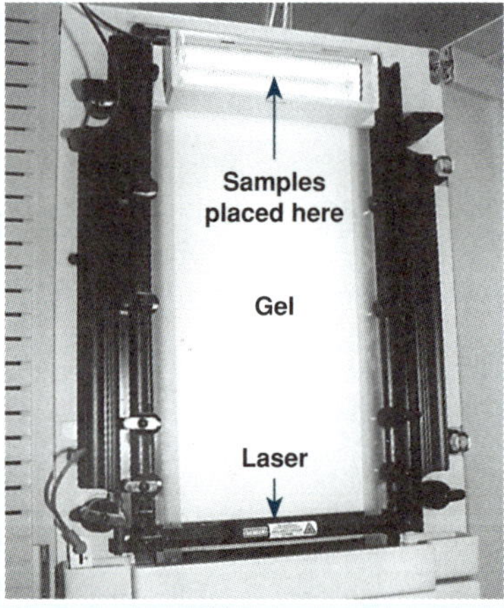

6. Acrylamide gel is loaded
The DNA sequencer is prepared by placing the gel (sandwiched between two sheets of glass) into position. A 36 channel 'comb' for receiving the samples is placed at the top of the gel.

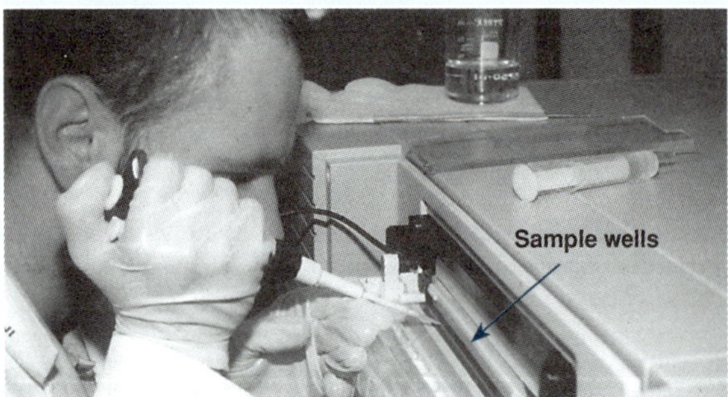

7. Loading DNA samples onto gel
Different samples can be placed in each of the 36 wells (funnel shaped receptacles) above the gel. A control DNA sample of known sequence is applied to the first lane of the sequencer. If there are problems with the control sequence then results for all other lanes are considered invalid.

8. Running the DNA sequencer
Powerful computer software controls the activity of the DNA sequencer. The gel is left to run for up to 10 hours. During this time an argon laser is constantly scanning across the bottom of the gel to detect the passing of dye-labeled nucleotides attached to DNA fragments.

© BIOZONE International 2013
ISBN: 978-1-927173-72-5
Photocopying Prohibited

REFER

Related activities: *Gel Electrophoresis, The Human Genome Project*

Weblinks: *Dideoxy DNA Sequencing*

How a DNA Sequencer Operates

The gel is loaded following preparation of the samples and the gel (see steps 1-7 and box, right).

Comb with 36 lanes into which different samples can be placed.

DNA fragments with dye-labeled nucleotides move down the gel over a period of 10 hours.

The smallest fragments move fastest down the gel and reach the argon laser first. Larger fragments arrive later.

DNA fragments separate into bands (see box below).

Argon laser excites fluorescent dye labels on nucleotides.

Lenses collect the emitted light and focus it into a spectrograph. An attached digital camera detects the light. See 'data collection' (below, right).

Negative terminal repels DNA fragments

2400 volts 50 mA

Acrylamide gel

Positive terminal attracts DNA fragments

Creating the dye labeled fragments

for gel electrophoresis is outlined in step 3. Key ingredients are:

(a) Original DNA template (the sample)

A C C G T A T G A T T C

(b) Many normal unlabeled nucleotides:

A   T   G   C

(c) Terminal nucleotides labeled with fluorescent dye (a different color for each of the 4 bases). The structure of the nucleotides is altered so they act as terminators to stop further synthesis of the strand:

Two examples of synthesized DNA fragments are shown below. One is relatively short, the other is longer:

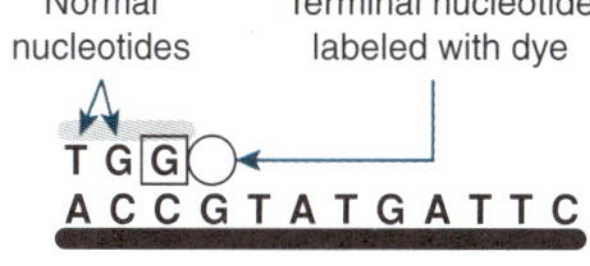

Data collection: The data from the digital camera are collected by computer software. The first of 23 samples is highlighted below in lane 1 with base sequences appearing on the far left.

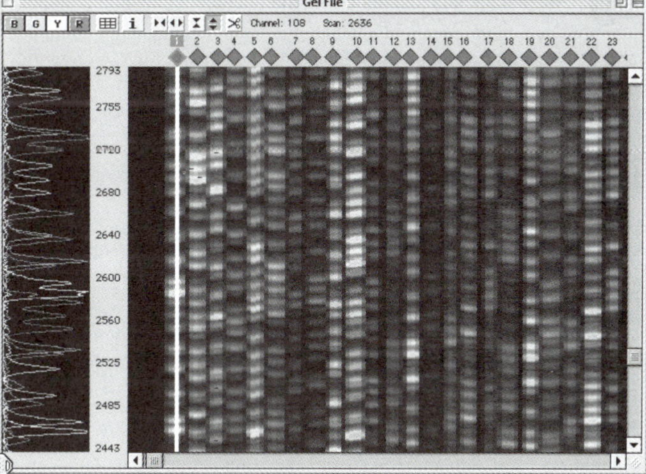

Data analysis: The data can be saved as a file for analysis by other computer software. Such software can provide a printout of the base sequence and perform comparisons with other DNA sequences (e.g. when looking for mutations).

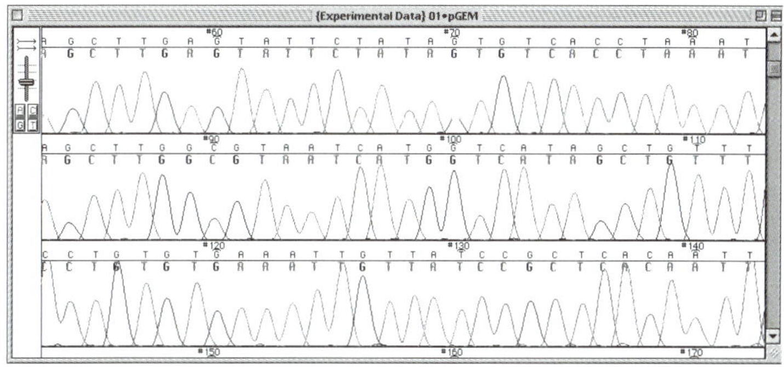

DNA fragments of different sizes are drawn down through the gel, separating into distinct bands of colour as they are illuminated by the laser:

Large fragments travel slowly down the gel

T G G C A T A C T A A G ◯ Yellow

T G G C A T A C T A A ◯ Green

T G G C A T A C T A ◯ Green

T G G C A T A C T ◯ Red

T G G C A T A C ● Blue

T G G C A T A ◯ Green

T G G C A T ◯ Red

T G G C A ◯ Green

T G G C ● Blue

T G G ◯ Yellow

T G ◯ Yellow

T ◯ Red

Small fragments travel quickly down the gel

Laser scans across the gel to detect the passing of each colored dye

Genome Analysis

Genome analysis involves determining the exact order of all of the millions of bases making up the DNA of an organism's **genome**. Genome analysis must also identify all the genes present, their correct and exact location in the base sequence, and the regions of DNA that control the activity of the genes. Chromosomes range in size from 50 million to 250 million bases; too large to handle for high resolution mapping and sequencing. They must be broken down into much shorter pieces, cloned, and sequenced. It is important to be able to assemble all of the sequenced fragments into a complete, continuous sequence for each chromosome. This is achieved by mapping known **genetic** **markers** at regular intervals along each chromosome. When DNA fragments are sequenced, the presence of DNA markers enables them to be correctly positioned in the overall sequence. A wide variety of applications are currently or potentially available for genome analysis, from the treatment and diagnosis of disease to ecological studies of diversity and phylogeny. Note that a small proportion of an organism's DNA occurs outside the nucleus, in the mitochondria, and is called the **mitochondrial genome**. Mitochondrial DNA (mtDNA) is often targeted in studies of phylogeny because it is highly **conserved** (it codes for vital functions and changes very little over evolutionary time).

Mapping and Sequencing the Genome

1 Chromosome cut into large fragments:

A human chromosome, consisting of 50-280 million base-pairs, is cut randomly into large fragments with **restriction enzymes**. Each fragment is 150,000 - 1 million base pairs long.

2 Create a clone library:

Each large fragment is inserted into a separate vector (yeast or bacterial plasmid) using DNA ligation. The plasmids are then cloned in cells to produce many copies of the fragments; known as a **clone library** (each type of DNA fragment resides in a separate culture).

3 Map fragment with DNA markers:

Each of the fragments are then mapped using **PCR** and **gel electrophoresis** to determine the position of **DNA markers** on each fragment.

4 Create a low resolution map of a chromosome:

Overlaps between the large fragments can be determined and a low resolution map of the chromosome can be built up. In reality, there would be many hundreds of large fragments created by the cutting up of a single chromosome (only four are shown here).

5 Each large fragment is cut into smaller pieces:

A large fragment is cut into smaller pieces (1500 - 5000 base pairs) with **restriction enzymes**. These smaller fragments are inserted into vectors using DNA ligation techniques. These vectors are then cloned to make copies; a **sub-clone library**.

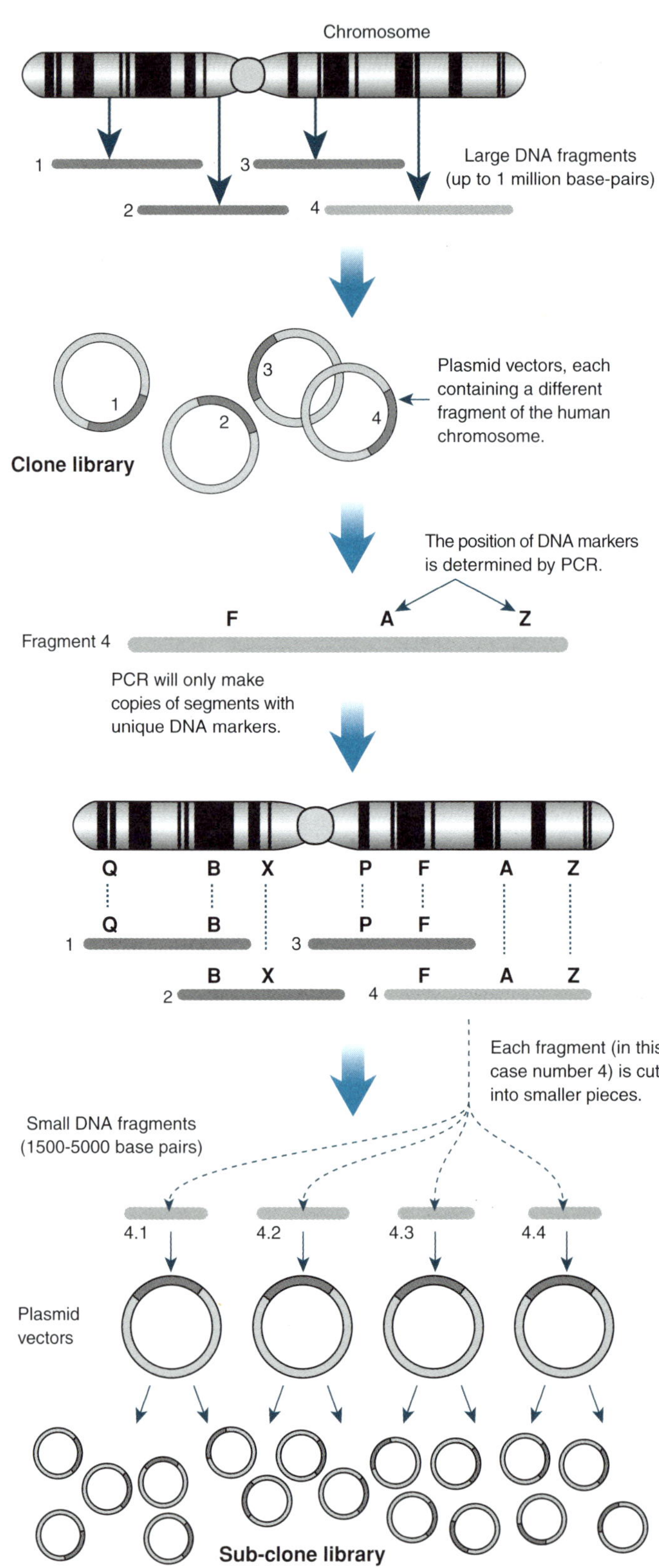

KNOW

Related activities: Automated DNA Sequencing, The Human Genome Project, Genome Projects

6 **Sequence fragments:**

The small fragments are then sequenced using gel electrophoresis to find the exact order of the bases. Note: the examples on the right show only 15 base-pairs in each small fragment. In reality, they would be 1500 to 5000 base pairs in length.

7 **Overlapping sequences are assembled:**

Overlapping sequences are assembled together using a computer to work out the sequence of the large fragment.

Steps 5-7 are repeated for all large fragments until the entire chromosome is sequenced.

8 **Assemble sequenced fragments on chromosome:**

The sequences of the large fragments are then assembled on the chromosome map to make a complete chromosome sequence.

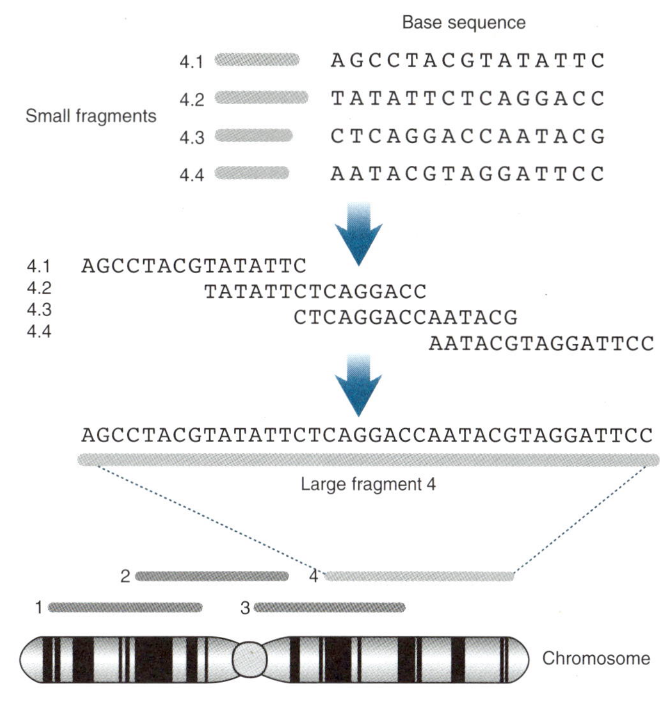

1. Explain how the following two main components of genome analysis contribute to the overall process:

(a) Genome **mapping**: ____

____

(b) Genome **sequencing**: ____

____

2. Explain the difference between a **clone library** and a **sub-clone library**, identifying their role in genome analysis:

____

____

____

____

____

3. Describe the steps in the genome analysis process where the following techniques are used:

(a) Restriction enzymes: ____

____

(b) Ligation: ____

____

(c) Polymerase Chain Reaction (PCR): ____

____

(d) Gel electrophoresis: ____

____

4. Explain the role that DNA markers play in genome analysis: ____________________________

____

____

Investigating Genetic Diversity

PCR and **DNA sequencing** can be used in assessing **genetic biodiversity**. For conservationists, large amounts of genetic variation within a species may indicate a greater ability to adapt to environmental change (e.g. climate shifts). The amount of variation between populations of a species is of particular interest. Sometimes the genetic variation found between populations is enough to warrant separating them into two or more '**morphologically cryptic**' species (containing populations that are identical in appearance, but different genetically). **Springtails** are abundant arthropods, closely related to insects, which live in soil throughout the world. One particular species, *Gomphiocephalus hodgsoni*, is the largest year-round inhabitant of the Antarctic continent. It is being studied in an area of

Antarctica known as the Dry Valleys, particularly in Taylor Valley. This region is largely ice-free, and the springtails survive in moist habitats such as at the edges of lakes and glacial streams. Springtails collected throughout Taylor Valley appear to be morphologically identical. However, after DNA analysis of a gene from springtail **mitochondrial DNA**, significant genetic biodiversity has been found between populations. This may indicate the presence of more than one species. As climate change and the presence of humans affect the habitat of Taylor Valley over time, it is important to understand and monitor the genetic structure of the springtail populations in order to ensure that biodiversity is conserved.

The springtail *Gomphiocephalus hodgsoni* (above) is a small arthropod, just over 1 mm long. Liam Nolan investigated the genetic relatedness of populations in and around Taylor Valley in Antarctica.

Taylor Valley, one of the Dry Valleys in Antarctica, is clear of snow much of the year. The ephemeral stream is ideal springtail habitat.

The Process of DNA Analysis of Springtails is Illustated Below

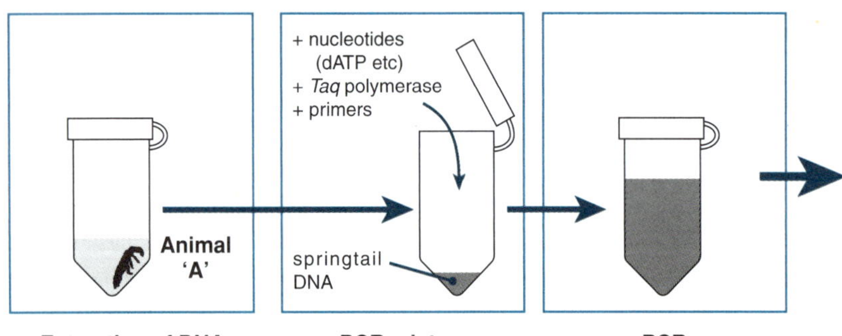

Extraction of DNA
Proteinase enzyme dissolves the tissues of the springtail to release DNA

PCR mixture
Primers anneal to the start and end of the gene in the mitochondrial DNA

PCR
DNA amplification 92°C, 45°C, 72°C 45 cycles

Source: Many thanks to **Liam Nolan**, teacher at Tauranga Girls' College, for supplying the information for these pages. Liam studied with the Centre for Biodiversity and Ecology Research (University of Waikato, Hamilton, New Zealand), whilst the recipient of a study award from the NZ Ministry of Education.

Conditions in Antarctica are harsh, even at the best of times. Members of the research group shared a tent at their camp in Taylor Valley, set aside as a field laboratory. Despite overnight temperatures well below freezing, the tent often became very hot during the day as the mid-summer sun heated it for most of the 24 hour cycle.

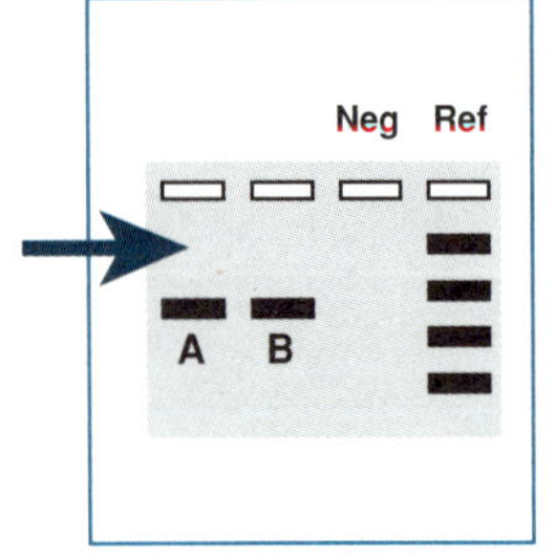

Gel electrophoresis of PCR product

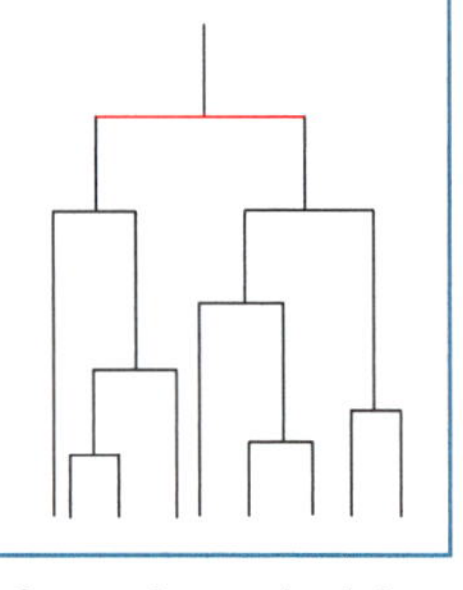

Sequencing of PCR product

Computers calculate relationships between springtail DNA

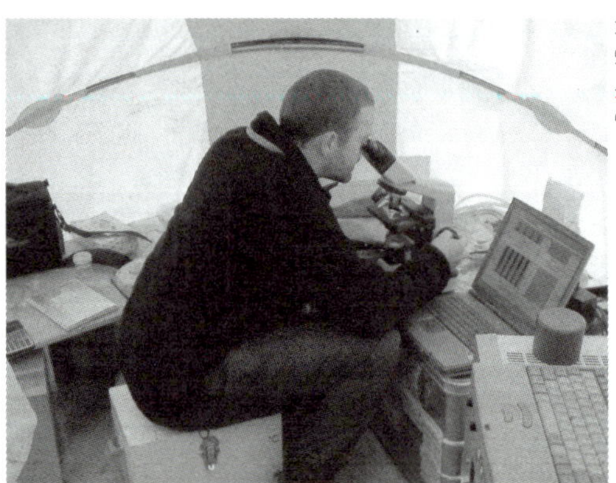

Expeditions in Antarctica are fraught with logistical problems. Apart from making sure that scientific equipment functions properly in freezing temperatures, just getting the equipment from Scott Base to the field station is difficult, requiring the use of helicopters.

Scott Base is the center for research scientists from around the world. They work mostly during the summer months, when there is perpetual daylight. There are facilities for carrying out some lab work, as well as recreational facilities for the expedition members.

Genome Research

1. Explain why a **proteinase** enzyme is helpful in the extraction of DNA from springtails:

2. (a) Describe the function of *Taq* polymerase in **PCR**:

   (b) Explain why nucleotides are added to the PCR mixture:

   (c) Explain the effect of different temperatures (used in PCR) on the DNA and primers:

3. (a) The **electrophoresis gel** is also loaded with a known '**negative**'; a substance that will produce a definite negative result, for comparison with samples A and B. Describe what would be put into the negative well:

   (b) A **reference**, which contains a mixture of DNA segments of known length, is also loaded onto the gel. Explain why such fragments are added into the reference well:

4. (a) The given DNA sequences (on the previous page) are taken from two different individuals. Describe the kind of mutation observed:

   (b) Mutations are most frequently found at the third base of a codon. Discuss the significance of this mutation in the springtails' DNA sequence:

The Human Genome Project

The **Human Genome Project** (HGP) is a publicly funded venture involving many different organizations throughout the world. In 2000, first draft of the human genome was obtained, and the entire genome is now available as a high quality (golden standard) sequence. In addition to determining the order of bases in the human genome, genes are being identified, sequenced, and mapped (their specific chromosomal location identified). The next challenge is to assign functions to the identified genes. By identifying and studying the protein products of genes (a field known as **proteomics**), scientists can develop a better understanding of genetic disorders. Long term benefits of the HGP are both medical and non-medical (see next page). Some biotechnology companies have taken out patents on gene sequences. This practice is controversial because it restricts the use of the sequence information to the patent holders. Other genome sequencing projects have arisen as a result of the initiative to sequence the human one. In 2002 the International HapMap Project was started with the aim of developing a haplotype map (HapMap) of the human genome. Initially data was gathered from four populations with African, Asian and European ancestry and additional populations may be included as analysis of human genetic variation continues.

Gene Mapping

This process involves determining the precise position of a gene on a chromosome. Once the position is known, it can be shown on a diagram.

X Chromosome

Equipment used for DNA Sequencing

Banks of PCR machines prepare DNA for the sequencing gel stage. The DNA is amplified and chemically tagged (to make the DNA fluoresce and enable visualisation on a gel).

Banks of DNA sequencing gels and powerful computers are used to determine the base order in DNA.

Count of Mapped Genes

The aim of the HGP was to produce a continuous block of sequence information for each chromosome. Initially the sequence information was obtained to draft quality, with an error rate of 1 in 1000 bases. The **Gold Standard** sequence, with an error rate of <1 per 100,000 bases, was completed in October 2004. This table shows the length and number of mapped genes for each chromosome.

Chromosome	Length (Mb)	No. of Mapped Genes
1	263	1873
2	255	1113
3	214	965
4	203	614
5	194	782
6	183	1217
7	171	995
8	155	591
9	145	804
10	144	872
11	144	1162
12	143	894
13	114	290
14	109	1013
15	106	510
16	98	658
17	92	1034
18	85	302
19	67	1129
20	72	599
21	50	386
22	56	501
X	164	1021
Y	59	122
Total:		**19,447**

Data to March 2008 from gdb.org (now offline)

Examples of Mapped Genes

The positions of an increasing number of genes have been mapped onto human chromosomes (see below). Sequence variations can cause or contribute to identifiable disorders. Note that chromosome 21 (the smallest human chromosome) has a relatively low gene density, while others are gene rich. This is possibly why trisomy 21 (Down syndrome) is one of the few viable human autosomal trisomies.

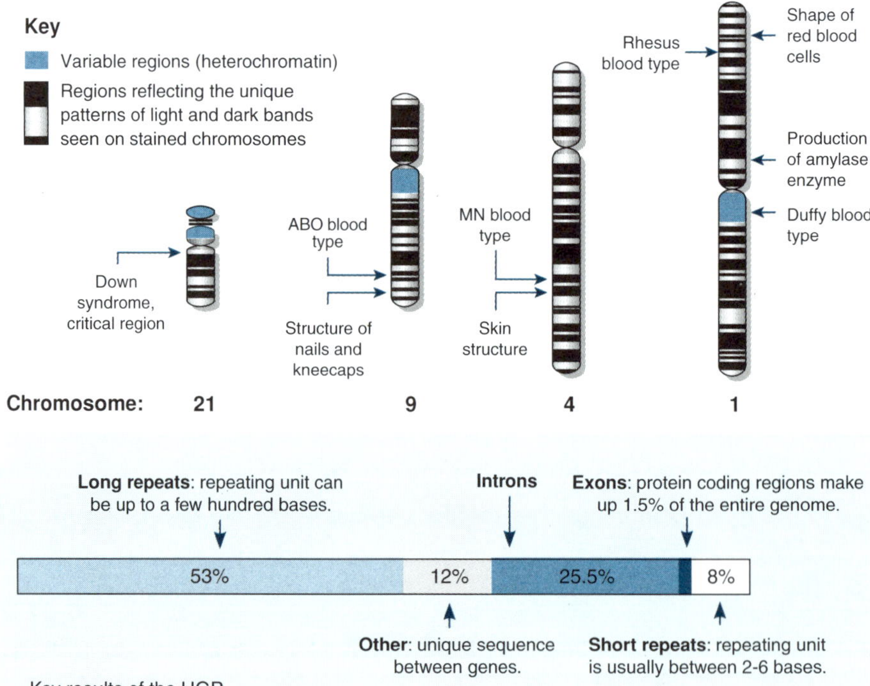

Key results of the HGP
- There are perhaps only 20,000-25,000 protein-coding genes in our human genome.
- It covers 99% of the gene containing parts of the genome and is 99.999% accurate.
- The new sequence correctly identifies almost all known genes (99.74%).
- Its accuracy and completeness allows systematic searches for causes of disease.

© BIOZONE International 2013
ISBN: 978-1-927173-72-5
Photocopying Prohibited

Benefits and ethical issues arising from the Human Genome Project

Medical benefits

- Improved **diagnosis** of disease and predisposition to disease by genetic testing.

- Better identification of disease carriers, through genetic testing.

- Better **drugs** can be designed using knowledge of protein structure (from gene sequence information) rather than by trial and error.

- Greater possibility of successfully using **gene therapy** to correct genetic disorders.

Non-medical benefits

- Greater knowledge of **family relationships** through genetic testing, e.g. paternity testing in family courts.

- Advances **forensic science** through analysis of DNA at crime scenes.

- Improved knowledge of the evolutionary relationships between humans and other organisms, which will help to develop better, more accurate classification systems.

Possible ethical issues

- It is unclear whether third parties, e.g. health insurers, have rights to genetic test results.

- If treatment is unavailable for a disease, genetic knowledge about it may have no use.

- Genetic tests are costly, and there is no easy answer as to who should pay for them.

- Genetic information is hereditary so knowledge of an individual's own genome has implications for members of their family.

Couples can already have a limited range of genetic tests to determine the risk of having offspring with some disease-causing mutations.

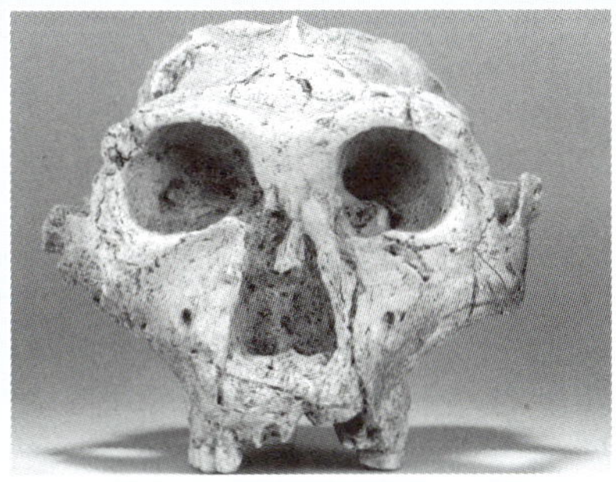

When DNA sequences are available for humans and their ancestors, comparative analysis may provide clues about human evolution.

Legislation is needed to ensure that there is no discrimination on the basis of genetic information, e.g. at work or for health insurance.

1. Briefly describe the objectives of the Human Genome Project (HGP): ______________________________________

____

____

2. Suggest a reason for developing a HapMap of the human genome: ____

____

____

3. Describe two possible **benefits** of Human Genome Project (HGP):

    (a) Medical: ____

    ____

    (b) Non-medical: ____

    ____

4. Explain what is meant by **proteomics** and explain its significance to the HGP and the ongoing benefits arising from it:

____

____

____

____

5. Suggest two possible points of view for one of the **ethical issues** described in the list above (top right):

    (a) ____

    ____

    (b) ____

    ____

Genome Research

Genome Projects

The aim of most genome projects is to determine the DNA sequence of the organism's entire genome. Over one hundred bacterial and viral genomes, as well as a number of larger genomes (including honeybee, nematode worm, African clawed frog, pufferfish, zebra fish, rice, cow, dog, and rat) have already been sequenced. Genomes that are, for a variety of reasons, high priority for DNA sequencing include the sea urchin, kangaroo, pig, cat, baboon, silkworm, rhesus monkey, turkey and even Neanderthals (prehumans). Genome sequencing is costly, so candidates are carefully chosen. Important factors in this choice include the value of the knowledge to practical applications, the degree of technical difficulty involved, and the size of the genome (very large genomes are generally avoided). Genome sizes and the number of genes per genome vary, and are not necessarily correlated with the size and structural complexity of the organism itself. Once completed, genome sequences are analyzed by computer to identify genes.

Artist's impression

Yeast
(*Saccharomyces cerevisiae*)

Status: Completed in 1996
Number of genes: 6000
Genome size: 13 Mb

The first eukaryotic genome to be completely sequenced. Yeast is used as a model organism to study human cancer.

Bacteria
(*Escherichia coli*)

Status: Completed in 1997
Number of genes: 4403
Genome size: 4.6 Mb

E. coli has been used as a laboratory organism for over 70 years. Various strains of *E. coli* are responsible for several human diseases.

Mouse
(*Mus musculus*)

Status: Completed in 2002
Number of genes: 30,000
Genome size: 2500 Mb

New drugs destined for human use are often tested on mice because more than 90% of their proteins show similarities to human proteins.

Fruit fly
(*Drosophila melanogaster*)

Status: Completed in 2000
Number of genes: 14,000
Genome size: 150 Mb

Drosophila has been used extensively for genetic studies for many years. About 50% of all fly proteins show similarities to mammalian proteins.

Chimpanzee
(*Pan troglodytes*)

Status: Draft, Dec. 2003, Completed, Sept. 2005
Genome size: 3000 Mb

Chimp and human genomes differ by <2%. Identifying differences could provide clues to the genetics of diseases such as cancer, to which chimps are less prone.

Rice
(*Oryza sativa*)

Status: Completed 2002 for two varieties (*indica* and *japonica*)
Genome size: 466 and 420 Mb

A food staple for much of the world's population. An international consortium is currently working on a third rice genome sequence, which will be the Gold Standard.

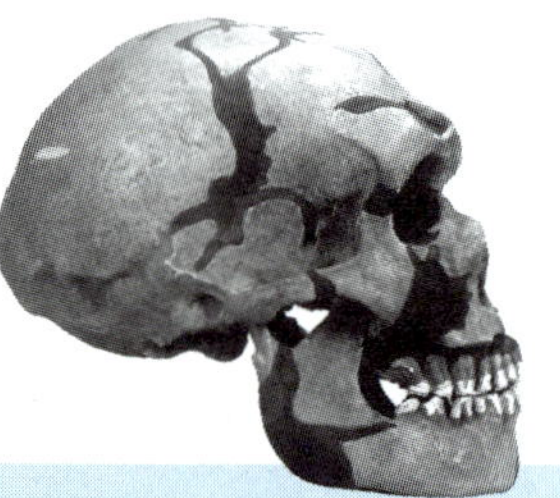

Neanderthal
(*H. neanderthalensis*)

Status: Draft completed May 2010
Genome size: 3000 Mb

Completion of this draft enables the first genome-wide comparison of the human and Neanderthal genomes. Researchers may now be able to identify the genetic variations that gave rise to humans.

Chicken
(*Gallus gallus*)

Status: Completed in Feb. 2004
Genome size: 1200 Mb

Various human viruses were first found in chickens making this species important for the study of human disease and cross-species transfers. It was the first bird genome to be sequenced.

1. Calculate the number of genes per megabase (Mb) of DNA for the organisms above:

   (a) Yeast: _________________   (b) *E. coli*: _____________   (c) Fruit fly: _______________   (d) Mouse: __________

2. Suggest why the number of genes per Mb of DNA varies between organisms (hint: consider relative sizes of introns):

   ____

   ____

3. Suggest why researchers want to sequence the genomes of plants such as wheat, rice, and maize:

   ____

   ____

4. Use a web engine search to find:

   (a) First **multicellular animal genome** to be sequenced: _____________________________ Date: ______________

   (b) First **plant genome** to be sequenced: _____________________________ Date: ______________

KNOW

Related activities: The Human Genome Project, GM plants–Golden Rice
Weblinks: Landmarks in Biotechnology, A Guide to Sequenced Genomes

DNA Profiling Using PCR

In chromosomes, some of the DNA contains simple, repetitive sequences. These *noncoding* nucleotide sequences repeat themselves over and over again and are found scattered throughout the genome. Some repeating sequences are short (2-6 base pairs) called **microsatellites** or **short tandem repeats** (STRs) and can repeat up to 100 times. The human genome has numerous different microsatellites. Equivalent sequences in different people vary considerably in the numbers of the repeating unit. This phenomenon has been used to develop **DNA profiling**, which identifies the natural variations found in every person's DNA. Identifying such differences in the DNA of individuals is a useful tool for forensic investigations.

In 1998, the FBI's Combined Offender DNA Index System (CODIS) was established, providing a national database of DNA samples from convicted criminals, suspects, and crime scenes. In the USA, there are many laboratories approved for forensic DNA testing. Increasingly, these are targeting the 13 core STR loci recommended by the FBI; enough to guarantee that the odds of someone else sharing the same result are extremely unlikely (less than one in a thousand million). The CODIS may be used to solve previously unsolved crimes and to assist in current or future investigations. DNA profiling can also be used to establish genetic relatedness (e.g. in paternity or pedigree disputes), or when searching for a specific gene (e.g. screening for disease).

Genome Research

Microsatellites (Short Tandem Repeats)

Microsatellites consist of a variable number of tandem repeats of a 2 to 6 base pair sequence. In the example below it is a two base sequence (CA) that is repeated.

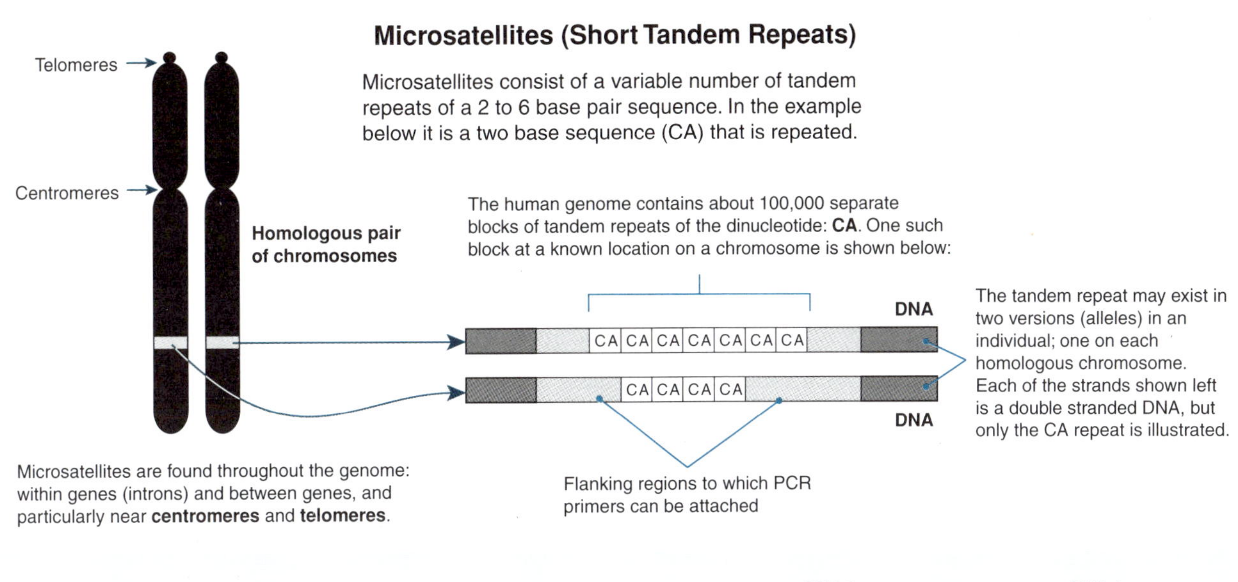

Microsatellites are found throughout the genome: within genes (introns) and between genes, and particularly near **centromeres** and **telomeres**.

How short tandem repeats are used in DNA profiling

This diagram shows how three people can have quite different microsatellite arrangements at the same point (locus) in their DNA. Each will produce a different DNA profile using gel electrophoresis:

❶ Extract DNA from sample

A sample collected from the tissue of a living or dead organism is treated with chemicals and enzymes to extract the DNA, which is separated and purified.

❷ Amplify microsatellite using PCR

Specific primers (arrowed) that attach to the flanking regions (light gray) either side of the microsatellite are used to make large quantities of the micro-satellite and flanking regions sequence only (no other part of the DNA is amplified/replicated).

❸ Visualize fragments on a gel

The fragments are separated by length, using **gel electrophoresis**. DNA, which is negatively charged, moves toward the positive terminal. The smaller fragments travel faster than larger ones.

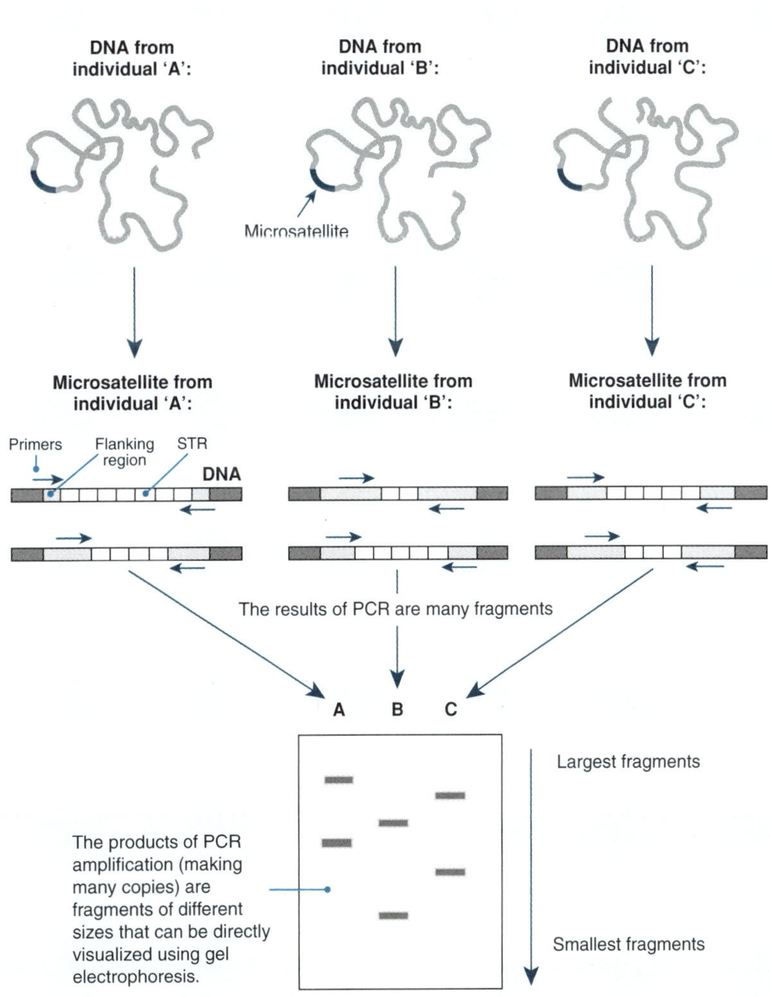

Related activities: *Gel Electrophoresis, Forensic Applications of DNA Profiling, Polymerase Chain Reaction*

KNOW

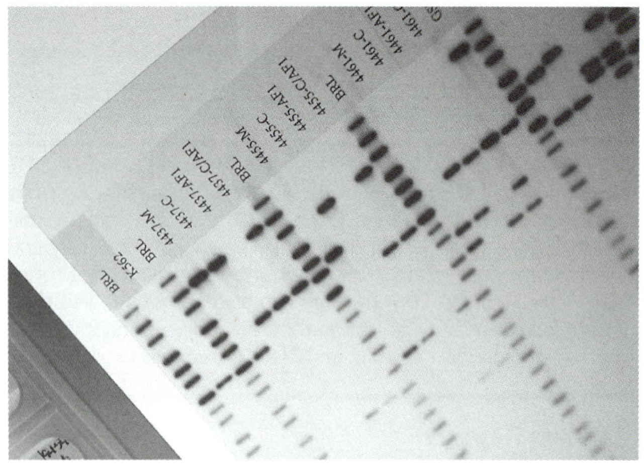

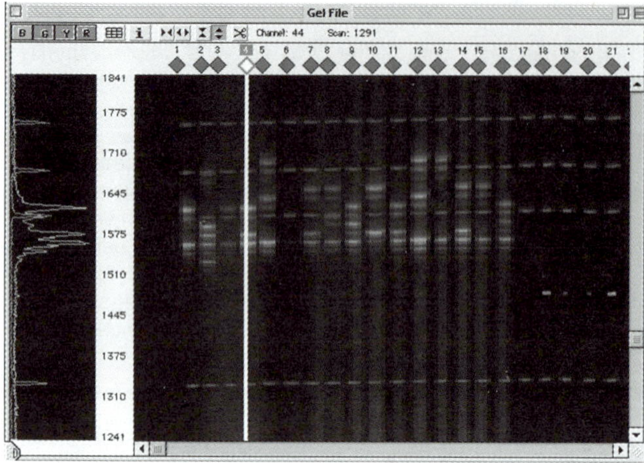

The photo above shows a film output from a DNA profiling procedure. Those lanes with many regular bands are used for calibration; they contain DNA fragment sizes of known length. These calibration lanes can be used to determine the length of fragments in the unknown samples.

DNA profiling can be automated in the same way as DNA sequencing. Computer software is able to display the results of many samples run at the same time. In the photo above, the sample in lane 4 has been selected. It displays fragments of different length on the left of the screen.

1. Describe the properties of **short tandem repeats** that are important to the application of **DNA profiling** technology:

2. Explain the role of each of the following techniques in the process of DNA profiling:

   (a) Gel electrophoresis:

   (b) PCR:

3. Describe the three main steps in DNA profiling using PCR:

   (a)

   (b)

   (c)

4. Explain why as many as 10 STR sites are used to gain a DNA profile for forensic evidence:

Forensic Applications of DNA Profiling

The use of DNA as a tool for solving crimes such as homicide is well known, but it can also be used to as a solution to many other problems. DNA evidence has been used to identify body parts, solve cases of industrial sabotage and contamination, for paternity testing, and even in identifying animal products illegally made from endangered species.

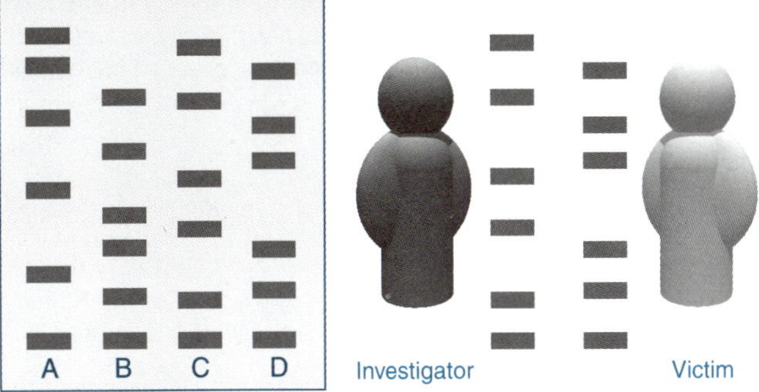

During the initial investigation, samples of material that may contain DNA are taken for analysis. At a crime scene, this may include blood and body fluids as well as samples of clothing or objects that the offender might have touched. Samples from the victim are also taken to eliminate them as a possible source of contamination.

1. In the above case two sets of DNA profiles are shown. Describe the purpose of lane A in each set of profiles:

2. Explain why DNA profiles are obtained for both the victim and investigator:

3. Use the evidence to decide if the alleged offender is innocent or guilty and explain your decision:

4. Explain how DNA profiling could be used to refute official claims of the number of whales being captured and sold in fish markets:

2 DNA is isolated and profiles are made from all samples and compared to known DNA profiles such as that of the victim.

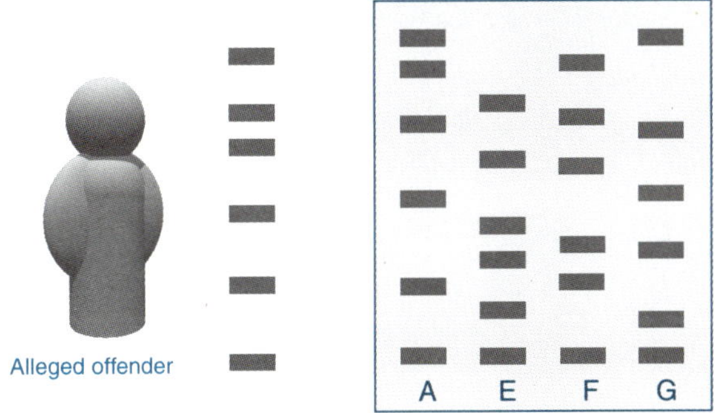

3 Unknown DNA samples are compared to DNA databases of convicted offenders and to the DNA of the alleged offender.

4 Although it does not make a complete case, DNA profiling, in conjunction with other evidence, is one of the most powerful tools in identifying offenders or unknown tissues.

Whale DNA: Tracking Illegal Slaughter

Under International Whaling Commission regulations, some species of whales can be captured for scientific research and their meat sold legally. Most, including humpback and blue whales, are fully protected and to capture or kill them for any purpose is illegal. Between 1999 and 2003 Scott Baker and associates from Oregon State University's Marine Mammal Institute investigated whale meat sold in markets in Japan and South Korea. Using DNA profiling techniques, they found around 10% of the samples tested were from fully protected whales including western grey whales and humpbacks. They also found that many more whales were being killed than were being officially reported.

Related activities: DNA Profiling Using PCR

KNOW

Finding the Connection

During the last decade, the study of **species relationships** has been revolutionized by the use of **DNA technology**. Through genomic analyses, many so-called species that were once thought to be separate have been shown to be one. Conversely, taxa that were thought to be monospecific have now been shown to include more than one genetically distinct group. In New Zealand, there are a number of different sheep breeds, each of which has been bred for a specific purpose (e.g. meat of wool production). While some of these breeds are very old, others are recent developments. As new sheep breeds are developed by selective breeding, older breeds become less profitable to farm and are eventually replaced. These older breeds are becoming increasingly important because they carry traits that could be valuable but are now absent in more recent breeds. The relationships between the older and newer breeds are important as they show the development of breeds and help farmers and breeders to plan for the future development of their flocks.

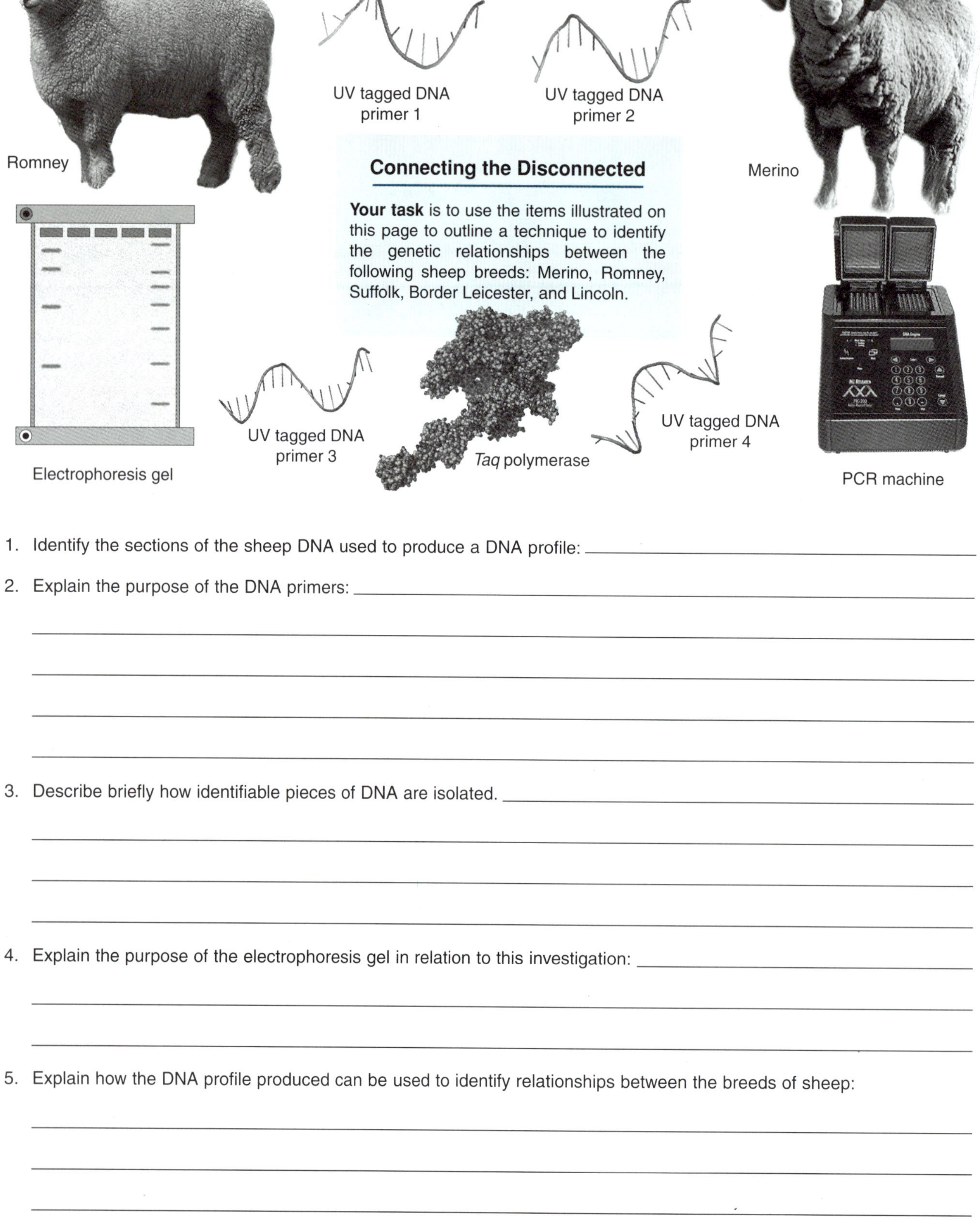

1. Identify the sections of the sheep DNA used to produce a DNA profile: ________________________________

2. Explain the purpose of the DNA primers: ________________________________

\
\
\
\

3. Describe briefly how identifiable pieces of DNA are isolated. ________________________________

\
\
\

4. Explain the purpose of the electrophoresis gel in relation to this investigation: ________________________________

\
\

5. Explain how the DNA profile produced can be used to identify relationships between the breeds of sheep:

\
\
\

TEST

Related activities: *Coning a Gene Ex Vivo, DNA Profiling Using PCR, Gel Electrophoresis*

Studying Gene Expression

DNA chips (also called microarrys or gene chips) are a progression of the technology used in DNA probes. They allow thousands of DNA sequences to be probed at once. DNA chips allow researchers to study which genes are expressed (turned on) in a cell. It is done by probing the mRNA content of a cell. If certain mRNA is present, then a specific gene is turned on and being expressed. The mRNA is extracted from a cell and then copied into **complementary DNA** (**cDNA**) using the enzyme reverse transcriptase. The DNA chip itself is covered with thousands of dots. In turn, each dot contains thousands of copies of a unique DNA sequence which corresponds to a known gene from the genome being probed. When the cDNAs are applied to the chip, they will only bind to their complementary sequence. Computer analysis of the chip determines which dots have DNA bound, and this tells researchers which genes are being expressed.

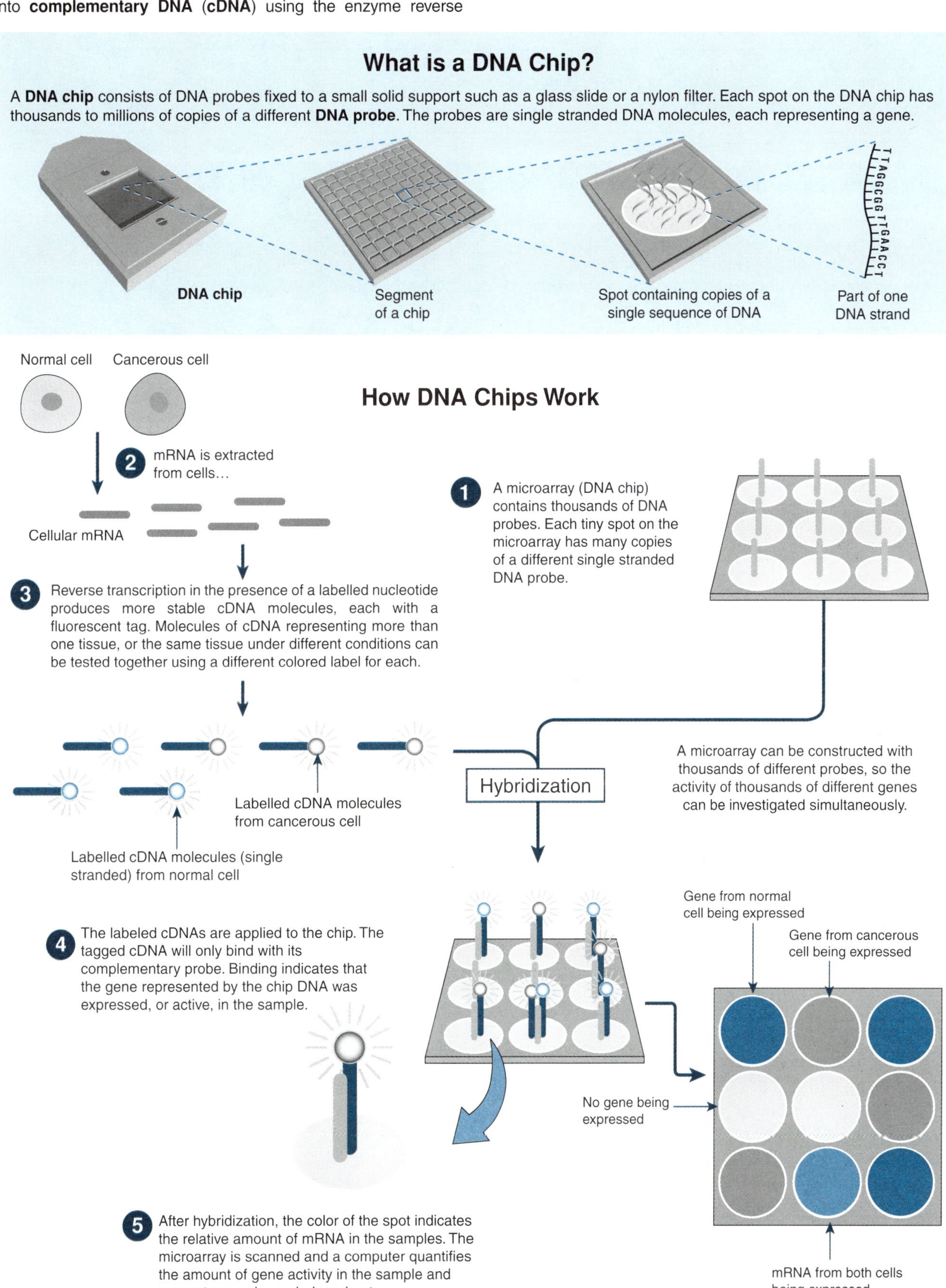

Genome Research

Related activities: Screening for Genes, Cloning a Gene In Vivo
Weblinks: DNA Microarray

KNOW

1. Describe one purpose of DNA chips: ____

____

____

2. (a) Identify the basic principle by which DNA chips work: ____________________________

____

____

(b) Identify the role of reverse transcription in DNA chip technology: ____________________

____

3. DNA chips (microarrays) can be used to determine which genes are being expressed in a cell. In one type of microarray, hybridization of the cDNA from cell 1 turns the dot red while hybridization of the cDNA from cell 2 turns the dot green. Hybridization of cDNA from both cells turns the dot yellow. In an experiment, cDNA derived from a strain of antibiotic resistant bacteria (cell 1) was labeled with a red fluorescent tag and cDNA derived from a non-resistant strain of the same bacterium (cell 2) was labeled with a green fluorescent tag. The cDNAs were mixed and hybridized to a chip containing spots of DNA from genes 1-25. The results are shown on the right.

1	2	3	4	5
6	7	8	9	10
11	12	13	14	15
16	17	18	19	20
21	22	23	24	25

No colour (no expression)

Red (Expression cell 1)

Green (Expression cell 2)

Yellow (Expression in cell 1 and 2)

(a) Discuss the conclusions you could make about which genes might be implicated in antibiotic resistance in this case:

____

____

____

(b) Suggest how this information could be used to design new antibiotics that are less vulnerable to resistance:

____

____

____

4. DNA chips are frequently used in diagnostic medicine to compare gene expression in cancerous and non-cancerous tissue. Suggest how this information could be used:

____

____

____

____

5. Suggest how the study of gene expression might help a genetic engineer produce new crops or manipulate model animals for further research:

____

____

____

____

____

Marker Assisted Selection

Selective breeding is the process of breeding together two individuals with desirable phenotypic traits. This is a relatively easy way to produce individuals with the desired phenotype in organisms that can be bred in large numbers, have short generation times, or have easily identified phenotypic traits. However, not all traits are easily identified and, in some cases, the trait may not appear for some time or its expression may be sex limited (e.g. high milk production in dairy cattle). **Marker assisted selection** (**MAS**) is a molecular technique in which the genotype of the individual is screened for genetic markers associated with genes for desirable traits. The technique can identify individuals with desirable genes early on and help direct breeding programmes by focusing breeding efforts on only those individuals with the most desirable combination of genes.

Quantitative Trait Loci

A **quantitative trait** is a phenotype (characteristic) that varies in its appearance, e.g. height, and is controlled by two or more genes (it is **polygenic**). This contrasts with discrete traits, e.g. attached or free earlobes in humans, which are controlled by only one gene.

The genetic analysis of a quantitative trait requires a researcher to identify the genes associated with the trait. The locations of these genes (or their markers) are called **quantitative trait loci**.

For any given individual from a breeding stock, there will be many phenotypic traits that have been identified as desirable. Each of these traits may have many QTLs and so will require many gene markers to identify them all.

What is a Gene Marker?

A **gene marker** is a length of DNA that is associated with a particular gene. It is not necessarily the gene itself, but it is linked to and inherited with the gene. A number of markers are used in marker assisted selection, each with advantages and disadvantages:

Restriction Fragment Length Polymorphisms (RFLPs): This was one of the first markers used to identify genes. It is a simple digestion of DNA using a restriction enzyme. The fragments are separated on a electrophoresis gel.

Microsatellites: Microsatelittes are short repeated sequences of DNA e.g. CACACA. They are highly variable between individuals, making them useful as markers.

Single Nucleotide Polymorphisms (SNPs): SNPs are changes to one base pair in a DNA sequence. They are useful when they occur within a gene (thereby producing a new allele). SNPs act as **direct markers** if they are directly related to a desired gene.

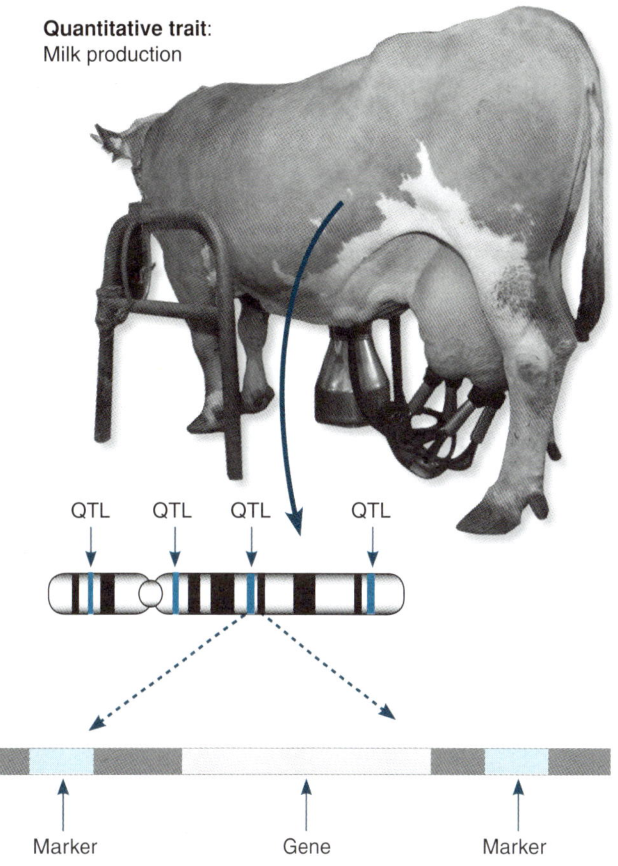

1. What is a gene marker? ____

____

____

2. (a) What is a quantitative trait? ____

____

____

   (b) Explain why a quantitative trait may have many gene markers: ____

____

____

3. Explain why marker assisted selection can speed up the process of selective breeding for particular traits:

____

____

____

____

____

Related activities: DNA Profiling Using PCR
Weblinks: Marker Assisted Selection

KNOW

Why MAS? Why Not Just Use Phenotypes?

There are two problems with using only phenotypic traits to select individuals for breeding. The first is that a breeder may have to wait many years before a trait becomes apparent in an individual. Secondly, some phenotypes are associated with multiple genes, and many of those genes have multiple alleles (versions of the gene). The effect of the alleles may not always be obvious. For example, a harmful allele may be hidden until it pairs up with another. Such a situation occurred in the late 1980s with the holstein bull **Osborndale Ivanhoe**, below.

In 1988 a problem was affecting the United States dairy industry. A disease specific to holstein cattle, bovine leukocyte adhesion deficiency (BLAD), was becoming more common in young calves. The disease affected their immune system's ability to fight off infection, and calves with the disease died. BLAD is a hereditary disease, caused by a recessive allele.

One bull, Osborndale Ivanhoe, produced offspring with high milk yields. It is estimated he sired 79,000 daughters and 1200 sons, which were then used to sire many more holstein calves. However, Osborndale Ivanhoe was a carrier for BLAD. By the time it was discovered, 20,000 calves with BLAD were being born in the United States each year. The disease spread quickly because artificial insemination was used to impregnate thousands of cows with Osborndale Ivanhoe's semen. This example demonstrates that undesirable, as well as desirable traits, can quickly spread through a population using selective breeding.

In 1991 a gene marker was developed for BLAD. It was found that two mutations in the CD18 gene were responsible. One mutation affected the recognition site for the restriction enzyme **Taq**1. In the normal gene, *Taq1* produces two fragments 26 bp and 32 bp long. In the affected gene, a recognition site is missing and only one 58 bp fragment is produced. MAS has identified BLAD carriers, and they have been removed from the breeding population. BLAD has virtually been eliminated from holstein cattle.

Profile of CD18 genes digested with Taq1

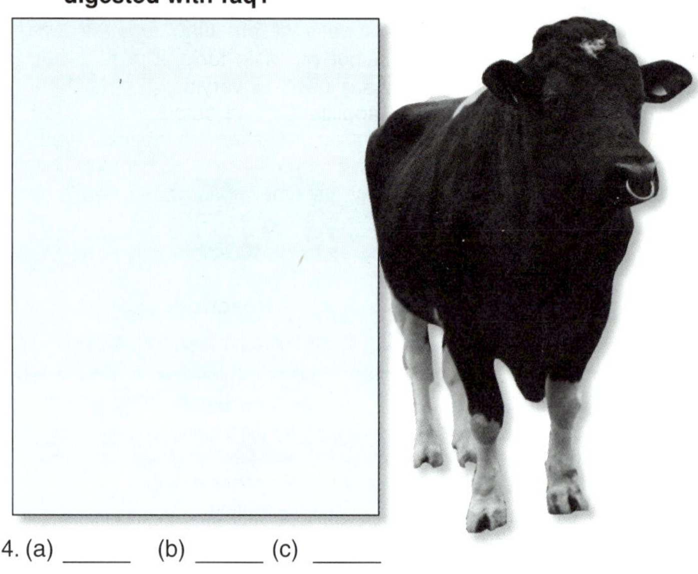

4. (a) ______   (b) ______   (c) ______

Section of DNA and amino acids from normal CD18 Gene

DNA strand 5'...GGC TAC CCC ATC **GAC** CTG TAC TAC ... 3'
Amino acids ... Gly   Tyr   Pro   Lle   **Asp**   Leu   Tyr   Tyr ...

Section of DNA and amino acids from the BLAD CD18 Gene

DNA strand 5'...GGC TAC CCC ATC **GGC** CTG TAC TAC ... 3'
Amino acids ... Gly   Tyr   Pro   Lle   **Gly**   Leu   Tyr   Tyr ...

4. The DNA sequences below show a single DNA strand for each allele of the CD18 gene. The three sequences show (in no particular order) a genotype that is homozygous normal, a heterozygous genotype (one normal, one BLAD allele), and a genotype that is homozygous for the BLAD allele. The *Taq*1 restriction enzyme cuts the DNA at the recognition sequence **TCGA** (cutting between the T and C). For each of the sequences below circle the recognition sequence on both DNA strands (if necessary). Then simulate an electrophoresis gel in the blue gel box (Question 4 (a), (b), and (c)) above showing the two homozygotes (NN, BB) and the heterozygote (NB), and the approximate positions of the bands on the gel:

(a)

```
GTGACCTTCCGGAGGGCCAAGGGCTACCCCATCGACCTGTACTACCTGATGGACCTCT
GTGACCTTCCGGAGGGCCAAGGGCTACCCCATCGACCTGTACTACCTGATGGACCTCT
```

(b)

```
GTGACCTTCCGGAGGGCCAAGGGCTACCCCATCGGCCTGTACTACCTGATGGACCTCT
GTGACCTTCCGGAGGGCCAAGGGCTACCCCATCGGCCTGTACTACCTGATGGACCTCT
```

(c)

```
GTGACCTTCCGGAGGGCCAAGGGCTACCCCATCGACCTGTACTACCTGATGGACCTCT
GTGACCTTCCGGAGGGCCAAGGGCTACCCCATCGGCCTGTACTACCTGATGGACCTCT
```

5. Why might it be risky to base a selective breeding programme solely on phenotypic traits? __________________________

____

____

____

6. Explain how marker assisted selection helped to remove BLAD from the holstein breed: _________________________

____

____

____

____

____

Some Common Tools in Genetic Engineering

Genetic engineering uses a set of basic tools to manipulate genetic material. The tools are used in varying combinations depending on the required application and outcome. Although other tools are used in genetic engineering, those described below are some of the most common. It is worthwhile becoming familiar with them.

Tools used in Genetic Engineering

Tool	Description	Application
Reverse transcriptase	An enzyme that catalyzes the formation of a complementary DNA (cDNA) from an RNA template by reverse transcription.	▶ Used in reverse transcription polymerase chain reaction where the polymerase chain reaction technique is applied to RNA. ▶ Reverse transcriptase is used to create cDNA libraries from mRNA.
Restriction enzymes	Enzymes that cut DNA at specific nucleotide sequences. The recognition sequences are usually about six nucleotides long.	▶ Allows DNA to be cut at specific locations, and produces sticky ends that can later be joined to other sequences.
DNA ligase	An enzyme that joins two DNA strands together by catalyzing the formation of a phosphodiester bond.	▶ Joins DNA sequences that were cut with a restriction enzyme. Allows DNA fragments to be joined together to produce recombinant DNA.
Plasmids	A small circular DNA strand that can replicate independently of the chromosomes. Found in bacteria and some yeast.	▶ Used in genetic engineering as vectors for the insertion of a target gene to produce recombinant DNA.
Taq polymerase	A thermostable DNA polymerase isolated from the thermophilic bacterium _Thermus aquaticus_. Stable at 95°C.	▶ Used in polymerase chain reaction (PCR), to amplifying short segments of DNA.
Single-Nucleotide Polymorphism (SNPs)	SNPs (pronounced snips) represents a difference in a single nucleotide between individuals in a population.	▶ Used for creating genetic maps. ▶ Can be used to see how likely it is individuals may get certain diseases, or how they might respond to drugs and medicines.

DNA is cut at a specific sequence

No break in DNA molecule

Nucleotides

Variation in a single nucleotide between individuals in a population

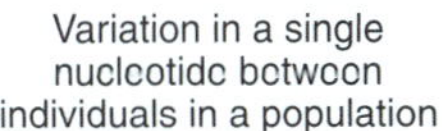

REFER

Some Common Techniques in Genetic Engineering

Some commonly used techniques in genetic engineering are described in the table below. Not all the techniques are necessarily used by researchers each time. Like the tools described on the previous page, these techniques can be used in various ways to achieve particular outcomes. As with many aspects of biotechnology the applications are vast.

Techniques used in Genetic Engineering

Techniques	Description	Application	
Recombinant DNA technology	A gene from one individual is placed into the genome of another individual. The inserted gene can be from the same species, or a different species.	▸ DNA cloning ▸ Biotechnology ▸ Medicine (including gene therapy)	Inserted DNA
Genetic libraries	A collection of DNA from a single organism or a particular source. The DNA library consists of DNA fragments that are inserted into a vector (e.g. plasmid) for cloning.	▸ Gene expression in each cell type can be catalogued. ▸ All the DNA sequences in a genome can be catalogued. ▸ Libraries can be screened to find sequences of interest.	Stored cDNA
DNA probing (screening a genetic library)	A labeled DNA fragment (probe) is used to find a specific sequence of nucleotides in a collection of DNA fragments.	▸ Allows researchers to find a particular DNA sequence within a DNA library.	DNA sequences / Probe / DNA hybridization
Polymerase chain reaction (PCR)	A technique used to amplify selected sections of DNA or RNA. It generates thousands to millions of identical copies of the sequence.	▸ Generates many identical copies of a nucleotide sequence. ▸ Can be used instead of *in vivo* gene cloning.	
Dideoxy screening (also called Sanger's method)	An *in vitro* DNA synthesis method used to sequence DNA. DNA is replicated in the presence of dideoxynucleotides (ddNTPs) which stops the replication process when they are incorporated into the growing strand of DNA. The DNA strand is then sequenced.	▸ Determine the nucleotide sequence of a gene or specific DNA sequence.	A T C T G G T C T T
Genetic mapping	A genetic map is created that assigns (locates) DNA fragments or genes to regions on a particular chromosome.	▸ Find the location of genes associated with certain phenotypes, diseases, or conditions.	Human chromosome 1 / Rh blood group / Alzheimer's disease / Glaucoma

KEY TERMS: Mix and Match

INSTRUCTIONS: Test your vocabulary by matching each term to its correct definition, as identified by its preceding letter code.

bioinformatics

DNA (gene) probe

DNA (genetic) profiling

DNA chip (microarray)

forensic

gel electrophoresis

gene marker

genomics

Human Genome Project

marker assisted selection

microsatellites (STRs)

polymerase chain reaction (PCR)

proteomics

quantitative trait

quantitative trait loci

recombinant DNA technology

selective breeding

SNPs

A   The process of identifying regions of a DNA sequence that are variable between individuals in order to distinguish between individuals.

B   Short sequence of labeled DNA (e.g. radioactively labeled) which is introduced to a DNA sample in order detect complementary DNA sequences for analysis.

C   The use of computer science and mathematics to analyze genetic material.

D   The scientific collaboration, now completed, to map the entire DNA that makes up the human genome.

E   The application of scientific ideas and techniques in order to answer questions about material of interest (often crimes).

F   The branch of molecular biology concerned with the structure, function, evolution, and mapping of genomes.

G   A length of DNA with a known location on a chromosome. It is not necessarily the gene of interest itself, but it is linked to and inherited with the gene of interest and can therefore be used to identify specific individuals.

H   The process of identifying regions of a DNA sequence that are variable between individuals in order to distinguish between individuals.

I   A phenotype (characteristic) that varies in its appearance, e.g. height, and is controlled by two or more genes.

J   A short (normally two base pairs) piece of DNA that repeats a variable number of times between individuals and so can be used for identification.

K   An enzyme based reaction that is used to amplify fragments of DNA.

L   Variation in the DNA sequence at a particular location, which occurs when a single nucleotide is altered.

M   The identification and study of the protein products of genes.

N   Technique used for the separation of nucleic acids or protein molecules using an electric field applied to a (buffered) gel matrix.

O   Stretches of DNA containing, or linked to the genes, for a particular quantitative trait.

P   The technology and procedures involved in the production and use of recombinant DNA (DNA possessing sequences not originally found in it).

Q   The process by which cultivated breeds with particular traits are developed over time (also called artificial selection).

R   A molecular technique used to identify individuals with desirable genes. The genotype of the individual is screened for genetic markers which are associated with genes for desirable traits.

VOCAB

Index